THE GREAT KOSHER MEAT WAR OF 1902

The Great Kosher Meat War *of* 1902

IMMIGRANT HOUSEWIVES AND THE RIOTS THAT SHOOK NEW YORK CITY

SCOTT D. SELIGMAN

Potomac Books
An imprint of the University of Nebraska Press

Library of Congress Cataloging-in-Publication Data
Names: Seligman, Scott D., author.
Title: The great kosher meat war of 1902: immigrant
housewives and the riots that shook New York City /
Scott D. Seligman.
Description: [Lincoln]: Potomac Books, an imprint
of the University of Nebraska Press [2020] | Includes
bibliographical references and index.
Identifiers: LCCN 2020010712
ISBN 9781640123588 (hardback)
ISBN 9781640124103 (epub)
ISBN 9781640124110 (mobi)
ISBN 9781640124127 (pdf)
Subjects: LCSH: Meat industry and trade—New York
(State)—New York—History—20th century. | Kosher food
industry—New York (State)—New York—History—20th
century. | Boycotts—New York (State)—New York—History—
20th century. | Jewish women—New York (State)—New
York—History—20th century. | Women immigrants—New
York (State)—New York—History—20th century. | Consumer
movements—New York (State)—New York—History—20th
century.
Classification: LCC HD9418.N5 S45 2020 | DDC
381/.45664909747109041—dc23
LC record available at https://lccn.loc.gov/2020010712

Set in New Baskerville ITC Pro by Laura Buis.

CONTENTS

ILLUSTRATIONS

Food riots have occurred throughout history when supply has been short or prices too high, most commonly in developing countries. Often they are caused when a staple like bread, rice, or meat is suddenly out of reach; at other times anger stems from poor economic conditions overall, when everything is suddenly too expensive or bellies are not full. At such times, consumers don't consider the costs of inputs or the logistics of getting their food to market. They care only about whether it is for sale at an affordable price.

But the Lower East Side of Manhattan was not starving in 1902 when thousands of Jewish women took to the streets in a quest for affordable kosher meat, nor was America a poor country. Although many immigrant Jews lived hand-to-mouth existences, their boycott was never really about hunger. Non-kosher meat was always available and more affordable. But to families that felt duty bound by history, culture, and religion to honor the commandments in Exodus, Deuteronomy, and Leviticus and the rulings in the Talmud that specified in exacting detail which foods were permitted and how and by whom they had to be slaughtered and processed, it was simply not an option.

This book tells the inspiring story of immigrant Jewish women in early twentieth-century New York who, certain of the righteousness of their cause, discovered their collective power and found their political voice. It is an early case study in consumer activism, all the more impressive because it involved mostly uneducated women, some barely conversant in English, with few resources at their disposal. That they managed to organize themselves overnight to challenge powerful, vested corporate interests in their new homeland is remarkable.

For most, it was their first foray into the political and economic arena, and they were treading new ground. Though they could look to the nascent labor movement for inspiration, community organizing was a broader and more complex task than unionizing, requiring educating vast numbers of their compatriots about supply and demand economics and persuading them of the value of short-term sacrifice. And despite the attendant violence, in the main they approached the task in a disciplined and strategic manner, never losing sight of their goal.

Whatever relevant experience these women might have brought with them when they crossed the Atlantic, resistance in America called for breaking out of traditional roles and employing unfamiliar tactics. And it was an America that was itself in the throes of rapid social change.

Here you will also find the very much related story of the Beef Trust, a cartel of greedy, Chicago-based packers colluding to corner the national market for meat. Behind closed doors, they cooperated to depress the prices they paid for cattle, pressure the railroads for kickbacks in shipping fees, manipulate the nation's supply of beef and other commodities, and, ultimately, gouge consumers.

At precisely the same time as the Lower East Side boycott, President Theodore Roosevelt set out to expose and break up their syndicate. His administration's prosecution of the beef barons provided the backdrop against which New York's Jews struggled to achieve their goal of affordable kosher meat.

Although the true villains in the drama were mostly gentile businessmen located hundreds of miles away, the local scene pitted Jew against Jew: housewives against butchers, butchers against wholesalers, the secular against the Orthodox, Eastern Europeans against Germans, honest rabbis against corrupt ones. It also exacerbated other frictions, such as those between the Jewish community and the police.

The women's need to build a coalition to help carry their water dictated reaching out to congregations, unions, mutual aid societies, philanthropic and political groups, all of which were male-dominated, and eventually—and probably inevitably—men assumed some control over leadership of the effort. But it was, at its outset at least, conceived, organized, and executed *entirely* by female homemakers.

Issues of authenticity and quality of the meat supply were also front and center during the boycott, and herein you will meet Jacob Joseph, brought to America at great expense and with great fanfare as the chief rabbi of New York. Charged with bringing order to a chaotic and corrupt system of kosher slaughter, he was ultimately no match for the forces marshaled against him.

But most importantly, you'll meet several extraordinary women who, facing a common, existential threat, rose to the occasion and pulled off an impressive feat of grassroots organization. Their pioneering efforts inspired later generations of activists who, in their own times, would heed the call to fight back when rents rose too high, staple foods became out of reach, women sought voting rights, or employers underpaid or mistreated workers.

This book nearly didn't get written. Not because I wasn't strongly drawn to the subject. Immigrant Jewish women not unlike my own female forebears, their backs to the wall, waging a battle for their way of life in an era in which it wasn't thought proper for women to demonstrate in the streets certainly seemed like a topic that merited further exploration. An excellent, seminal article written about their struggle in 1980 by the late Dr. Paula E. Hyman, a professor of Jewish history at Yale, had intrigued me. Later writers had also taken note of their strike, but no one since Professor Hyman had dug more deeply into it than she had.

I realized that, if told in depth, the story of the strike needed to address a number of questions, not all of which had been within the scope of Hyman's groundbreaking research. *Why* did the price of meat rise so suddenly and substantially? Who was behind it? Why were Orthodox Jews affected more than others? What went into getting kosher meat to the tables of the immigrants on Manhattan's East Side, and how is it that the women came to blame fellow Jews for the price rise? Why did they point fingers at their own retail butchers, and not the slaughterhouses, packers, or cattlemen?

I also resolved to dig into some issues Dr. Hyman did address. How did these women, unsophisticated and foreign, decide on a boycott as the means to solve their problem? Who were they, and what influenced them? Where did they get the organizational skills to execute such a massive undertaking with so little preparation and so few resources? And finally, why is their story important? Were their efforts merely a flash in the pan, or did they yield lasting effects?

It seemed that the story would best be told from these women's point of view and in the context of what was going on in their lives, but I was foiled by the fact that a century had passed and materials about them as individuals were scarce. Nor did any of them leave memoirs or go on to greater achievements. On the contrary; to a woman they sank right back into the obscurity from whence they had come when it was all over.

In the face of these obstacles to creating accurate, three-dimensional portraits of the women and their inner lives, others might have turned to fictionalization. But because I'm a historian and not a novelist, the idea of fabricating *anything* about them was anathema to me. I enjoy creating narrative nonfiction, but I've always been averse to inventing dialogue that was never spoken or projecting thoughts or feelings onto people who may never have thought or felt them. I don't judge other writers who choose this route; it's just not for me.

So reluctantly, I let them go and moved on to another project.

. Two years later, unable to put them entirely out of mind, I decided to revisit the topic. This time, I turned to the tools of genealogical research. I consulted city directories, ship passenger manifests, and court and census records in addition to books and newspaper reports. I also traced and contacted descendants of several of the movement's leaders.

With help, I obtained access to a rich vein of sources that had previously eluded me. The contemporary Yiddish press provided more detail and nuance than the English-language papers, and many insights into how the Jewish community itself viewed the events. Papers representing both socialist and Orthodox Jewish points of view survive for that period, and their coverage offered up much compelling material. The Yiddish newspapers provided another window into the personalities of the women who led the boycott, and helped depict the novelty, creativity, and power of their common efforts.

My American-born maternal grandmother, Celia Sternrich Abrams, only ten years old at the time of the strike, was living with her family on Orchard Street. I'd like to think that her mother, Austrian-born Mollie Zimmerman Sternrich, joined the boycott and stopped buying kosher meat, as most Jewish women of the neighborhood did. My paternal grandmother, Belarus-born Gussie Rudbart Seligman, would not arrive in America until 1907, but she was in nearby Newark in time for some of the later, copycat strikes.

I would like to dedicate this book to my female immigrant ancestors and, more broadly, to the immigrant Jewish women who, when it looked as if they could not feed their families and remain true to their religious beliefs, took matters into their own hands in 1902, brazenly forcing their way into the public sphere and launching a brave and successful effort to shape their own future in their new homeland.

ACKNOWLEDGMENTS

This is first and foremost a book about women, and so it's fitting that so many women have offered me generous help in the conception and writing of it. I am deeply grateful to:

Dr. Pamela Nadell, Patrick Clendenen Chair in Women's and Gender History at American University. She has been a valued friend and constant source of wise counsel who helped me frame the subject, pointed me to many valuable sources and reviewed the entire manuscript.

Dr. Jenna Weissman Joselit, Charles E. Smith Professor of Judaic Studies and Professor of History at the George Washington University, who helped me think about the broader issues raised in the work and improve the book immeasurably.

Dr. Miriam Isaacs, former Visiting Associate Professor of Yiddish Language and Culture at the University of Maryland, who led me expertly and enjoyably through several dozen contemporary Yiddish-language articles about the boycott.

I also thank Dr. Elissa Sampson, Visiting Scholar and Lecturer, Cornell University; Dr. Judith Rosenbaum, executive director of the Jewish Women's Archive; and Dr. Annie Polland, executive director of the American Jewish Historical Society, for their advice and counsel.

For help with the finer points of Jewish law and religious customs I turned to two childhood friends, Rabbi Yisroel Finman and Levi Rosenhand; to two cousins, Jennifer Shaw Racz and Yehoshua Racz; and to two aunts, Frieda Friedenberg and the late Silvia Seligman, all of whom were generous with their time and assistance. Another cousin, Mara Sokolsky, graciously corrected the Yiddish spellings in the book.

I am indebted to descendants and relatives of several of the women profiled in this book. They include Addie Edelson, Stanley Edelson, Rosalyn Edelson, Walter Rybeck, Carole Haber, Peter Snyderman, Matthew Snyderman, Joyce Braunhut, Ted Astor and Eric Lurio.

Many friends and family members read all or portions of the manuscript and gave me valuable feedback on it. Harvey Solomon has been a faithful sounding board and cherished friend. I'm also indebted to Dr. James Banner, Chris Billing, Lawrence Gotfried, Rita Gotfried, Daniel Grossman, Steven Herman, Susan Levine, Stephen Mink, Sara Sill, and Suzanne Zunzer. Others, including Marsha Cohan, Natalie Lichtenstein, Erica Ling, Dr. Cynthia Rohrbeck, Madelyn Ross, Deborah Strauss, Dr. Philip Wirtz, and Dori Jones Yang have been constant sources of support throughout the process.

Thanks also go to Laura Apelbaum, former executive director, and Wendy Turman, deputy director of the Jewish Historical Society of Greater Washington, and Arianne Brown, senior cantor of Adas Israel Congregation, all of whom have pointed me in useful directions.

Many others helped gather materials. My thanks to Rivka Schiller of Rivka's Yiddish; Melanie J. Meyers and Boni J. Koelliker of the American Jewish Historical Society; Ilya Slavutskiy of The Center for Jewish History; Patrizia Sione and Melissa Holland at the Kheel Center for Labor Management Documentation and Archives at Cornell University; and Chelsea Dowell of the Museum at Eldridge Street. Also to Tina Mullins, Joseph P. Healey Library, University of Massachusetts, Boston; Dr. Beverly Bossler, professor at the University of California, Davis; and Kenneth Cobb, assistant commissioner of the New York City Department of Records and Information Services.

And, finally, my heartfelt thanks to my literary agent, Peter W. Bernstein, who has consistently offered wise counsel on the structure and direction of the book and who shepherded me expertly through the proposal process; to copyeditor Amy Pattullo, for her skilled guidance and gentle touch; to Judy Staigmiller, indexer; and to Tom Swanson, Ann Baker, Anna Weir, Andrea Shahan, Tish Fobben, Emily Wendell, and their colleagues at Potomac Books and the University of Nebraska Press, for their belief in the manuscript and in me.

CHRONOLOGY

1872   The refrigerated boxcar is invented, revolutionizing meatpacking by enabling slaughter in one city and sales in a distant one.

1879   A first, unsuccessful effort to recruit a chief rabbi for New York is launched.

1888   Rabbi Jacob Joseph, hired by Orthodox congregations as chief rabbi of New York, arrives from Vilna.

A secret agreement among the large midwestern meatpackers establishes what comes to be known as the "Beef Trust."

1890   The Sherman Antitrust Act is enacted.

1893   The New York–based managers of the Beef Trust's constituent companies begin weekly meetings to set local retail prices.

1902   SUNDAY, MAY 4 More than four hundred members of the East Side Hebrew Retail Butchers' Kosher Guarantee and Benevolent Association convene to discuss how to respond to a rise in wholesale prices that has driven many out of business.

MONDAY, MAY 5 Lower East Side retail butchers vote to close the following Saturday night to pressure wholesalers into lowering prices.

SATURDAY, MAY 10 Most butchers refuse delivery of meat and do not open for business. Those who do are harassed by their cohorts.

U.S. Attorney Solomon H. Bethea files a complaint in the U.S. Court of Appeals in Chicago against the Beef Trust companies, accusing them of colluding to control the nation's beef trade.

SUNDAY, MAY 11 Fifteen hundred Lower East Side kosher butchers vote to stay closed at least until the following Tuesday.

MONDAY, MAY 12 Pledges of solidarity are received from kosher butchers in Brooklyn and Newark. Consumers, too, are generally supportive. A delegation of 350 butchers meets with representatives of the wholesalers, who insist they are powerless to lower prices.

TUESDAY, MAY 13 Wholesalers offer modest concessions to placate retail butchers who, having earned no income for several days, decide to pocket the concessions and reopen.

WEDNESDAY, MAY 14 Retail butchers reopen, but raise meat prices as high as twenty-five cents a pound. Infuriated Jewish housewives attend an impromptu mass meeting organized by Sarah Edelson. Feeling betrayed by their local butchers, they resolve to boycott them until prices fall.

THURSDAY, MAY 15 Women picket kosher butcher shops in the Jewish quarter. Those who cross picket lines are assaulted and their meat confiscated. Butchers are attacked and shops are damaged. Many are arrested and brought before a magistrate, who issues stiff fines.

An ex-justice appointed by the New York State Supreme Court hears testimony to determine whether prosecution of meatpackers is warranted.

Sarah Edelson calls a meeting that attracts five thousand people. Zionist activist Rabbi Joseph Zeff and labor leader Joseph Barondess deliver fiery speeches, as violence is directed outside against butchers who refuse to close. More arrests are made.

FRIDAY, MAY 16 A local magistrate fines ninety people; twenty-five are jailed.

Paulina Finkel, Clara Korn, and Caroline Schatzberg call on Mayor Seth Low to seek a demonstration permit and ask that police not molest protestors. They are referred to police headquarters.

An envoy sent by New York Attorney General John C. Davies in Albany is unable to serve Manhattan managers of Beef Trust companies with subpoenas because all have fled the jurisdiction.

SATURDAY, MAY 17 Women set out in pairs to exhort congregants at synagogues and prayer halls to support the boycott. Things go smoothly in most places, save the People's Synagogue of the Educational Alliance, where they are insulted and treated rudely.

Police Commissioner John N. Partridge denies the women a demonstration permit and orders a local hall to bar their entry, forcing droves of protestors onto the streets. There is violence against butchers in Lower Manhattan, Brooklyn, Harlem, and the Bronx.

SUNDAY, MAY 18 The *Chicago Tribune* and the *New York Herald* publish purloined documents that confirm collusion among the Beef Trust companies. This revelation forces them to admit the allegations against them, but they insist they have not violated the Sherman Antitrust Act.

Members of the East Side Hebrew Retail Butchers' Kosher Guarantee and Benevolent Association vote not to reopen.

Five hundred people vote to establish the Ladies' Anti–Beef Trust Association and elect officers; Caroline Schatzberg is chosen to head the group. Some men are also selected for leadership positions.

The new association establishes committees to recruit supporters, reach out to adjacent communities, seek support from labor unions, and explore the establishment of cooperative shops.

MONDAY, MAY 19 Unrest continues, but most butcher shops have closed. The real drama takes place at a meeting of the new Ladies' Association, when Sarah Edelson contests the election of Caroline Schatzberg and storms out, vowing to set up a rival group.

TUESDAY, MAY 20 U.S. Attorney Solomon H. Bethea presents evidence against the Beef Trust to federal judge Peter S. Grosscup, who enjoins the companies from further collusion.

A rally in Rutgers Park gives rise to a false rumor that the Ladies' Association is a socialist group.

A mob of one hundred Boston kosher butchers attacks butcher shops aligned with the city's principal kosher wholesaler. Much property is destroyed and shots are fired.

WEDNESDAY, MAY 21 Representatives of the East Side Butchers' Association negotiate with the wholesalers, but no agreement is reached.

Delegates from Jewish congregations, unions, lodges, benevolent associations, and newspapers establish a coalition to spearhead the boycott. The new Allied Conference for Cheap Kosher Meat is led by men and women.

THURSDAY, MAY 22 Despite nascent efforts at mediation, violence continues unabated, especially in Williamsburg. In Boston, women attack butcher shops.

SATURDAY, MAY 24 Boston butchers resume business following a meeting with local rabbis.

The Allied Conference votes to permit independent butchers who agree to sell meat at a reduced price to reopen. The controversial plan cedes control to Orthodox rabbis, many of whom had hesitated to join the boycott.

MONDAY, MAY 26 About 150 kosher butchers sign an agreement to sell meat at thirteen cents a pound; fifty others reopen without agreements and sell little meat.

TUESDAY, MAY 27 Upstate New York witnesses testify against the Beef Trust in Albany.

THURSDAY, MAY 29 Six hundred members of the East Side Butchers' Association agree to close and work with the Allied Conference.

TUESDAY, JUNE 3 Wholesalers agree to drop their price to nine cents a pound, enabling retailers to sell kosher beef at a small profit for fourteen cents per pound.

WEDNESDAY, JUNE 4 New York State Supreme Court justice Alden Chester enjoins Beef Trust companies from colluding on prices.

The Allied Conference seeks pledges from all butchers to sell meat at fourteen cents a pound for a sustained period. Although there is no formal announcement, the boycott seems no longer to be in effect. Caroline Schatzberg, unhappy that so many shops have reopened without signing pledges, pleads for its continuation.

TUESDAY, JUNE 10 Two cooperative meat shops open, undercutting most butchers. One, run by Sarah Cohn, is under the auspices of the Ladies' Anti–Beef Trust Association; the other is managed independently by Sarah Edelson. Business is brisk.

THURSDAY, JUNE 12 The Ladies' Association discusses plans for more cooperative shops.

MONDAY, JUNE 16 Rabbi Jacob Joseph dies.

WEDNESDAY, JUNE 18 Workers in a printing press factory attack thousands of mourners as Rabbi Joseph's funeral cortege passes in the worst outbreak of antisemitic violence the city has ever seen. Police set upon the mourners rather than their attackers and cause many injuries. The Jewish community is incensed and demands an investigation. The mourners are ultimately exonerated, but the officers involved are merely reprimanded or fined a few days' pay.

1903   Several Beef Trust members form the National Packing Company for the purpose of aggregating their assets to permit continued collusion.

The U.S. Circuit Court for the Northern District of Illinois issues a final order barring the Beef Trust from anticompetitive practices.

Beef Trust companies appeal their case to the U.S. Supreme Court.

1904   The New York Rent Protective Association is established to fight rising rents. It initiates a rent strike in the Lower East Side, borrowing many tactics from the 1902 meat boycott.

1905   The U.S. Supreme Court hears arguments in the Beef Trust case and rules that the Trust is an illegal combination in restraint of trade.

Upton Sinclair's *The Jungle,* an indictment of the meat industry, is published in serial form. It is deeply damaging to meatpackers.

1906   Women lead a second kosher meat strike on the Lower East Side that spreads to Harlem and Brooklyn.

1907   A second rent strike occurs on the East Side and spreads to Brooklyn, Harlem, and Newark.

1909   The New York shirtwaist strike, the largest strike of female workers to date, breaks out. At issue are wages, working conditions, and working hours. The strike is not settled until the following February.

1910   A meat riot breaks out in Harlem. It is notable for the leadership of forty-eight-year-old Anna Pastor, mother of well-known columnist and socialist Rose Pastor Stokes.

1912   Another price rise causes meat riots in Brooklyn, which spread to the East Side and then to Chicago, Philadelphia, and Boston before enthusiasm ebbs over the summer.

        The National Packing Company is dissolved under the direction of the Justice Department.

1916   Butchers take on wholesalers again after a rapid rise in the retail prices of all foodstuffs in the run-up to World War I. Many close shops or sell only poultry. Socialists organize cost-of-living protests.

        Protest meetings are held with the mayor and the governor but the boycott loses steam after the Passover holiday.

1919   Anna Pastor presides at a meeting in the Bronx at which yet another boycott is announced. It soon spreads to Harlem but never gets much traction.

1935   Led by radical activist Clara Lemlich, who rose to prominence during the 1909 shirtwaist strike, New York Jewish women urge kosher butchers to close in response to rising prices. Against the backdrop of the Great Depression their boycott extends to non-kosher meat dealers in Harlem and to half a dozen other cities.

DRAMATIS PERSONAE

Joseph Barondess (1867–1928) Jewish activist who helped form many labor unions and who played a leading role in the kosher meat boycott.

David Blaustein (1866–1912) Superintendent of the Hebrew Educational Alliance who helped organize the Allied Conference for Cheap Kosher Meat.

Isaac Blumenthal (1846–1906) President of the United Dressed Beef Company.

Abraham Cahan (1860–1951) Editor of the socialist *Forward* who wrote frequently in support of the boycott.

Sarah Zucker Cohn (1871–1955) Activist in the meat boycott and proprietress of New York's first kosher cooperative retail butcher establishment.

John C. Davies (1857–1925) New York State attorney general from 1899–1902 who investigated the Beef Trust for violations of state antitrust law.

Sarah Zimmerman Edelson (1852–1931) Initiator of the meat strike whose efforts led to the establishment of the Ladies' Anti–Beef Trust Association.

Paulina Wachs Finkel (1868–1960) Early organizer of the meat boycott and treasurer of the Ladies' Anti–Beef Trust Association.

Joseph Goldman (1848–1927) President of the East Side Hebrew Retail Butchers' Kosher Guarantee and Benevolent Association.

Peter Stenger Grosscup (1852–1921) U.S. Court of Appeals judge who presided over *United States v. Swift & Co. et al.*

William Travers Jerome (1859–1934) New York County district attorney, 1902–9.

Frederick Joseph (1851–1931) Vice president of Schwarzschild & Sulzberger, a New York–based meat wholesaler, and son-in-law of its founder.

Jacob Joseph (1840–1902) Chief rabbi of New York City, 1888–95.

Philander C. Knox (1853–1921) Attorney general of the United States, 1901–4.

Fanny Levy (1867–?) One of the early organizers of the meat boycott.

John Nelson Partridge (1838–1920) Police commissioner of the City of New York, 1902–3.

Adolph Moses Radin (1848–1909) Rabbi employed by the Hebrew Educational Alliance who was unsupportive of the boycott and insulting to its female organizers.

Caroline Zeisler Schatzberg (1851–1928) Early activist in the meat boycott and president of the Ladies' Anti–Beef Trust Association.

Adolph Spiegel (1869–1957) Rabbi of Congregation Shaare Zedek, who helped negotiate an end to the meat boycott.

Joseph L. Stern (1833–?) President of Joseph Stern & Sons, a New York–based meat wholesaler.

Ferdinand Sulzberger (1854–1933) President of Schwarzschild & Sulzberger, a New York–based meat wholesaler.

A NOTE ON LANGUAGE

The Yiddish, Hebrew, and Russian terms included in this work, with minor exceptions, are romanized according to the pronunciation favored by Litvak Jews—those originating in present-day Lithuania, Belarus, Latvia, and northeastern Poland—who made up the majority of the Lower East Side Jewish community at the turn of the twentieth century. In some cases, these spellings deviate from common, modern spellings.

PROLOGUE

A Modern Jewish Boston Tea Party

In the wee hours of Thursday, May 15, 1902, female pickets took up positions on all the blocks of the Lower East Side of Manhattan on which kosher butcher shops were located. Some three thousand souls, Jewish women recruited by their peers the previous night, had assembled in the pitch black and formed squads of five by the time the stores opened at 7:00 a.m. Although they had trusted their butchers and bought meat from them for years, that faith had all but evaporated.

Rather than buy from these men, they were now intent on shutting them down.

The proximate cause of the conflict was a sudden spike in the retail price of kosher meat, on which these women, mostly immigrants from Russia and Eastern Europe, depended to feed their families. The price of a cheap cut of beef, twelve cents a pound a few months earlier, had abruptly risen 50 percent. At eighteen cents a pound—$5.25 in today's dollars—kosher beef was now beyond the reach of families that had to pinch pennies to make ends meet. And for most, buying the nonkosher variety was unthinkable.

The kosher butchers had seen the problem coming. When the local slaughterhouses from which they bought meat raised wholesale prices, the owners of many retail shops, envisioning passing the increase on to customers who could ill afford it, had shut down for several days to pressure their suppliers into lowering them. And the wives and mothers of the Lower

East Side had fully supported them in this effort, dutifully doing without meat for several days.

But when the retailers reopened and actually *raised* prices a few cents a pound, the East Side women felt betrayed. Persuaded that their butchers, even as they loudly pinned all the blame on the wholesalers, were taking advantage of a bad situation and profiteering at their expense, they decided to take to the streets.

The demonstrations were supposed to be nonviolent, but they did not stay that way for long. Customers who insisted on patronizing the butchers were assaulted and their purchases thrown into the gutter. Sometimes meat was doused with kerosene so it could never be eaten. Butchers who refused to close were attacked, their windows smashed, their stock ruined, and, in many cases, their fixtures destroyed. There were even reports of arson. Police, summoned to the neighborhood by the hundreds, viciously attacked the pickets. The brutal blows from their nightsticks sent many to local hospitals and many more to jail.

To several newspapers reporting on the boycott at the time, it was nothing less than a modern Jewish Boston Tea Party. New York had never seen anything remotely like it, and where it would all end was anyone's guess.

How all hell broke loose on the Lower East Side in May of 1902 is the story of a cartel of mostly gentile midwestern beef barons colluding to restrict competition and control the price of meat, and of trust-buster President Theodore Roosevelt and his Justice Department, hell-bent on stamping out their anticompetitive business practices. It is the story of a handful of greedy and disingenuous German-Jewish slaughterhouse operators determined to maximize their profits. It is the story of six hundred or so retail kosher butchers, many struggling to eke out a living, caught between avaricious wholesalers and hard-up consumers. And it is the story of New York's first and only chief rabbi, imported from Europe at great expense, and his quixotic efforts to rationalize the corrupt system of kosher slaughter in the city.

Most importantly, though, it is the story of Sarah Edelson, Caroline Schatzberg, Paulina Finkel, Sarah Cohn, and countless other forgotten immigrant Russian and Eastern European Jewish women who, with steely determination and a laser-like focus on their goal, took to the streets to right a perceived wrong and remained there until their cause was won. In the process, they would set a pattern that future generations could employ to address injustice wherever and whenever they experienced it.

THE GREAT KOSHER MEAT WAR OF 1902

1

A City within a City

Sarah Edelson was a force of nature. For one thing, she was physically quite imposing. Although of medium height, she was broad shouldered and bulky: by more than one account she weighed nearly 250 pounds. But apart from her girth, there was gravitas in her bearing. Her large, hazel eyes flashed when she spoke, and when she did it was in a booming voice that rang with authority. People listened to Sarah, who had been blessed with both a moral compass and a winning smile. A natural leader and a born organizer, she seldom shrank from a fight.

Born Sarah Zimmerman in 1852 somewhere in the Russian Pale of Settlement, she was among the earliest Russian Jews to leave for to New York, arriving in 1868, the same year as her husband-to-be, Joel Edelson. Joel, also Russian-born, became a peddler and they married four years later. In 1876 he naturalized as an American citizen, a process that required little more than proving he had been in the country for at least five years and in New York State for one, and renouncing any residual loyalty he might—improbably—have felt for the czar. Given that the Edelsons had fled a virulently antisemitic Russia, this latter consideration was a low bar. Joel's naturalization meant that Sarah automatically became a citizen as well, since under U.S. law until 1922 wives were deemed to derive their nationality from that of their husbands.[1]

Most Russian Jews who came to America had been town-dwellers in the old country. They were not farmers, but largely skilled and unskilled laborers and craftsmen, and so settling in a city like New York made sense because there was employment to be had there. Joel worked as a butcher on New York's Lower East Side for much of the 1880s and 1890s. By the turn of the century, however, he had given up the meat business and amassed enough capital to open Monroe Palace, a saloon located at 88 Monroe Street.[2]

The family lived down the street at number 104. By 1900 Sarah had given birth to six children, only four of whom had survived to adulthood. Three were already grown and out of the house, but the requirements of motherhood had never kept her homebound. She kept house, helped out at the bar, and derived additional income by working as a *shadchen*, a matchmaker, helping young Jewish lonely hearts find one another and, presumably, happiness.

Sarah could be contentious. In 1893, at the wedding of a couple she had united, she had fallen through a trap door accidentally left open by a careless bartender and been seriously injured. She sued the owner of the hall for $20,000 in damages. When a jury awarded her only fifty dollars, she went on to pursue the man into bankruptcy.[3]

Like most of the half million or so Jewish immigrants on the Lower East Side from the Russian Pale—an area that includes modern-day Belarus, Lithuania, much of Ukraine, and eastern Poland—Sarah was deeply observant. Coming to America in no way signaled an abandonment of Jewish tradition. Attending services at the synagogue on the High Holidays of Rosh Hashanah and Yom Kippur and observing *Shabbos*, the Jewish Sabbath, were only small signs of their devotion. They lived their religion every hour of every day of their lives. Even their relationship with food was fraught with cultural and religious significance. Inextricably related to their historical identity as Jews, it involved strict obedience to Jewish law.

Like most of her neighbors, Sarah kept a strictly kosher home, which meant, among other things, serving only certain cuts of meat from animals with cloven hoofs that also chewed the cud, slaughtered under strict rabbinical supervision, soaked, salted, and drained of lifeblood. Meat and dairy-based foods were never eaten together—or even within a few hours of each other—due to a broad interpretation of the commandment in Exodus and Deuteronomy never to cook a young goat in its mother's milk. Observing this commandment meant that even a family without a carpet or a comfortable chair in their home would almost certainly possess two sets of dishes, cookware, and cutlery and a cupboard in which to store them. Nor was seafood ever eaten in her home except for creatures with both fins and scales, the only types allowed by Leviticus and Deuteronomy. This firmly ruled out all kinds of shellfish, among other species. And only specific types of fowl were permitted.

Sarah cut her hair short and wore a *sheitl*, or a wig, on her head when outside her home in obedience to the Talmudic requirement that Jewish women dress modestly in public. This was thought to de-emphasize their sexual attractiveness to men other than their husbands. She would surely have visited a local *mikveh*, such as the one in the basement of Norfolk Street's Beis Hamidrash HaGadol, the city's leading Eastern European Orthodox *shul*, or synagogue. There she would immerse herself in a pool of stationary water from a naturally running source before her marriage, after childbirth, and each month, a week after menstruation ended, to render herself ritually pure and able to resume sexual activity.

Six blocks from the Edelsons, in a five-story walk-up at 204 East Broadway, lived fifty-year-old, recently widowed Caroline Schatzberg. Born Chaia Zeisler in Romania, she had married in Bucharest and emigrated to the United States in 1885. Her husband, Simon, a cloak maker, had died in September 1901, leaving her in widow's weeds with two of her seven children still at home. Sigmund, age twenty, was already working, but six-year-old Dora was still at school. Somewhat more refined than Sarah Edelson, Caroline was also better off financially; she had a live-in, Polish-born servant in her home. White haired but with a youngish face, Caroline had

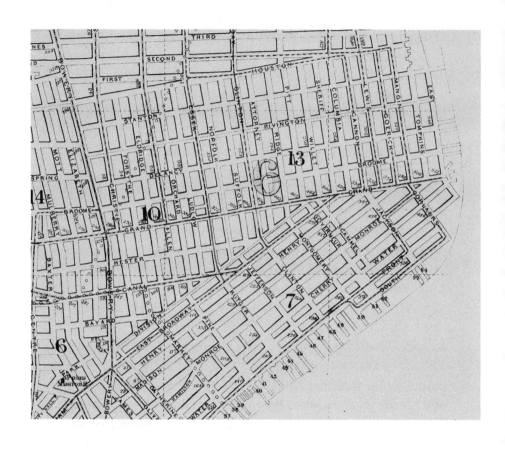

1. The Lower East Side. Source: Map of New York and Vicinity.
[New York: M. Dripps, 1867]. Library of Congress Geography
and Map Division, LC-2015591056.

learned English well in her eighteen years in America, and was thoughtful and almost eloquent in the language. There was a quiet strength about her.

Most housing that immigrants like the Edelsons and the Schatzbergs could afford was communal and offered few amenities. Life in the tenements—New York had some eighty thousand of them in 1900—was a dark, crowded, stifling affair. Several families generally crowded into spaces not designed for multiple occupancy.

Lacking central heating, the occupants relied on wood- or coal-burning stoves for heat, which made the kitchen the only warm room in winter. Summer nights could be unbearable. If the bedbugs didn't get you, the heat and humidity would. Benzene and kerosene were available to kill the vermin, but many abandoned their mattresses entirely and headed for the tenement roofs to catch whatever breeze might be blowing.

Early buildings, five-story brick structures constructed on twenty-five-foot lots, might house ten to twenty families in flats of two or three rooms, only one or two of which typically faced outside and boasted windows. A ten-by-ten-foot room was considered spacious. Toilets were outside in a tiny back-yard or in the basement, one assigned for use by the tenants on each floor. Each had two openings: a large one for adults and a smaller one for children. There was no toilet paper per se; any paper would do, and you had to bring your own. Nor were there any flush mechanisms. "Night soil," collected periodically, was dumped in the city's waterways.

If there was running water in the building at all, it would be available via a communal tap in the hallway on each floor. That enabled tenants to wash clothes indoors, first by boiling them, then by scrubbing them on a washboard, and finally by hanging them out to dry on a clothesline suspended between a window and a tall pole in the yard. Scrubbing the common stairways that led to the apartments was a shared responsibility; tenants would take turns doing it.[4]

After 1879, thanks to the efforts of social reformers, build-ers of new tenements were required to provide natural light in every room, a problem managed on New York's narrow lots with interior light wells, shafts that ran from the ground to the roof but were generally too narrow to offer much in the way of fresh air or illumination. Number 88 Monroe, the six-story, brick dwelling between Pike and Pelham Streets where the Edelsons' saloon was located, had been built with such wells in 1888, though the two-story brick walk-up where they lived was likely an earlier structure that had not.[5]

Not until 1901 did the New York State Tenement House Act mandate that new buildings be built with larger light shafts, artificial illumination in stairwells, fire escapes, and private toilets in each flat, and that old ones be retrofitted to provide at least one flush toilet for every two families. But that didn't mean all landlords complied.[6]

Storefronts occupied the ground floors of most tenements, offering baked goods, meats, groceries, and apparel for sale, and pushcarts laden with other useful merchandise lined Orchard Street, Hester Street, and several other blocks of the Lower East Side. Although the Jewish quarter was big—as the largest concentration of Jews in the world at the time and the most densely populated neighborhood in the nation, far too big for all its occupants to know one another—it was also a remarkably trusting place. Mounds of merchandise and food-stuffs might be stacked on sidewalks while the owner tended to other business, but there was little theft. "The goods outside lie within the reach of all," the *New York Sun* observed, "yet the visitor can walk through the 'ghetto' and never see man or child take so much as an apple or a plum from the piles placed so temptingly within reach."[7]

Russians and Eastern Europeans like the Schatzbergs and the Edelsons were hardly the first Jewish people America had ever seen. Jews had been in America since the seventeenth century, beginning with Sephardim from Holland and the Iberian Peninsula. They had fled poverty and persecution and sought opportunity, and although their numbers were minuscule, it had taken them little time to assimilate and achieve success in America.

2. Tenements on Orchard Street at the turn of the century.
Source: New York Public Library, Image ID: 416563.

Jews from German-speaking lands began to arrive in sizeable numbers in the 1840s, pushed out by persecution and economic hardship. Many of them settled in the Midwest, but a goodly number remained in New York, where they prospered and became Americanized. They, too, had begun life in America on the Lower East Side, but by the turn of the twentieth century many had gravitated uptown. It was they who planted Reform Judaism in America, and once established, they built synagogues like Temple Emanu-El, then an imposing Moorish revival building at Forty-Third Street and Fifth Avenue.

The Edelsons were outliers as far as immigration was concerned; the flow of Jewish arrivals from Russia and Eastern Europe did not gain momentum until the 1880s, when the Schatzbergs, followed by millions of others, crossed the sea. Between two and three million would arrive in the late nineteenth and early twentieth centuries. In 1880 Russians had accounted for only 10 percent of the Jews in America, but by 1906 their numbers had grown substantially to make them about 75 percent of the total.[8]

Economic, political, and demographic developments had conspired to push these Jews out of Europe. Poverty was a major factor in the decision, often by whole families, to leave lands in which their ancestors had dwelled for generations. Religious persecution played a role also. Official and popular antisemitism on the part of Russians, Poles, and others during the last two decades of the nineteenth century had led to pogroms, violent antisemitic riots in which Jews were murdered and their property was destroyed. Many were expelled from their villages and their occupations and had to find new livelihoods.

America was the favorite destination.

Most of New York's Russian Jews congregated on the Lower East Side of Manhattan, a quarter the *New York Sun* considered self-sufficient and self-contained, since everything its people might need could be bought from the local shops, pushcarts, and peddlers, and since it did not contain any thoroughfares vital to the life of the city. "As the famous ghetto of old Frankfurt once was walled in with structures of masonry," the paper observed, "the ghetto of modern New York is walled in with natural conditions that make it a land so unknown to the mass of the rest of the population that it might as well be in Siberia."[9]

As early as 1875 the *Sun* had taken its readers on a rather disapproving tour of that quarter. The paper saw the Jewish newcomers as a group that "have their own religious institutions, halls of learning and courts of justice." Years later, the *Forward*, one of the daily Yiddish newspapers that served the community, referred to the insular neighborhood as a "city within a city," which was not much of an exaggeration. Many sought to lead lives similar to those they had led in Europe, and make as few compromises as possible with the customs of their adopted land. They had left Russia to escape poverty and persecution, not to change their culture.[10]

These Jews would have felt entirely out of place in the uptown Reform synagogues of the German Jews. The specter of a pipe organ, or of men with heads uncovered seated together with women during worship looked for all the world like a Christian church to them, and it frankly appalled them. But the condescension was mutual. The uptown Jews saw the newcomers as paupers, beggars, and bumpkins, embarrassing throwbacks who resisted assimilation and thus threatened their own, hard-won but precarious acceptance by non-Jews. The Russians were not welcome in the German Jews' synagogues or their clubs.

Yiddish was the lingua franca of the East Side ghetto. It was the native tongue of most of the Russian, Polish, and Eastern European Jews, and those who had not spoken it in the old country learned it quickly in America. The Yiddish of the Litvaks—Jews from present-day Lithuania, Belarus, Latvia, and northeastern Poland—differed somewhat from that of the Galitzianer Jews from western Ukraine and southeastern Poland, but it was more a matter of accent than dialect. Yiddish's similarity to German also meant that Jewish newcomers not conversant in English could communicate fairly effectively with earlier arrivals from German-speaking lands. Nuance might be lost, but basic facts were relatively easily understood.

By the turn of the century, newcomers had their choice of several newspapers, each representing a distinct point of view. They mirrored ideologies that had been doing battle for some time in their native lands. The *Yidishes Tageblatt* and the *Morgen Journal* offered an Orthodox religious perspective. The *Forward* was unabashedly socialist. The *Freie Arbeiter Shtime* was an anarchist paper. For those few who preferred to get their news in English, there was also the New York–based *American Hebrew*, representing a conservative point of view; the Zionist *Jewish Exponent*, published in Philadelphia; the *American Israelite*, a Reform Jewish weekly published in Cincinnati; and the anti-Reform *Jewish Messenger*, published twice a month in New York. These latter journals, however, were far more popular among assimilated, uptown Jews than Russians or Eastern Europeans.

New York's Jewish community was too large and diverse for any one umbrella organization to play the role that the *kohol*—the governing body of a local Jewish community—had played in the towns and villages of Europe. Instead, the East Side was host to a kaleidoscope of associations that ministered to the people's spiritual, intellectual, and social needs. Apart from the congregations, there were clubs, fraternal lodges, political groups, and trade unions. And most notably, mutual aid societies called *landsmanshaftn* provided members who hailed from the same European regions with a variety of social services, such as short-term loans and proper burials for the deceased, which were expensive propositions.

Few Russian Jews arrived with much money. Even if they had saved for the trip to America, their funds were usually depleted during an arduous journey by train or wagon, or on foot to Hamburg or Bremen, for example, where they boarded New York–bound ships. There they soon discovered that if the city's streets were paved at all, it was with cobblestones rather than gold, and too often covered in horse manure.

Men and women with skills found employment easily, often in the growing ready-made garment industry. It was harder for the unskilled; sometimes they were hired fresh off the boat to work in farms or sweatshops, or brought in as scabs to toil in factories whose employees were on strike. Working conditions were typically dreadful. Overcrowded, unhealthy, and unsafe workplaces and, of course, low wages were the rule. Even working fifteen- to eighteen-hour days, most struggled to make ends meet.

Labor unions had preceded the arrival of Russian Jews, and those who entered the trades were welcomed. They represented not only those in the needle trades, but also cigar makers, typesetters, and other skilled workers. The Jewish laborers sometimes formed all-Jewish unions of their own as well, although these frequently did not outlast a strike, whether successful or not. Socialists were particularly active in organizing the new immigrants.[11]

An East Side husband, if employed, might bring home something like two dollars a day and would typically turn the entire sum over to his wife to manage the household. She might supplement it with proceeds from peddling or taking in washing or sewing; from sending a daughter to work in a sweatshop; or, commonly, from rent collected from a boarder, who would pay about fifty cents a week for a bed in a corner, a peg on which to hang his clothing, and maybe a cup of coffee in the morning.

Just over thirty cents a day would go to rent, which ran about ten dollars per month for an average flat. Food for a family of six would require fifty or sixty cents a day. Potatoes cost two cents a pound in 1902; beets fetched seven. A pound of onions cost a nickel, the same as a head of cabbage. A loaf of pumpernickel bread went for three cents; carp, a favorite, along with pike, for making gefilte fish—poached, minced fish balls—sold for a nickel a pound.

Immigrant Jewish women had more latitude than they

had had in Europe, where traditions were deeply rooted and social pressure made convention hard to ignore. It was up to them to decide how to balance tradition with the realities of life in a Christian country, and many felt the tension inherent in the position they occupied between the two worlds. Shopping for and preparing food generally fell into their bailiwick, and they were responsible for decision making in this important area.

Some, seduced by lower prices or convenience, and less susceptible to the judgments of neighbors in a small community, became lax in their piety, and in their observance of the dietary laws in particular. They might be tempted by nonkosher beef, though few likely went so far as to embrace pork. But for most, and even many who were desperately poor, certain corners simply could not be cut. They considered themselves bound by all the commandments in the Hebrew Bible, of which they counted 613. Fully twenty-six of them related to diet. By contrast, Reform Jews probably seemed to them to obey only those biblical directives that suited them.

Many Russian Jews in New York in 1902 were not only strict in their adherence to the dietary laws; they observed all the holidays and fast days on the Jewish calendar. They did no work on *Shabbos* if it could be avoided, nor did they travel or light fire on that day. Preparation for *Shabbos* began on Friday, or even Thursday. It was the busiest time of the week. Challah, a braided, glazed egg bread traditionally eaten on the Sabbath, had to be baked or purchased for a few pennies a loaf.

Cholent also made frequent appearances on *Shabbos* lunch tables. A stew consisting of some combination of meat, potatoes, onions, beans, barley, and whatever else was on hand, it was actually a solution to the conundrum posed by the prohibition against lighting a fire on the Sabbath on one hand and the desirability of eating a hot meal on the day of rest on the other. Before sundown on Friday, the ingredients would be assembled and boiled, and the pot then either brought to a local bakery and inserted into an oven still hot from baking challah, or placed on a metal plate on the stovetop at home and kept warm there. This was crock-pot cooking, 1900s-style. The dish would slow-cook over a low flame until the next day, when all the flavors had commingled into a tasty stew.

Russian and Eastern European Jewish society was both patriarchal and chauvinistic. With few exceptions, roles were assigned according to gender. Educating sons was mandatory; with daughters, it was optional. Most women had domain over their kitchens, but were not expected to play a role in public life, and most did not. It was their husbands who were the principal breadwinners, who worked outside of the home, and who joined unions and political and mutual aid associations. They were the titular heads of the household.

But anyone who took that to mean that the women were homebound, shrinking violets who deferred meekly to the authority of their spouses didn't know much about Jewish women, and *surely* hadn't met Sarah Edelson or Caroline Schatzberg. Women like them were far more influential than their husbands in important decisions that affected their families. They often shared responsibility for managing family businesses, and many were born organizers, extremely hard driving when it came to protecting and caring for their loved ones.

If life in America presented immigrant Jewish women with new challenges, it also afforded them new opportunities for involvement in the public sphere that had not been easily attainable in Europe. They were still primarily mothers and wives, but many worked at home or helped run family enterprises, and these had contact with the larger community. Many of their daughters had begun to work outside the home in tenement sweatshops or in factories. Labor unions opened their ranks to them, as did political organizations peddling ideologies from socialism to anarchism to Zionism. Americanization was a slow process that affected some more rapidly than others, but it offered numerous possibilities for growth and change, and for life beyond the four walls of depressing tenement apartments.

The big news in the spring of 1902, with the Passover holiday just around the corner, was that the price of kosher meat had skyrocketed. A pound of *flanken,* or short ribs, which had cost twelve cents only a few months earlier, had risen a whopping 50 percent and was now selling for eighteen cents. Sarah and Caroline and other Lower East Side *balebostes*—housewives—had been feeling the pinch for months, but 1902 saw a sudden, most unwelcome spike. Eighteen cents a pound, for many families struggling to make ends meet, was simply beyond reach.

Since eating cheaper, nonkosher meat was out of the question, choices were few. What would happen if kosher meat became unaffordable, which was where it seemed to be heading, was everybody's worry. And anybody's guess.

2

Greater Power Than Ten Standard Oil Companies

The wave of immigration that brought Sarah Edelson and Caroline Schatzberg to America was unlike anything the country had ever seen. Whether seeking economic opportunity, fleeing persecution, or both, nearly twelve million men, women, and children—the vast majority of them Europeans—found their way to America's shores between 1871 and 1901. This was more than had arrived in the previous three centuries combined. And New York is where most landed and many remained.[1]

Before the Civil War, America had been predominantly rural, but by 1880 the northeast was already majority urban, and the whole country would follow suit before 1920. The changes were palpable and profound, and you didn't have to venture much beyond New York's Lower East Side to appreciate them. Culturally, the Jewish immigrants were only one strand in the tapestry. They lived cheek by jowl with Italian, Polish, German, Irish, Chinese, and African-American people in the crowded tenements, managing to coexist despite profound differences in language, culture, and customs.

Politically, the long arm of Tammany Hall, the corrupt Democratic political machine that controlled New York politics, was very much in evidence as it doled out jobs, food, fuel, and money to newcomers in exchange for their ballots. Or, if your tastes ran to socialism, communism, or even anarchism, you could find like-minded people at a political rally on the East Side nearly every week. Some Jews had already had a taste of these ideologies in the old country and remained passionately committed to them.

Economically, the rapid development of industry was evident from the proliferation of factories in which men labored for paltry wages and sweatshops that gave young women piecework in the garment industry. And vibrant commercial development was everywhere: in East Side saloons like Joel Edelson's Monroe Palace; in the shops of tailors like Caroline Schatzberg's late husband; or among the butchers, fishmongers, cutlers, bakers, haberdashers, grocers, and pharmacists of the quarter. One step lower down the ladder were the pushcart vendors and the door-to-door peddlers who hawked everything from fruits, vegetables, and pickles to combs, pins, thread, scissors, watches, and knives.

As America's cities industrialized—New York, the largest of them, grew from 1.7 million souls in 1870 to 4.3 million in 1900—so did their need for raw materials like steel, oil, and, of course, food. To meet demand, cities had to reach beyond their immediate hinterlands. Supplies had to come from other parts of the country where they were mined, grown, or fabricated. Fortunately, urban growth after the Civil War went hand in hand with the construction of a national rail network. And this not only served the cities, it also shaped them.

The first transcontinental railroad, completed in 1869 thanks in large part to the toil of Chinese immigrant laborers, shaved travel time between New York and California from six months to a week. But it was only the beginning of the story. By the turn of the century, railroad companies, aided by land grants from the federal government, had multiplied fourfold the forty-five thousand miles of track that had existed in 1871. New locomotives rushed goods from one coast to the other at the previously unheard of speed of one hundred miles per hour, a fact that essentially turned the entire nation into a ready source of supply for its urban areas.

It's hard to overstate the profound changes this national rail network brought. It expedited the settlement of the West and served growing urban populations in the Midwest and the East. It tied the countryside more closely to the cities. And it created something entirely new: a unified, national market.[2]

In so doing, the rails not only provided a foundation for development of new businesses; they also enabled the scaling up of traditionally local industries to levels theretofore unseen. Beginning in the 1870s, for example, industrialist John D. Rockefeller transformed his oil refining partnership into a dominant position in the industry by buying up competitors, sometimes drastically lowering his prices to force them to sell out, and then absorbing them or closing them down. By the 1880s he had merged several dozen properties and affiliates into the Standard Oil Trust, a holding company that used economies of scale aggressively to set prices and dominate the industry.

Rockefeller soon controlled nearly 90 percent of the nation's petroleum business and was the largest shipper of oil and kerosene in the country. Standard Oil was such a large customer, and was so dominant in the marketplace, that railroads bent over backwards to compete for its business. And Rockefeller, in turn, used his market power to pressure them for secret, preferential shipping rates in the form of rebates.

Standard Oil made Rockefeller the richest man in the world. It was the first of the great corporate trusts, which were essentially arrangements whereby corporations in the same or related industries were centrally controlled or coordinated for the purpose of monopolizing a market. Their goal was to eliminate, or at least neutralize, competition.

The vast expansion of railroads increased demand for steel—for tracks and for trains, but also bridges and buildings. Here, too, one man came to dominate an industry. Andrew Carnegie made a fortune in steel through technological advances and vertical integration. By the late 1880s he became the world's largest manufacturer of pig iron, steel rails, and coke. In 1901 he was bought out by J. Pierpont Morgan, who incorporated his holdings into United States Steel, another major industrial trust.

Trusts emerged in many industries and used their market power to eliminate competition in myriad ways, some legal, some clearly not. They lowered prices to hurt competitors and then bought competitors' assets at bargain prices. They entered into noncompete agreements to divide markets and set prices that did not fluctuate according to supply and demand. They forced unfavorable terms on customers and extorted rebates from suppliers. They developed complex legal structures to make their methods impervious to public scrutiny. They bought off members of Congress to secure favorable legislation. And, when other methods failed, some employed intimidation and violence to get their way.

Charles Darwin's theories of evolution had been pressed into service to describe these distinctly nonbiological activities of men like Rockefeller and Carnegie, who came to be called "robber barons." But was survival of the fittest the way the American experiment ought to play out? The rise of the trusts helped spawn a backlash in the Progressive movement, which emerged in the late nineteenth century and whose advocates rejected social Darwinism. Progressives believed government had an important role to play in improving society, solving social problems, protecting consumers, and reigning in the excesses of unbridled capitalism. They felt sure government could and should help solve the vexing social problems caused by industrialization, urbanization, and corruption.[3]

One key area that came under their scrutiny was the treatment of the labor force. Little of the wealth generated by the trusts—or, for that matter, other businesses—trickled down to workers, who had precious little power to wield in their relationships with employers. Long hours, unsafe working conditions, and low wages were the rule, and with the supply of labor growing by leaps and bounds, individual workers were viewed as expendable. Business had little incentive to ameliorate dangerous working conditions or even to pay a living wage.

Since the laws provided little protection for workers, it fell to them to stand up for themselves through collective bargaining. Strikes in America dated to the eighteenth century, but it was not until the second half of the nineteenth that the nation would see the rapid rise of trade unions. Individual unions formed, sometimes around a strike, and these, in turn, often affiliated with national umbrella organizations such as the Federation of Organized Trade and Labor Unions and the American Federation of Labor. The unions pushed—and struck—for recognition and for such improvements as safer working conditions, standard and higher wages, shorter hours, and overtime pay.

The federal government did little to advance the cause of laborers during this period, but intense public resentment fueled by the Progressives did lead Congress to pass two pieces of landmark antitrust legislation within three years of each other. The first, enacted in 1887, was the Interstate Commerce Act. It was aimed squarely at the railroads, which had themselves become a trust, consolidating and cooperating to divide traffic and gain control over shipping rates to the detriment of those dependent on them to get their goods to market.[4]

The act drew its authority from the commerce clause of the Constitution, which reserved for Congress the power to regulate trade among the states. It made railroads the first private industry subject to federal regulation. It aimed to level the playing field between large and small shippers by requiring shipping rates to be "reasonable and just," mandating that the railroads publicize them and forbidding price discrimination based on length of the haul or volume shipped. It established the nation's first independent regulatory body, the Interstate Commerce Commission, which was charged with ensuring the railroads' compliance.

A second law, passed in 1890, was the Sherman Antitrust Act, Congress's first effort at outlawing monopolistic business practices. It prohibited not only monopolies, but trusts, in which the business decisions of separately owned companies were centrally coordinated to hinder or prevent competition across state or international borders. The Sherman Act was fuzzy on some important distinctions—between mergers and trusts and between large corporations and monopolies, for example—but despite its flaws, it authorized the federal government to sue trusts in order to dissolve them.[5]

Agricultural producers were not immune to becoming cartels or monopolies, and the first significant legal case the government prosecuted under the Sherman Act was actually about sugar. But unlike steel and oil, food was often resistant to scaling up, in large part because so little of it could be hauled long distances and stay fresh, and so it remained a local industry as cities fed themselves with nearby agricultural products. This, of course, meant that consumers were hostage to the calendar; produce was available only in season.

All of that began to change, however, with the invention in 1872 of refrigerated boxcars. Suddenly fruit could be brought to New York from California in perfect condition and vegetables could make their way from the temperate south even in wintertime, all with minimal spoilage. New Yorkers could eat the same produce as Floridians at more or less the same time, at low prices due to economies of scale.

And cattle could be slaughtered in one city and its meat sold in another.

Because the land in the southwest and far west was suitable for grazing but not especially arable, those areas of the country became dominant cattle producers. But the fertile Midwest was where hay and corn grew, and so cattle were transported there to be fattened for sale. This is how the cities of the region—Chicago, Kansas City, St. Louis, and others—became the nation's principal cattle markets. Livestock was shipped there to be readied for sale and purchased by the meat packing houses.[6]

The biggest consumer markets, however, were back East, and it was the advent of the refrigerator car that permitted Chicago to become what writer Carl Sandburg famously labeled the "hog butcher for the world." Regular trains could transport live animals, but it took cold cars to ship carcasses long distances. Strategically situated, with multiple rails con-

3. Leaders of the Beef Trust. From left, Gustavus Swift, Philip Armour and George Hammond. Not pictured: Nelson Morris. Sources: Wikipedia (Swift and Armour), Historic Detroit (Hammond).

necting it with points east and west, Chicago emerged as the nexus of the meat industry. Well into the twentieth century, its Union Stockyards, which had opened in 1865, processed more meat than any other place on earth.[7]

As beneficial as the new boxcars were for fruit and vegetable producers, who now had access to vast new markets, they affected no industry more profoundly than meat packing. Cattle had to be fed and watered on long trips; meat didn't. It did have to be kept cool, so the new cars required the railroads to set up icing stations at various points along their routes to refresh the cars. But there was no arguing with the economics: the cost was more than made up for by the profits. A fifteen-hundred-pound steer could lose as much as two hundred pounds during the journey from Chicago to New York, and under the stress of long journeys, some 6 percent of cattle, on average, died in transit, something that was not a problem with carcasses. These took up far less space than live steers and contained much less in the way of unusable body parts.[8]

Slaughtering of East Coast–bound cattle in Chicago caused some abattoirs in New York to shut down, but it made the midwestern companies even more profitable, putting them in a position to invest heavily in this new technology. Five rose to prominence in the second half of the nineteenth century, each the creation of a gifted businessman. What John

D. Rockefeller was to petroleum and what Andrew Carnegie and J. P. Morgan were to steel, Gustavus Franklin Swift, Philip Danforth Armour, George H. Hammond, Nelson Morris, and Michael Cudahy became to meat packing.

Swift was not the actual inventor of the refrigerator car, but it was one of his engineers who came up with the design of a rail car with ice tanks, ventilators, and insulated sides, bottoms, and tops. Grasping its potential immediately, he financed the world's first line of cold cars. Armour followed Swift's lead and built the Armour Refrigerator Line into the nation's largest private refrigerator car fleet.[9]

Hammond set up a cold car production line in the early 1870s in the Indiana city that bears his name. When he died in 1886 the G. H. Hammond Company owned more than eight hundred such cars and slaughtered and shipped one hundred thousand head of cattle a year. Morris, born in Germany to a Jewish family, had gotten rich by supplying meat to the Union Army during the Civil War. His corporation boasted nearly a hundred branches across the country by the turn of the century. And Cudahy, sometimes considered a member of this group, set up a packing plant in South Omaha, Nebraska, with Armour's backing, eventually buying out Armour entirely.[10]

A "gentleman's agreement" among these large packing houses, run by their founders or their close relatives, made them a formidable force in the marketplace. Collectively, they became known as the Beef Trust, a term that entered the nation's lexicon in 1888, though it operated so much in the shadows that exactly *which* companies composed it depended on who was doing the accusing. Most of the time the alliance was referred to as the Big Four, or the Big Five if Cudahy was included. Sometimes, however, Schwarzschild & Sulzberger, a New York-based, German Jewish–owned concern that had expanded westward in the 1890s, was also counted, and it was the Big Six that came under scrutiny.

In addition to developing efficient slaughtering operations and monetizing meat byproducts, all the important slaughterhouses bought their own refrigerator cars as, eventually, did the railroads themselves. And it was the financial arrangements that came to govern the use of these vehicles, as much as the technology that permitted their development, that allowed these companies to prosper.

Because of stiff competition, the rails did not initially charge extra for the use of cold cars, just the normal rates for freight. Soon, however, they began assessing nominal charges for replenishing the ice along any given route. This added cost to the shippers, who, in turn, figured out a way to use their collective might to push back. They demanded what was euphemistically called a "private car charge" of three quarters of a cent per mile for the *privilege* of hauling their cars. And to the rails, it was a privilege that could be revoked at their peril. Any line that did not cooperate would soon find that the shippers had made other arrangements with its competitors and left it out in the cold, so to speak.

The railroads' published rates remained the same, which permitted them to pretend to be charging a flat rate to all comers. But they offered rebates to select customers, remitted as secret kickbacks, though over time their existence became an open secret. Small competitors of the large packing houses, many of which had no refrigerator cars of their own and were forced to use the railroads' cars, were offered no such concessions, which meant that their operating costs were higher than those of the Big Six. This, in turn, made it difficult for them to compete. Some went belly up; others were gobbled up at bargain prices by the midwestern packers, whose control over the marketplace grew with each acquisition.

As they were cornering the market, the members of the Beef Trust were also doing all they could to suppress the prices they paid for livestock. They accomplished this by fixing prices and agreeing not to compete against one another. At the various stockyards of the Midwest, if the agents of one company offered a price to a cattle producer, no other firm would offer anything different. And cattlemen who made the mistake of selling to independent buyers would find that no Trust company would do business with them again.

The Beef Trust achieved market domination by positioning itself between the cattle raisers and the consumers and pickpocketing both. Contemporary muckraking journalist Charles Edward Russell described it as promising "greater fortunes and greater power than ten Standard Oil Companies." It was so successful that by the turn of the century, New Yorkers were getting most of their meat from its Chicago slaughterhouses.[11]

But not Sarah Edelson or Caroline Schatzberg. Whatever cut of beef these women planned to put on their Passover tables in the spring of 1902, the steer from which it came would likely be handled by one of the Trust companies and come to New York on a train. But it was a sure bet it would make the journey alive.

3

The Conscience of an Orthodox Jew Is Absolute

The pressure the Beef Trust put on cattle prices, coupled with the efficiencies of its giant packing plants and the rebates it extorted from the railroads, meant that beef butchered in Chicago could be sold more cheaply in Manhattan than that killed locally. Western-dressed beef thus came to fill most of New York's needs quite handily. Carcasses were delivered to storage houses in Manhattan and New Jersey, where they awaited sale and delivery to city butchers. By 1902 nearly two-thirds of the beef sold in New York had been slaughtered before it arrived.

The market for that last third had three important components. The first consisted of high-end hotels like the Waldorf, the Holland House, and the Hotel Manhattan, as well as the city's finer dining establishments, where quality and freshness trumped price. Western-dressed beef might sit in the cooler of a midwestern slaughterhouse for three or four days before transport. It took two or three *more* days to get to the East Coast. Even then it might hang in a storage locker in Weehawken or Jersey City for a week or more before being ferried across the Hudson River for final sale. And some of it was treated with boric acid, a preservative, to make it appear fresher than it actually was. It was far easier to guarantee the freshness of "city-dressed beef," as New Yorkers called the locally killed variety. And that's what mattered most to the upper class diners at the Waldorf, for whom an extra two to four cents a pound for choice cuts was not a consideration.[1]

The second market for such beef was the international one. The New York Central Railroad maintained stockyards at Sixtieth Street and the Hudson River for livestock bound for Europe, principally England. Some foreign-bound cattle, shipped on the hoof from the Midwest, came from holding pens in New Jersey. It would be loaded onto ships for Liverpool, London, and Hull and ports on the continent.

The third and largest component of the market for cattle brought to New York alive was the Jewish community.

One of the many rules governing kosher meat, apart from the species of the animal and the method of slaughter permitted, mandated that no more than seventy-two hours elapse between the killing of an animal and the *kashering*—soaking and salting—of its flesh, a final purification procedure generally performed in the home during this era, designed to drain it of all vestiges of blood. This was because after that interval, blood becomes too congealed to extract.

For this reason, the Orthodox—the majority of New York's estimated 585,000 Jews in 1902—could not avail themselves of western-dressed beef. Even if it were properly slaughtered in Chicago by qualified, observant Jews, it simply took too long to get to their kitchens for New Yorkers to render it kosher. A secondary factor was that keeping track of meat that changed hands many times over a long distance was difficult, and the risk of forbidden meat being substituted for the kosher variety, whether accidentally or deliberately, was substantial. Locally slaughtered kosher meat had a far shorter chain of custody between supplier and consumer, and was thus more likely to be the genuine article.[2]

The lion's share of the animals that would become city-dressed beef, whether for the kosher market or otherwise, were purchased in Chicago or Kansas City, brought in by rail, and delivered to the Jersey stockyards. Because the journey took a toll on the animals, they were permitted a day of rest before being inspected by government officials and sold at auction. Buyers for the wholesalers would journey from New York to examine and bid on them while they were

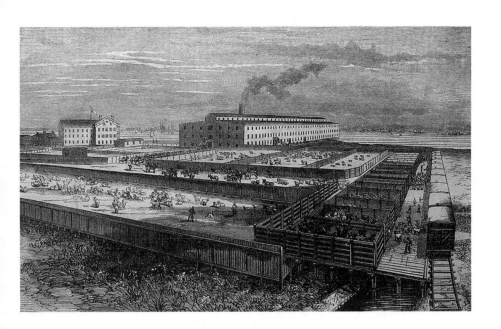

4. The Communipaw Stockyards at Jersey City, New Jersey.
Source: *Frank Leslie's Illustrated Newspaper*, November 17, 1866.

still in the pens. Those chosen would be tagged and driven aboard double-decker barges and unloaded on Manhattan's or Brooklyn's shores.[3]

The next stop for most of them was one of Manhattan's East River slaughterhouses. The two dominant concerns were located on First Avenue between East Forty-Third and East Forty-Sixth Street. Schwarzschild & Sulzberger occupied two city blocks and United Dressed Beef Company was immediately south of it. Both establishments backed up to the river, facilitating the transfer of livestock from the barges. A third wholesaler, Joseph Stern & Sons, was located at Thirty-Ninth Street on the Hudson. All of these engaged in both regular *and* kosher slaughter, and all were owned and operated by Jews of German extraction.

At United Dressed Beef, about three thousand steers were killed each week, fully 80 percent of them in the kosher manner. At Schwarzschild & Sulzberger, the number was thirty-five hundred per week, but there only about a third of the cattle were slaughtered according to Jewish law.[4]

Ritual slaughter could be undertaken only by a *shoychet*, a pious and usually burly Jewish butcher with a steady hand. He would have learned the codes of Jewish law pertaining to kosher meat and apprenticed as well. In the old country he would have been accredited and appointed by the chief rabbi of a community; in New York, most any Orthodox rabbi might do. In Europe, he would work under the supervision of a *mashgiach*, a rabbinical inspector, who represented the community rabbi and was vested with broad responsibilities over all types of food, not just meat. In America, however, the *shoychet* might work independently and be paid a flat salary by the slaughterhouse. To avoid corruption, he was not to profit from the volume of cattle he killed.[5]

A non-Jewish slaughterer might strike a steer on its head with an axe to stun it before dispatching it, but such a method was forbidden to a *shoychet* for two reasons. First, because an animal had to be without blemish, broken bones, or wounds to be kosher. And second, because a single stroke

The Conscience of an Orthodox Jew

5. A turn-of-the-century postcard view of Manhattan's East River slaughterhouses. Schwarzschild & Sulzberger occupied two city blocks and United Dressed Beef Company shared the block immediately to the south. The United Nations currently stands on this land.
Courtesy of Curt Gathje.

of a sharp knife was believed to be the quickest way to render a beast senseless, and therefore the most humane means of slaughter available. It was also considered a more hygienic method.

Of vital importance to the *shoychet*'s craft, therefore, was a razor-sharp, blunt-nosed steel knife about two feet in length. Once an animal had been selected—and the *shoychet* was bound to reject any that appeared unhealthy—ropes looped around both horns and the legs and run through a ring on the wall or the floor would be tightened slowly to coax it down until its head and shoulder touched the floor. A muzzle would then be placed over its snout and its neck would be bent sideways. In the meantime, the *shoychet* would run his fingernail over the edge of the knife to ensure there were no notches or rough patches on the blade, which might tear the flesh and add to the animal's suffering. Any imperfections would have to be ground out on a sharpening stone before he could proceed.

Once satisfied the blade was razor sharp and completely smooth, he would splash water across the animal's throat, recite a Hebrew blessing and then slash its windpipe, cutting the trachea and esophagus in a single stroke. Any interruption in this motion would immediately render the animal *treyf*, or unacceptable. The cut would cause both the carotid artery and the jugular vein to bleed profusely, sending the animal immediately into shock. The rapid loss of blood was understood to cause the beast to lose consciousness within two or three seconds.

After the animal had bled out, it would be hung from a hook for examination of its entrails. A second, shorter knife was used for disemboweling. If posthumous inspection of the heart, lungs, liver, or other vital organs revealed any foreign bodies or any hint of disease, the animal would be rejected and the carcass diverted to be sold as regular city-dressed beef or, in extreme cases, presumably discarded. The lungs were examined especially carefully for any sort of pleural disease, and in case of doubt were removed, bathed in water,

The Conscience of an Orthodox Jew

and inflated by mouth to reveal any subtle abnormalities. If they held air, the animal would be considered kosher.

Only about 65 percent of the cattle killed passed this internal inspection. Of those that did, only about a third of the meat on their carcasses—the forequarters as far as the thirteenth bone of the rib cage, including the breast, shoulder, and the first four ribs—might be certified as kosher. The hindquarters, although technically edible, were typically branded as *treyf.*

This rule proceeded from chapter 32 of Genesis, in which Jacob wrestles with an angel of God and suffers damage to his hip and thigh, interpreted as his sciatic nerve. Jewish law insisted that kosher meat not contain certain blood vessels or nerves, which had to be plucked out by hand. It was difficult enough to do this to the forequarters of the animal, but especially tedious—and not cost-effective in America, at least—to do it to the rear parts, which contained more tough, fibrous tissue and multiple small veins. Not for New York's Orthodox Jews were the porterhouse steaks or the tenderloins. In principle, even this part of the steer *could* be made kosher with enough effort, and sometimes had been in Europe, but in America it was far more expedient to sell it to non-Jewish consumers as regular, city-dressed beef.

The entire process was thus one of winnowing out so-called unclean meat. Obviously unhealthy animals were excluded at the start. Fully 35 percent of those slaughtered by *shoychtim* were classified as unkosher. Only the forequarters of the 65 percent that passed inspection could qualify, and even that meat was reduced in weight by as much as a fifth by the process of draining blood and removing bones, sinews, and forbidden fats. What this meant, in practice, was that nearly 80 percent of the meat of those animals slaughtered according to Jewish law had to be sold to gentiles, nonobservant Jews, or nonkosher sausage factories, or else discarded.

Naturally, this made kosher beef more expensive than other city-dressed beef, which itself cost a penny a pound (or an average of seven to eight dollars per carcass) more than Chicago-killed beef because it was shipped on the hoof. Kosher slaughter added another penny a pound to defray the salaries of the slaughterers and supervisors, who took home anywhere from eighteen to twenty-five dollars per week ($530 to $730 in today's currency). But this did not dissuade observant Jewish consumers, who were compelled by their religious beliefs to buy it if they wanted meat on the table. Nor did it deter a smaller number of non-Jews who preferred it because they believed it cleaner and more wholesome than other available meat.[6]

After a carcass was declared kosher, a seal bearing the signature of the *shoychet* and the date of slaughter was affixed to it. This served as a guarantee to local butchers that the meat on it was properly killed, and a signal as to how much time had passed since then. Then it would be shunted off into a cooler and hung, neck down, and stored with others at thirty-six degrees Fahrenheit. Later in the day, the forequarters would be severed from the rest of the carcass and prepared for sale and delivery to the kosher markets.

The next link in the chain was the retail kosher butchers. In 1902 there were an estimated six hundred of them in Manhattan, Brooklyn, and the Bronx. Typically, they would tend to their customers in the morning and visit the slaughterhouse coolers early in the afternoon to select their purchases, though the abattoirs also sent salesmen to visit those who couldn't spare the time to make the trip. Different grades of meat fetched different prices. If more than one butcher set his sights on a particular animal, a bidding war might ensue.[7]

Given the time pressure imposed by the fixed interval between slaughter and final preparation, the slaughterhouses' salesmen had a strong incentive to sell all kosher beef on the day the animal was killed. Meat left over from the day before was still marketable, but older carcasses had to be sold at a discount of a few cents a pound.

The industry was also prey to speculators, who generally got to the wholesalers earlier than the butchers and bought up the choice carcasses. Retail butchers, finding the best

The Conscience of an Orthodox Jew

grades already sold, were then faced with the choice of buying poorer quality meat from the wholesalers or paying a few cents a pound more to speculators, whom they resented very much.

Once a sale was made, a tag noting the name and address of the customer was affixed to the carcass and notice of the sale would be sent to the credit department for approval. Butchers, often cash-poor, were granted a two- to three-day grace period to enable them to use proceeds from the resale of meat to reimburse the slaughterhouse, but only if they were in good standing. If not, it was strictly cash on the barrel. Those retailers with their own trucks might haul away their purchases; meat would be delivered to others by the wholesalers' or speculators' wagons, often in the wee hours when the stores were closed. This required a measure of trust, because it necessitated letting the deliveryman know where the key to the shop was kept. He would be permitted to enter the store and place the cargo in the butcher's icebox.[8]

Most killing for the kosher trade took place on Fridays and Mondays. Because the *shoychtim* couldn't work on the Jewish Sabbath and the retail kosher markets were closed during the daytime on Saturdays for religious reasons and all day on Sundays because of state law, Friday was a high-volume day. Friday-slaughtered meat was delivered after sundown on Saturday, when demand among Jewish households was high for late Saturday and Sunday consumption. Retailers took care not to order too much of it, however, because if it was not sold by Monday night the window between slaughter and *kashering* would have closed. Hence Mondays marked another big slaughter day for the kosher market.

The task of the retail butchers was to extract bone and gristle from the meat, and of course to chop it into the various cuts that the forequarters of the beast provided. Most of those in New York in 1902 were located on the Lower East Side, often several to a block. Some sold both kosher and unkosher meat, and if they did, had to be trusted to keep them separate. If not, they would not be able to build lasting relationships with local Jewish women, who made up most of their customers and who, if they kept kosher homes, would not dream of serving *treyf* meat to their families.

Poultry, more expensive than beef, traveled a different route. Most of that consumed in New York was raised within a radius of a couple of hundred miles from the city. Wholesalers brought it by truck into town, where it was slaughtered by *shoychtim* and sold by local butchers. Because of the popularity of chicken as a Sabbath meal, the biggest business day of the week for kosher poultry was Thursday. The wholesaler would endeavor to get it to the retail butcher while the body was still warm, as the women of the Lower East Side much preferred to purchase just-killed fowl. In 1902 kosher chicken fetched anywhere from eighteen to twenty-five cents a pound.[9]

No particular rule governed the killing of fish; there was just an absolute restriction against eating any aquatic creature without both fins and scales. The shops and pushcarts on Hester Street sold fish at anywhere between eighteen and thirty cents a pound, with pike commanding the highest prices. Haggling with the vendors was de rigueur.[10]

"The conscience of an orthodox Jew is absolute when it comes to kosher meat," a First Avenue butcher told the *New York Tribune*. By this he meant that observant Jews would not accept any short cuts in this area. Jewish housewives typically chose butchers who were observant themselves; no one would buy from one who did not follow the religious laws in his personal life. He would be expected to belong to a synagogue, attend services regularly, and, of course, keep a strictly kosher home.[11]

Most of New York's kosher butcher shops were small affairs that required relatively modest investment. Expenses included rent, wages (a typical butcher needed an assistant), utilities, ice, packaging materials, delivery charges, and, of course, wholesale meat and poultry. A chopping block and a few benches were the only furniture necessary. Equipment included knives, cleavers, and saws; a cash register, a scale, a grinder, paper for wrapping purchases; and an icebox, usu-

The Conscience of an Orthodox Jew

6. A typical turn-of-the-century New York kosher butcher shop.
Pictured behind the counter are butchers Abraham (*left*)
and Max Farber. Source: Old NYC Photos.

ally located in the rear of the store. Poultry, cuts of beef, and organs would often be suspended from hooks and displayed in a shop window. The benches were used for extracting forbidden parts and trimming meat to the customer's specifications; the block was necessary for chopping thicker, bone-in cuts. A typical establishment was long on functionality and short on ambience.[12]

Lower East Side women typically patronized butcher shops within walking distance of their homes, often on the same block. They bought meat frequently and in small quantities; economies of scale from larger purchases were out of reach for most, not only because of a shortage of cash, but also a lack of iceboxes. The bond between the butcher and the housewife was an important one: there had to be trust, and there often had to be credit as well. Good customers known to the shopkeeper could maintain accounts and pay for purchases later. Uncollected debts put pressure on butchers' balance sheets, but extending credit was absolutely necessary for many to stay in business, because so many of their customers lived payday to payday.

One more hurdle had to be cleared before meat was considered fit to eat. When a Jewish housewife like Sarah Edelson bought a rib roast or a piece of poultry from her butcher, she had to *kasher* the meat by soaking it in water for half an hour and then sprinkling it with coarse salt—known today as "kosher salt"—to rid it of impurities and residual blood. Then, and *only* then, could she cook it and serve it to her family.

The rules governing kosher meat were matters of religious law, and the Orthodox Jews of the Lower East Side were served by providers who were themselves observant people.

But this, alas, did not mean that corners were never cut.

The Conscience of an Orthodox Jew

4

Each One Is an Authority unto Himself

If this system of devout Hebrews in New York City strictly discharging their duty to their fellow Jews to produce and sell kosher meat sounds like a well-oiled machine programmed to do God's work, it was actually anything but.

As early as 1863 an anonymous letter in the *Jewish Messenger*, a weekly Orthodox newspaper, had decried the lack of supervision over the *shoychtim*. The system was corrupt, the author asserted, and as a result, many Jews who thought they were obeying the dietary laws were, in fact, not eating kosher meat at all.

At the time, there were a dozen or so Jewish slaughterhouses in the city and the *shoychtim*, the paper complained, "are neither authorized by the congregations nor by the ministers." Although some were certified in Europe before they emigrated, they were never re-examined to determine whether they remained competent. The only judgment of their proficiency was made by those in the meat business who paid them, people with a vested interest in keeping the price of meat high and who didn't ask too many questions. It was to their benefit for the slaughterers to bend the rules because kosher meat fetched higher prices.

The solution, the writer asserted, lay in cooperation among the Orthodox congregations, which were urged to band together and select two or three local rabbis to supervise the slaughterers on a rotating basis. If paid by their congregations and not by the butchers or the slaughterhouses, they would have only the interests of their fellow Jews at heart, and would lack incentive to look the other way if they detected transgressions.[1]

Nothing happened, however, and not much had changed sixteen years later when the *Messenger* itself called for a solution. If anything, the situation had gotten worse. "Uncleanliness, over-charges, incapacity, roguery have combined to render suspicious nearly every butcher who hangs out the sign '*kosher*,'" it complained. "Our own self-respect and sense of duty should lead us to unite in a movement to uphold the purity and Jewish character of our households."[2]

But self-respect and sense of duty were in short supply. Hungarian-born Rabbi Moses Weinberger, in a dark portrayal of Jewish life in New York written for his fellow Orthodox Jews in 1887, had a lot to say about problems with the local kosher meat supply. Since the *shoychtim* were engaged by the slaughterhouses, there was no religious authority to ensure quality control over who was hired, as there might have been had the synagogues engaged the men directly. Some were reputable slaughterers who had been vetted in Europe, but others had been removed from office there and decided to start anew in America, where their pasts would not follow them. Still others were simply poorly schooled in ritual law. And in America, nobody supervised them.

Then, too, the relationship between the slaughterers and the retail butchers was often fraught. "Not a day goes by without screams and quarrels between *shoychtim* and butchers," Weinberger wrote. "Each side composes and spreads libelous documents about the other, stinging and battling, while Israel looks on, its sight failing, helpless."

Weinberger was equally critical of retail butchers, many of whom he was certain were corrupt. "There are those who are not embarrassed to take improperly slaughtered meat and to sell it publicly to innocent people, notwithstanding the fact that their stores are anointed in huge, gilded letters with the words 'KOSHER MEAT,'" he wrote. And some split

Each Is an Authority unto Himself

the difference, selling properly killed *flanken* but at the same time passing unkosher organ meat off as kosher.[3]

It wasn't as if kosher meat production in the old country had been immune to fraud or corruption, but there misbehavior had been more easily controlled. Civil authorities in many Eastern European countries had delegated legal responsibility for Jewish affairs to the *kohol*, or governing body, which was therefore in a position to penalize transgressions with fines, excommunication, and even corporal punishment.[4]

When a *kohol* paid a slaughterer a fixed salary that did not fluctuate with the kosher meat yield from the animals he killed, and when it forbade him from participating financially in the meat trade, his incentive for corruption was diminished, if not removed entirely. And when it possessed the authority to punish him, he thought twice about skirting the rules.[5]

But the *kohol* system had never taken root in New York. The city was simply too big, and its Jewish community too numerous and too balkanized. The system that had served smaller Jewish communities in Europe well would not do in Manhattan. But to several Orthodox congregations on the Lower East Side, that did not mean that a chief rabbi could not bring order to the out-of-control slaughtering business. Jews in Britain had appointed such a man in the 1840s, and the idea had been raised in America before. In mid-1879 it had looked as if it might come to fruition when several congregations raised funds and recruited a noted Eastern European talmudist, but he had declined and the effort had come to naught.[6]

Another attempt was made in 1887 after the death of the rabbi of the Beis Hamidrash HaGadol, the Orthodox shul that had been established in 1852. That congregation took the lead in founding an Association of American Orthodox Hebrew Congregations that consisted of itself and seventeen other Russian and Eastern European synagogues on the East Side. Money was pledged and a new search was organized.

The perceived need for a chief rabbi was actually about much more than the chaos reigning in kosher slaughter. Orthodox Judaism, Eastern European style, was not standing up as well to the pressures of life in America as many wished, and some of its leaders were feeling besieged. The children of the Orthodox were becoming Americanized and beginning to eschew many traditions. The Reform Judaism favored by many uptown German Jews offered an alternative, if alarming, model. So, for some, did secularism.

Even within the Orthodox community there was little discipline. Tiny congregations—*shtieblach*—sprang up and then dissolved into factions. Many were lay led and could not afford rabbis, who were desirable, but not necessary, for formal Jewish worship, where a quorum of ten men sufficed. And even where there *were* rabbis, few commanded the respect enjoyed by those in the old country. Because Jewish law was not binding in America, their decisions could safely be ignored by any who chose not to recognize their authority. Some were unqualified for their positions. There were even occasional charlatans among them.[7]

A new chief rabbi might unify at least the "downtown" Jews, represent them to the larger community, oversee Jewish education for the young and preside over a *beis din*, or religious court, to adjudicate disagreements. But it was clear his principal task would be to bring order to the system of *kashrus*— dietary laws—and this was written into his job description: "His mission would be to remove the stumbling blocks from before our people and to unite the hearts of our brethren, the house of Israel, to serve God with one heart and soul, and to supervise with an open eye the *shoychtim* and all other matters of holiness to the House of Israel, which to our deep sorrow are not observed nor respected, because there is no authority nor guide revered and accepted by the whole community, and each one is an authority unto himself."[8]

In 1887 the Association of American Orthodox Hebrew Congregations recruited a European luminary to assume the newly created position of Chief Rabbi of New York. Jacob

Each Is an Authority unto Himself

Joseph of Vilna (Vilnius) was a well-regarded talmudic scholar, but one who had amassed substantial debt. He was offered a six-year term at the princely salary of $2,500 per year—about $66,000 in today's currency—plus a large apartment and a travel allowance for himself and his family. Joseph was amenable if he were granted a signing bonus that would permit him to settle his obligations before he left Europe.[9]

There was much excitement on the Lower East Side on July 7, 1888, when the ss *Aller* docked at Hoboken, New Jersey, with forty-eight-year-old Rabbi Joseph on board. But it was *Shabbos*, and so the reception committee from the association, in their best black suits and tall silk hats, had to bide their time until sundown before the learned man would disembark. They themselves had arrived from Manhattan before dusk on Friday to avoid forbidden travel on the Sabbath.

At nearly 10:00 p.m., well after the sun had safely set, a compact, bright-eyed man with a full beard and a winning smile appeared alone. He had left his family behind until he was certain his decision to come was a sound one. The streets were lined with people who had assembled to welcome him as he was escorted to a hotel for prayers and subsequently taken across the river to 179 Henry Street in New York, where an apartment had been rented for him at a cost of $1,300 per year ($35,000 today). Another $4,000 ($106,000 today) had been spent fitting it out for him and his family.[10]

It was an auspicious beginning to what would turn out to be a very sad story.

Even before he arrived, it was clear Rabbi Joseph would not speak to, or for, all of New York's Jews. Most uptown Jews saw his appointment as beneficial to their downtown brethren, especially if he could rationalize the kosher food supply. But for the most part they did not intend to accept his authority themselves. Adolph L. Sanger, one of the officers of Temple Emanu-El, the flagship Fifth Avenue Reform temple, told the *New York Herald* that "the question as to whether certain congregations put themselves under Rabbi Joseph's control lies with themselves and is entirely voluntary. It is not

7. Rabbi Jacob Joseph, the chief rabbi of New York—or some of it.

at all likely that any of the uptown congregations will recognize him at all, although possibly some of the more orthodox may."[11]

Even many downtown Jews had their doubts. An unnamed Russian Jew who had lived in America for six years put it this way: "No matter how great the respect and admiration commanded by Rabbi Joseph is, his power scarcely extends beyond the older element of the Hebrew community."[12]

Nor could Joseph count on support even from those downtown Orthodox congregations that had not joined the association that hired him. As one leading member of such a shul told the *New York Sun*, "I am opposed to the enterprise, not because I am averse to having a learned rabbi and an able preacher . . . but because the power vested in the new rabbi extends far beyond mere preaching and expounding the laws about religion. The plan to bring all the Jewish butchers under his jurisdiction . . . won't work here. Our butchers and their customers are aroused by the intended reform, and I fear it will give rise to serious conflict."[13]

It was a prescient remark.

Rabbi Joseph's first address to his new flock came on July 21 at the Beis Hamidrash HaGadol on Norfolk Street. Its sanctuary could seat a thousand, but twice that number showed up, necessitating the presence of twenty-five policemen to close the street and let no more worshipers in. To the devout Jews assembled in the pews, galleries, and aisles, the rabbi spoke in Yiddish, directing some of his remarks to the women present.

> To you, fair daughters and good mothers of our race, I appeal to keep this house inviolate. Whatever may be your influence on mundane affairs, I speak to you on behalf of the religion based exclusively on domestic virtue, on sublime truth and on the sanctity of family relations.
>
> You who have upheld the religion of your fathers with more strictness even than your husbands and sons and brothers, I beseech to aid, encourage and induce those male members of your family, to . . . keep intact the structure known as the

8. Beis Hamidrash HaGadol Synagogue on Norfolk Street, early 1900s.
Source: Wikipedia.

House of Israel. That is your mission. Lift them up then also to the higher spheres of the religion which have kept forever the homes of the Israelites sacred. And may God bless you for such undertaking.[14]

Singling out the women was no accident. Joseph knew that in most Jewish households, responsibility for observing religious laws fell on the wives and mothers. Implied, but not stated overtly, was their sacred responsibility to keep kosher homes.

In September, he visited some slaughterhouses to ascertain whether the knives being used to kill cattle passed muster. His first serious effort to assert his authority, however, was not in beef, but poultry. Late that month, he sent two hand-picked *mashgichim*—supervisors—to Fleischhauer's slaughterhouse on East Seventy-Sixth Street to determine whether fowl was being killed properly there. Charles Wolf, the *shoychet*, did not take kindly to unannounced supervision and ordered the men off the premises. But not only did they refuse to leave; they broke the leg of each chicken that did not appear to them to have been slaughtered correctly. Wolf had them arrested for disorderly conduct and they were taken to the Essex Market Police Court, where the judge eventually discharged them.[15]

This may have been all the reconnaissance Rabbi Joseph needed to hatch his first scheme, which was designed to combat the problem of ersatz kosher poultry being sold as the real thing. As he wrote to the association that had hired him, now twenty-three congregations strong:

We have appointed men, learned and skilled in the profession, to supervise the work of the slaughterers, that it be done in accordance with our sacred law. But this is not sufficient, for we are unable to inquire into the trustworthiness of all the butchers selling kosher meat. We have authorized our own butchers to put our seal upon the meat that is prepared under the supervision of our men. Thus the pious, who will be guided by our teachings, may be perfectly assured that the meat which they buy is kosher beyond a doubt if it is stamped with our seal, and that we do not hold ourselves responsible for the perfect fitness of meat that is not so stamped.

The seal, called a *plombe*, was a small, lead tag that could be attached to fowl or meat that testified to the fact that it had been slaughtered under the supervision of one of Joseph's *mashgichim* and that indicated the date of slaughter. But the *plombe* scheme would have to be financed. Rabbi Joseph received a salary from the association's constituent congregations in order to avoid any conflict of interest, but his coterie of *mashgichim* would also need to be paid if the new system were to be self-sustaining.

The association's solution was to charge buyers an extra penny for each bird with a *plombe* attached to its leg. That way, those who benefited from the new system would finance it. Joseph objected to this; he believed the *plombe* would aid the entire community and that the association should foot the bill. He eventually agreed to charge fowl purchasers for a *plombe*, but he drew the line at charging beef buyers for one, because beef was a staple of poorer Jews, and chicken, which was more expensive, was more likely to be bought by the affluent.[16]

It all sounded logical, but there were vested interests at stake, and it didn't take long for the long knives to be drawn. The rabbi's instincts were correct. Many butchers objected to the new rules, and Jewish housewives resented the extra charge. Brickbats came from rabbis who had overseen the meat business before Joseph showed up and were now disenfranchised. And even those not directly affected—secular socialist Jews, and some uptown German Jews who didn't keep kosher homes—criticized the new arrangement.

The rabbi took on his butcher critics head on. "The very fact that the butchers object to regulations about kosher meat shows that they wish to sell other meat in its stead," he asserted. "If they were honest in this matter, what difference is it to them whether the meat prepared according to the regulations of our law is marked or not?"[17]

Equally worrisome, though, was the reaction of many house-wives. The *plombe* had an analogue in a hated practice many immigrant Jewish women remembered all too well from Russia. It seemed for all the world like the *karobke*, a punitive tax on kosher meat administered by the *kohol* ostensibly to support the Jewish community, but sometimes diverted by the government for use to their detriment.[18] To them, the penny tax seemed less a service fee than an attempt at gouging. Rabbi Joseph was accused of adding a layer of corruption to an already crooked system, and one that worked to his own benefit and that of his cronies.

The *plombe* was no more popular with *mashgichim* who were not under Joseph's supervision, who would not only not profit from it, but stood to lose business because of it. And of course, the slaughterers and butchers who played fast and loose with the rules were dead set against it. Forty-six butchers who refused supervision even set up their own organization, the Hebrew Poultry Dealers' Protective Benevolent Association, to fight the new scheme, and they had the support of three rabbis from congregations not under Rabbi Joseph's authority. After they heard a rumor that Joseph had ordered members of his association's synagogues to boycott butchers whose poultry failed to display his *plombe*—something Joseph denied ever doing—it seemed to them that they were fighting for survival.

In January 1889 Samuel Pincus, the head of the Poultry Dealers' Association, sought a sit-down with Rabbi Joseph to try to come to some sort of accommodation, but the rabbi refused to meet with him. In retaliation, Pincus's fellow members voted to declare all meat sold by those "who made common cause with the charlatans who impose the *karobke*" to be *treyf.* He told the *New York Sun* they were considering legal proceedings against Joseph, and a representative of his association even paid a call on the District Attorney's office to discuss the possibility.[19]

Some uptown Jews were also critical of the *plombe*. "It is said that the taxes are excessive, illegal and stamp the whole movement as a business. It is not a question of kosher, but of a tax," the *Jewish Messenger* opined.[20] A letter to the same publication criticized Joseph for being in the pocket of the businessmen who had helped him discharge his debts in Europe and were paying his salary. The writer maintained that Joseph "is making the poorer class suffer for the benefit of his favorites. The quicker he abandons his imported Russian method of taxation, the better it will be for all concerned."[21]

But uptowners from some Orthodox German and Sephardic congregations, many of them rabbis themselves, were supportive, even though they didn't accept Joseph's jurisdiction. In an open letter published in the *Jewish Messenger* on February 15, twenty-six prominent uptowners appealed to all observant Jews to "assist in order that the good work may be extended, and those difficulties removed which hinder uptown Hebrews in obtaining meat and poultry kosher beyond suspicion." They even convened a public meeting and invited Joseph to address them.[22]

Far from being cowed by the criticism, Joseph pressed on with more reforms. He attempted, with some success, to assert authority over the abattoirs that supplied kosher beef, hounding out *shoychtim* who did not meet his standards and certifying new ones, expanding inspections and extending use of the *plombe* to beef, although in this case no extra charge was assessed. By early 1889 fully eighty-six slaughterhouses and butchers were operating under his supervision. Those butchers were licensed with a *hechsher*, a certificate bearing the rabbi's signature placed conspicuously in their workplaces that testified to their adherence to the laws of *kashrus*. For this, he charged them four dollars per month ($106 today).[23]

In March, however, Joseph backed down from charging for supervision certificates. After all, his independence had stemmed from the fact that he, at least, was paid by the congregations and not by anyone in the meat business. But this move cut into revenues. To make up the difference, he decreed that flour used to make *matzoh* for the following

Each Is an Authority unto Himself

month's Passover holiday would be subject to an inspection charge of one dollar a barrel. It was another unpopular move that was interpreted as a money grab.[24]

By most accounts a pious and sincere man, Rabbi Joseph was utterly trounced in the court of public opinion. With the wide acceptance of the equation between the *plombe* and the *karobke*, he had lost the battle. A greenhorn who spoke no English, he had failed to appreciate the differences between America and Eastern Europe, and he turned out to be no match for those in its fragmented Jewish community with vested interests. "New York is not Vilna, and America is not Russia," the *Jewish Messenger* declared derisively.

It was all downhill from there. Reviled by a sizable contingent of the community, Rabbi Joseph was left with the support only of those Orthodox congregations that had invited him in the first place, and even they eventually began to balk at how much he was costing them. By the early 1890s they did not feel able, nor did they feel it was fair to them, to finance kosher supervision for the entire city. To extricate themselves from the sizable financial commitment their association had made to the rabbi, they negotiated a new arrangement whereby butchers would pay a portion of his salary and those of the *mashgichim* who were working for him.

This, of course, thoroughly undermined not only his perceived objectivity, but his authority. And when a contingent of Hungarian and Galitzianer congregations named their own "chief rabbi," his influence declined even further. Then a third "chief rabbi" emerged in 1893 to preside over a few Hasidic congregations. Asked who had endowed him with the title, the man replied sheepishly, "the sign painter."[25]

Even Joseph's new compensation scheme dissolved in 1895 when one of his rivals offered butchers cheaper supervision. Joseph was deposed from his position. He did not return to Europe, however; he was simply left to fend for himself as a *mashgiach*.[26]

After this, New York's kosher meat industry more or less reverted to its original chaotic state. The system Rabbi Joseph had failed to fix remained divided and broken. But soon the Lower East Side would face a new existential threat to its supply of permitted meat that would revolve around price rather than quality. The culprits would also be men in the meat business. But this time they would not, for the most part, be local butchers, but rather a handful of men in Manhattan who did the bidding of gentile businessmen eight hundred miles away in Chicago.

5

A Despotic Meat Trust

Throughout 1901 the East Coast had experienced a gradual rise in the price of beef, but in early 1902 there was a quantum jump in the rates. By the end of March the wholesale price had climbed from seven to ten-and-a-half cents a pound (from two to almost three dollars in today's currency), a 50 percent increase. This increment, of course, was passed on to consumers by their butchers. Early 1902 therefore saw a lot of hand-wringing, but there was little mystery about who was responsible.

"The beef business in this country amounts annually to something like $600,000,000," ($17.6 billion today) the *New York Sun* told readers, "and it is almost entirely controlled by four firms: Swift & Company, Armour & Company, Nelson Morris & Company and G. H. Hammond & Company. It is alleged that these firms have an agreement which makes it possible for them to boost the price of fresh meats whenever they want to."[1]

Butchers certainly felt the effects of the price hikes; hotels and restaurants did, too, but unevenly. Large hotels suffered the least; they had signed long-term, fixed-price contracts with suppliers. But smaller establishments were hit hard. "I have stood it about as long as I can without losing money," one restaurateur told the *New York Tribune.* "In a few days, I shall have to charge my customers more for their meat. I am forced to do so by the unreasonable men back of the Trust," he said, adding, "they ought to be dragged before a jury of householders."[2]

Tammany Hall, the Democratic machine with an iron grip on New York City politics, saw an opportunity to hang the problem on the Republicans in Albany and Washington. Citing several nefarious practices attributed to the Trust—the blacklisting of dealers attempting to act independently, the manipulation of prices through secret agreements, the cornering of the market, and the signing of illegal, discriminatory freight contracts with railroads—it called on the Republican attorneys general of the state and the nation to take action against it.[3]

New York State did get into the act. Governor Benjamin Odell instructed Attorney General John C. Davies to look into the causes of the steep rise in beef prices. As Davies told the New York *World*, "the Governor is very much opposed to any high-handed proceedings by the Trust, and he is willing to endorse any legal steps to protect the interests of the people." He added, "it is criminal for any body of men to create a monopoly on a commodity that is essential to the maintenance of life, and if I find that this is really the case, I shall proceed against them on the ground of restraint of trade and of carrying on a business injurious to public policy."[4]

Many others joined the chorus. The Board of United Building Trades, which represented seventy-five thousand workers, passed a resolution in early April condemning the "selfish and grasping policy of the Beef Trust." The New York City Board of Aldermen strongly condemned "the inhuman action of the combination known as the Beef Trust" and demanded intervention by federal and state authorities. The assemblymen of Hudson County, New Jersey, debated asking the state legislature to nullify the charter of one of the Trust companies domiciled in the state. And Newark, New Jersey, butchers resolved to buy their own cattle and bypass the Trust entirely.

Nor did all the criticism come from the New York area. The Central Labor Union of Boston adopted an anti-Trust resolution. Kansas farmers organized to fight. And congressmen from Tennessee introduced a bill to abolish all duties on foreign meat imports to give the Trust some competition. The list went on and on.[5]

The grumbling did not go unnoticed in Washington. The situation seemed so blatant, and the protests so widespread and vehement, that President Theodore Roosevelt, who had suddenly ascended to the presidency the previous September upon the assassination of President William McKinley and who was suspicious of big business and no friend of trusts, attempted to put the brakes on meat prices. "President Roosevelt," the *St. Louis Republic* told readers, "is making this his personal fight for the 'full dinner pail.'" It was a reference to a slogan the 1900 McKinley campaign had employed to appeal to working class voters.[6]

Early in April, under instructions from Roosevelt, Attorney General Philander C. Knox ordered the U.S. Attorney for the Northern District of Illinois to open a secret investigation to determine whether the Beef Trust was violating federal antitrust law. It didn't take long. Before the month was out, Knox had gathered enough evidence against the Trust to satisfy himself that it was acting as a "combination in restraint of trade."

On April 24, after calling at the White House to brief the president, he directed the filing of simultaneous lawsuits under the Sherman Antitrust Act against Swift & Company, Armour & Company, the G. H. Hammond Company, and Nelson Morris & Company in Chicago; the Cudahy Packing Company in Omaha; and Schwarzschild & Sulzberger in New York. The goal was to put a stop to their anticompetitive practices—specifically creating monopolies, fixing prices, and dividing territory.[7]

The meat packers, of course, had their own version of why prices had risen so steeply. In an article in *National Provisioner*, their industry journal, they denied working in concert and argued that there was no such thing as a "Meat Trust" in the first place.

The Beef Trust—Don't shoot, I'll come down.

9. A cartoon by Charles L. Bartholomew showing Pres. Theodore Roosevelt holding a gun while a cow labeled "Beef Trust" sits on the moon reading a newspaper (ca. 1902). The headline reads: "Beef Is Way Up." The caption reads: "The Beef Trust—Don't shoot, I'll come down." Source: Library of Congress, Prints and Photographs Division, LC-DIG-ppmsca-37841.

It has been charged that five big packing concerns form a despotic Meat Trust that drives all competition to the wall, puts up prices at will, and that this combine, by one stroke of the pen, so raised prices as to take $100 million [nearly $3 billion today] extra out of the helpless consumers' pockets and added it to its already profitable greed. There is no such Trust. . . .

The price of live cattle makes the wholesale price of beef. The raisers of cattle make the price in the market. . . . Cattle are high. That makes beef so. They are also scarce and our export as well as home demand being great, the price of livestock goes up.[8]

Ferdinand Sulzberger, president of Schwarzschild & Sulzberger, which had been established in New York in 1853 and was considered the sixth member of the "Big Six," also defended the packers. He told the *Daily People*, the official organ of the Socialist Labor Party of America, that companies like his were actually *losing* money, and blamed it on an anemic corn crop that had depressed the population of livestock and raised its purchase price. "Last year, a 1,500-pound bullock cost five and a half cents a pound alive; today he costs seven cents. It costs $6 to get the beef killed and laid down in New York; we get $15 for the hide, fat and offal. The cost, then, is close to ten and a half cents a pound in New York. The margin between cost and selling price today is less than it was last year. Then we could make $2 on each live beef of 1,500 pounds. Now that margin has shrunk so there isn't any margin left."

In other words, he claimed his firm wasn't making *any* money on city-dressed beef.

"There is nothing like an agreement between the different large packing houses to stifle competition," he insisted. "There is *no* agreement to fix prices." But when pressed, he more or less admitted collusion. "Well, of course we may not compete so much at some times as others. Not to fight is a different thing, isn't it, from working together?"[9]

10. Ferdinand Sulzberger, president of Schwarzschild & Sulzberger.
Source: *Notable New Yorkers of 1896–1899* (New York: M. King, 1899).

In fact, it wasn't. A St. Louis meat dealer, speaking with the same publication, gave the lie to Sulzberger's claim. "The packers buy cattle on successive days so that each can buy at his own price. There is very little independent buying. The big packers keep others out by telling the cattlemen that if they sell *any* cattle to the independent buyers, they must sell *all* to them."

"The cooler managers meet every Wednesday afternoon and on Saturday. I do not know who fixes prices for them, but they are fixed the last day of the week for the week following. When a man does not sell his cattle in East St. Louis and ships them elsewhere, the packers send a dispatch ahead of him, instructing the buyers to only offer so much."[10]

The nefarious activities of the Beef Trust were so widespread and so egregious that it was inevitable its methods would be exposed in the press. The *New York Herald* quoted materials obtained surreptitiously from a Cudahy manager that decried the fact that Armour was shipping beef outside its "territory," explained how offering rebates only to large dealers was crushing smaller ones and described how members of the Trust were fined for violating the price agreement. The revelations were so damning that a senator from Oregon read them into the *Congressional Record.*[11]

A former employee of Swift & Company gave an insider's view of the situation to the New York *World.* "The wail of the packers that they cannot buy the cattle as cheaply as formerly is bosh," he asserted. "The packers pay the raiser just what they want to and no more. There *is* no competition in buying cattle."

"For instance, Armour's buyer will come along and offer the cattle-raiser three and a half cents a pound on the hoof. The raiser will refuse to take it, believing that Swift's buyer will pay four cents. But Swift's man will only offer just what Armour's man offered. These buyers are instructed by the big four packers in Chicago to pay just so much for cattle. If the raisers refuse to accept it they cannot sell their cattle, so they are forced to accept in the end."[12]

The meat packers had the cattlemen exactly where they wanted them. They were using their combined marketplace might to squeeze them as hard as they could by refusing to bid against one another and retaliating against any who tried to go around them. There *was* no cattle shortage, and producers were no more responsible for the rise in meat prices than were the housewives who bought *flanken* on Hester Street. The culprit was the Trust, which stood between them, operating behind the scenes to depress the cost of cattle and raise the price of meat in the cities.

And denying it all.

With a federal lawsuit pending against them, one might have expected the Trust companies to have lain low for a while, but in April they made another brazen and aggressive move. In response to the steep rise in beef prices, consumers were turning to alternate sources of protein. Many had switched to poultry, veal, mutton, lamb, eggs, and, in the case of non-Jews, pork and lard. Determined to frustrate this move, which cut into profits, the Trust also effected a price rise for some of these commodities, something it was able to do because many of them also passed through its slaughterhouses or came to New York in refrigerator cars it owned or controlled.

It was able to raise pork two cents a pound (nearly fifty cents in 2019 currency) and mutton, veal, lamb, and lard a half to three quarters of a cent (about thirteen to twenty cents today). Swift and Armour began to buy up and stockpile eggs to depress the supply in the market. Fifteen cents a dozen ($4.40) in 1901, they now sold for eighteen cents ($5.25). By one estimate, eggs alone increased Swift's profits by $36,000 (just over one million in 2019 dollars) with every one-penny rise.[13]

"Among the homes of the workingmen on the West Side, the effect of the rise in the price of a meal is painfully apparent," the *World* reported. "Families which have been accustomed to having meat on the table twice a day are now forced to get along with a meat stew once a day. To them, steaks are

A Despotic Meat Trust

barred. Roasts are out of the question. A roast of beef for a family of six costs $1.75 [fifty-one dollars today]. Steak, rump or shoulder cuts, for the same family for one meal, cost sixty-five cents [nineteen dollars]."[14]

But things were even worse on the East Side. Everyone was feeling the pinch, but the Jews, with fewer options, were feeling it more acutely than others. Kosher meat had always been more expensive, and many Jewish families were living so frugally that they simply couldn't spare the extra pennies. Nor was the situation helped by the imminent arrival of the Passover holiday on April 21. It was common for meat to be served with the ritual *seder* meal, and so demand was likely to rise and put further upward pressure on prices. With the price of a pound of brisket now hovering around eighteen cents, Jewish housekeepers were approaching the normally festive holiday with a good deal of anxiety.[15]

Passover's arrival was governed by the Jewish lunar calendar. In 1902 the eight-day holiday was to begin on April 21, a fact that raised an additional problem for Jewish families because the first and last day both fell on Mondays. Jewish law forbade butchers from working on Saturdays, but the state's blue laws, which prohibited the sale of alcohol and closed bars on the Christian day of rest, had been amended the previous year to prohibit butcher shops from doing business on Sundays as well. As a practical matter, Sunday closure laws were often honored in the breach in New York City, where a gratuity could persuade a corrupt policeman to look the other way. But the police had been especially aggressive lately. On April 13 they had arrested fifty-eight shopkeepers and pushcart salesmen, many if not most of them Jews, for doing business on a Sunday.

The reason the new law was problematical was that it meant that Orthodox Jewish housewives would have only a very brief window—a few hours after sundown on Saturday, after *Shabbos* had officially ended—to purchase meat slaughtered the previous Friday for their Passover tables.

Simon L. Adler, a Jewish state assemblyman, had tried to get the law amended to permit kosher butchers to open for a few hours on Sundays, but his effort failed. The arguments marshaled against it included the fact that no *civil* law required the Jews to close on *their* Sabbath, and that permitting them to remain open on Sunday would give them a monopoly on Sunday sales to the detriment of gentile butchers.[16]

A hue and cry arose on the Lower East Side as the community anticipated the difficulty of celebrating the coming holiday with meat on the table, and the matter came to the attention of Mayor Seth Low, who decided to offer relief, even though the problem was a state law, not a local one. Surely with an eye on the Jewish vote, which had helped elect him, the Mayor wrote Police Commissioner John N. Partridge:

> I am reminded that the Jewish Passover festival begins this year on Monday next, and lasts until, and including, Tuesday, April 29. The Monday and Tuesday of both weeks with the Jews are holy days, as well as the Saturdays, and upon these days the devout among them keep their shops closed. In the meanwhile, it is a requirement of their religion that they secure meat specially prepared, which under the circumstances, can only be had upon the two Sundays for use upon these days, thus compelling the devout Jew to choose between obeying the dictates of his conscience and the letter of the statutes of the State.

He essentially ordered the police not to enforce the state law.

The kosher butchers were grateful for the respite, but permission to open for an extra day did not solve their larger problem. They still had to pay much higher prices for meat, and worse, they were also now being forced by the slaughterhouses to pay cash on the barrel; the customary two- to three-day grace period was no longer being extended. They had no choice but to raise prices, but many of their patrons couldn't afford to pay more. As one butcher put it to a reporter, "We are entirely discouraged. Our customers cannot do as they do across town or uptown—merely grumble a little, pay more, and go on buying. No, they cannot do that, for they do not have the money to buy with."

11. New York City mayor Seth Low. Source: Library of Congress, Prints and Photographs Division, LC-USZ62–36674.

The butchers were feeling the heat. Kosher butchers generally operated from month to month and did not have significant reserves to enable them to weather a lengthy downturn. Many had already gone out of business; others whose leases would expire on May 1 knew they wouldn't be able to renew them.

It was time for a concerted effort. If they wished to stay in business, there was really no other choice but to fight back.

6

As Scarce around Essex Street as Ham Sandwiches

"When the holidays of the feast of Passover have ended next week, 150 to 200 meat markets on the East Side will go out of business," the president of the East Side Hebrew Retail Butchers' Kosher Guarantee and Benevolent Association, which represented the neighborhood's kosher butchers, predicted on April 17, 1902.

The Lower East Side butchers were hurting, and more than their nonkosher counterparts. Citywide, sales of kosher meat had plummeted from six hundred thousand pounds a week to about half that amount. Even at sixteen cents a pound there was no profit in meat, and most, if they were selling at all, were doing so at a loss.

"Three months ago my sales amounted to $55 a day," Max Rosen of Ludlow Street reported. "Today I have sold $1.90 worth of meat." And Jacob Bacharach, who operated on Hester Street, complained that he had not sold *any* meat in more than a week.[1]

But the poor were hurting even more. The papers were full of poignant stories. "The sights to be seen at some of the small butcher shops are pathetic," the *New York Tribune* wrote. "Women whose husbands allow them 30 or 40 cents a day to provide the family food for the day wistfully price the different scraps of meat and bone, trying to find some piece so undesirable that their scanty funds can secure it. The refuse in the shops is greedily snapped up at from ten to fifteen cents a pound. Women hasten back to the tenements closely grasping the few ounces of meat they have secured. Even the children are sent out to haggle with dealers in the hope of getting better terms."[2]

The New York *World* published the plaintive story of a babushka-clad woman with an infant in her arms and three other children in tow. Her Essex Street butcher was now obliged to charge her seventeen cents a pound for a piece of soup meat. She had gone into his shop to plead for a dime's worth of scraps to make a broth for her consumptive husband.[3]

"The attitude of the East Side to this situation is one of protest—not violent, for the people are too used to oppression to be deeply moved," the *Tribune* observed. "The factory work man who has had meat for one meal in the day will be obliged to subsist without it. Men are working 14 and 16 hours a day in factories and in sweatshops and subsisting from week's end to week's end without meat. Canned goods to some extent supply the place. Vegetables are introduced into the meager bill of fare, but East Side vegetables are neither very fresh, since they come from pushcarts, nor likely in the long run to be very healthful."[4]

At least one manufacturer of processed foods saw opportunity in the crisis. The Quaker Oats Company took out advertisements in the Yiddish press touting the health benefits of rolled oats. "If you begin the day with Quaker Oats you'll work better, sleep better and be in the best health and spirits," it told Jewish readers in an ad entitled "Stop! Don't Eat Meat for Breakfast," though it's far from clear how many Jewish families actually *were* eating meat for breakfast.[5]

New York's Jewish butchers had actually seen this problem coming since at least 1896, when their association, formed to represent the interests of the kosher butchers to the slaughterhouses and the speculators, first passed resolutions condemning the emerging "Beef Trust," a term by which they meant *local* abattoirs. The association president at the time had told the *Tribune* that prices had risen as a result of collusion among these slaughterhouses. The five hundred butch-

12. "Stop! Don't Eat Meat for Breakfast" read an advertisement aimed at Jewish readers that touted the health benefits of substituting Quaker Oats for meat in the morning. Source: *Yidishes Tageblatt*, May 6, 1902.

ers he represented had been refused an explanation for the hike. They believed the slaughterhouses were not only fixing prices, but also planning to dispense with competition by dividing the local butchers among themselves and permitting each to buy from only one house.[6]

By 1902 New York was home to three principal kosher slaughterhouses: Schwarzschild & Sulzberger, United Dressed Beef, and, to a lesser extent, Joseph Stern & Sons.[7] All three were German-Jewish owned, a fact that did not go unnoticed by the rabbi at Henry Street's B'nai B'rith Synagogue, who complained to the *World* that "if they have conspired against the people to raise the price of meat unwarrantably, they have transgressed the teachings of their faith." It was a shot across the bow at the likes of Ferdinand Sulzberger, Joseph L. Stern, and Isaac Blumenthal (the president of United Dressed Beef), who were suspected of being part of the conspiracy.[8]

Meat prices had risen for everyone, of course, and the nonkosher butchers were also agitated. They mused about bypassing the Trust entirely by purchasing cattle in quantity from the West and bringing them to New York themselves. It was a naïve idea, because the Trust would never have permitted the railroads to service them, and it had the clout to impose its will. But in any event, the Hebrew butchers, whose shops were now closing at the rate of a dozen a day, were in need of more immediate remedies.

"The Jewish butchers in greater New York can no longer sustain the yoke of the harmful Meat Trust," the Orthodox *Yidishes Tageblatt* opined. "The Trust has taken away from them every possibility to make a living. . . . Many have had to give up their shops, and those who are still struggling are hanging by a thread."[9]

It was obvious the time had come for their association to take action.

The group, now six hundred strong, was headed by Joseph Goldman, a fifty-three-year-old, Russian-born butcher who had been in America just over a decade. He had a shop on Suffolk Street, a narrow, six-floor stone and brick walk-up, and

As Scarce as Ham Sandwiches

lived above the store with his wife and seven children. Goldman also served as secretary of a small Orthodox congregation on East Broadway. He had petitioned for naturalization in 1896 but had not yet been sworn as an American citizen.

At a meeting at Broome Street's New Irving Hall, Goldman denounced the Beef Trust to an audience of four hundred of his cohorts. The members also heard from butchers Abraham Perlman and Jacob Andron and from two former Swift employees who knew the slaughterhouse business from the inside.

Polish-born Andron, in the country for thirteen years, gave voice to the irony of the dilemma the Trust had foisted on them. "Once we wanted to obtain all the customers we could. Now we are glad when the customers go by the door. We don't *want* to sell, for we have to sell at a loss, and yet we must dispose of the meat if we have it on hand. Better not to do business at all than to do it under the present conditions."[10]

Andron shared an accounting of the proceeds from 130 pounds of chuck he had sold at sixteen cents a pound. After allowing for expenses, he calculated his total profit at a mere seventy-seven cents. And apart from the rising costs, he pointed to the withdrawal of credit as another serious obstacle. The kosher butchers had formerly received their bills on Friday, but been given until Monday, when the meat would presumably have been sold, to pay up. The previous Friday he had been refused this amenity for the first time. When he demanded the reason, a salesman at the slaughterhouse observed, "If meat costs so much more than it did, how can you pay for it?"[11]

Several possible courses of action were discussed at the meeting. The former Swift employees advocated butchers closing their doors to exert pressure on the wholesalers; they thought a two-week shutdown would probably suffice to bring prices down. A less draconian option would be to close down the coming Saturday night. A third would be to cut back drastically on purchases, each butcher ordering only one chuck a day.[12]

Yet another possibility considered was to establish cooperatives. Instead of three or four butchers competing on a single block, several might join together to keep just *one* shop open, reducing overhead and sharing profits. Such a plan could cut costs drastically, while still meeting the needs of the community for affordable beef.

That idea, in fact, was not new. It had been considered as early as 1891, when a couple of hundred kosher butchers had met to discuss turning over their businesses to a unified company and receiving stock in return, with profits divided among all the shareholders. But nothing had come of it.[13]

The majority seemed to favor a shutdown, but Goldman did not put the question to an immediate vote. Instead, he appointed a committee of thirty butchers representing various streets on the East Side to draw up resolutions. He also called for a second meeting the following day to which representatives of the Allied Butchers Association of Brooklyn and the Hungarian Jewish butchers would be invited in solidarity.[14]

The next day, the committee of thirty recommended the popular and more expedient option of closing down. Then, at a contentious session that lasted three hours, a vote was taken and it was decided to shut all of the kosher butcher shops in Manhattan, Brooklyn, and the Bronx beginning the following Saturday night, and to hold a mass meeting the day after.[15]

When Saturday came, however, all did not go smoothly. It was asking too much to expect *all* of New York's kosher butchers to act in concert, and indeed, there were holdouts. Forty-three-year-old David Kesper of Essex Street was one. He couldn't afford to close.

Kesper, who lived behind his store with his wife of twenty years, four children, and two assistants, had emigrated from Lithuania in 1880. He was not a member of Goldman's association. When the wholesale wagon pulled up at 6:00 p.m. on Saturday, he accepted his usual order. A half hour later, association representatives passed his store. When they saw that he was open for business, they tried to talk him into

As Scarce as Ham Sandwiches

closing, but when that failed, things got violent. Stones were thrown at his windows. Fifty butchers converged on his shop and ruined much of his inventory, and several dragged Kesper into the street, shouting at him in Yiddish as his wife and children looked on in horror.[16]

Kesper might have been seriously injured had his son not run to the Eldridge Street police station to summon help. A group of officers and detectives arrived in time. They arrested several of his attackers and drove the mob out of the store, though stragglers continued to heckle the butcher from across the street. Although he stubbornly remained open, no one dared enter his establishment for hours afterward because the pickets shooed all comers away.

Kesper initially maintained that he had not heard of the boycott, but later revealed that he had stayed open because his wholesaler had threatened that if he closed on Saturday night, he would be raised two cents a pound the following Monday.

He had been damned if he'd closed, and damned if he'd stayed open.[17]

Police were also called to break up altercations at nearly a dozen other shops that had refused to shut their doors. But in the main, the boycott was successful in sending a signal to the abattoirs in that most of the wagons dispatched to the Lower East Side that night went back as full as they had come.

The mass meeting Goldman had promised occurred on Sunday, May 11, when fifteen hundred men crowded into New Irving Hall. Many ideas were discussed, but in the end everyone present agreed not to buy an ounce of meat from the wholesalers for at least two more days. "So kosher meat," the *New York Sun* observed wryly, "is likely to be as scarce around Essex Street as ham sandwiches."[18]

Several of those present had already selected their meat for Monday delivery, however, so after the decision was reached, they rushed back to the slaughterhouses to cancel their orders. Many went so far as to tear the identifying tags off the carcasses they had chosen earlier and leave explicit instructions that any meat the wholesalers attempted to deliver would be refused. They also asserted that they would buy no more until prices were lowered.[19]

At a second gathering that evening, a thousand people tried to jam into New Suffolk Hall, which could accommodate only six hundred. Goldman introduced the president of the Brooklyn butchers, who announced that his group had received notification of the decision of their Manhattan brethren too late to rescind their own Monday orders, but that his organization would meet the following morning to endorse the action.

Amid occasional cries of "Let the Beef Trust know what we want," some important business was conducted. To mitigate the loss those individual butchers with remaining inventory would suffer, a committee was designated to buy up unsold meat and send it out of town to be made into sausage. And there were loud cheers when it was decided that the butchers would sell only poultry for the next two days.

Henry Schumacher, a salesman for Schwarzschild & Sulzberger, was present and asked to address the group. After some grumbling, he was permitted to speak.

"Messrs. Schwarzschild and Sulzberger did not get any notification of the intention of the butchers until after they had killed the usual amount of cattle today," he said. "They were surprised to find that no one called to purchase their meat. When Mr. Sulzberger learned what had happened, he asked me to tell you that if a committee were sent to him he, for the firm, would grant all reasonable demands."[20]

It was an opening. Or seemed to be.

Both the *World* and the *Times* reported that the butchers enjoyed the hearty support of the East Side Jews, who were willing to go without meat because they believed their butchers that nothing short of a boycott would bring the wholesalers to terms. Goldman made this same point to the *Sun* later. "People will have to eat bologna if they can't afford chickens," he said. "The people are with us and we are fighting for them as well as for ourselves in this matter."[21]

As Scarce as Ham Sandwiches

13. A kosher butcher shop on the East Side that had not yet been closed down. Source: Library of Congress, Prints and Photographs Division, George Grantham Bain Collection, LC-DIG-ggbain-04488.

The people *were* with them. But there was some question as to whether they were fighting the right enemy.

To the retail butchers, the slaughterhouses on First Avenue and at Thirty-Ninth Street were the face of the Beef Trust. The fifteen hundred men who assembled at New Irving Hall were convinced that it was their greed that had caused the crisis, and that they had it in their power to lower prices if they so chose.

The United States Justice Department, however, saw things differently. Attorney General Philander C. Knox, for one, thought there were bigger fish to fry.

As Scarce as Ham Sandwiches

7

Let the Women Make a Strike,
Then There Will Be a Strike!

At 5:00 p.m. on May 10, 1902, U.S. Attorney Solomon H. Bethea filed the federal government's complaint against the members of the Beef Trust with the United States Court of Appeals for the Seventh Circuit in Chicago. The documents had been prepared by the Justice Department in Washington and approved by Attorney General Knox and President Theodore Roosevelt.

Based on the Sherman Antitrust Act, the complaint was a wholesale indictment of the Big Six meat packers, and it named not only the companies, but the men in charge. It accused them of being parties to an agreement to control the U.S. beef trade by manipulating the price of beef to the "manifest injury of the people of the United States and in defiance of law."

Among the accusations against them were that they had:

conspired to restrain competition by refraining from bidding against one another;

bid up prices to induce owners to ship livestock to Trust-controlled stockyards, glutting markets and enabling Trust members to obtain the livestock at their own prices;

conspired to raise, lower, and establish prices and to maintain uniform prices, which they determined at secret meetings;

kept and shared a blacklist of delinquents and collectively refused to sell to them; and conspired with the railroads to obtain unlawful transportation rates through rebates and other devices to the disadvantage of competitors.

Named in the complaint were the companies Swift, Hammond, Cudahy, Armour, Nelson Morris, and Schwarzschild & Sulzberger, as well as twenty-three individuals who constituted a veritable who's who in meat packing. Several were the firms' founders or their close relatives. Among them were J. Ogden Armour; Gustavus, Louis, and Edward Swift; Michael, Edward, and Patrick Cudahy; and Ferdinand Sulzberger.

The petition sought an injunction against further operation of the so-called Trust, its dissolution, its adoption of measures to prevent recurrence of collusion, and an immediate hearing. The judge scheduled arguments for Tuesday, May 20.[1]

At the same time, Attorney General Knox quietly issued an order to U.S. attorneys across the nation to collect local evidence against the Beef Trust. This was unprecedented, but Knox knew that the more proof he could garner against this hydra-headed cabal, the better prepared he would be.[2]

Nor was the federal government the Trust's only adversary. In Albany, New York State Attorney General John C. Davies, whose office had been investigating it for several weeks, had been awaiting federal action before filing a complaint of his own. On Monday, May 12, the *New York Herald* reported that he had amassed a list of more than a hundred witnesses who had been "unfairly used" by the Beef Trust and had collected a trove of documents pointing to arbitrary regulation of prices, division of territory, and restraint of trade, and that such an action was imminent.[3]

That same morning, the butchers' boycott on the Lower East Side appeared to be gaining steam, thanks to new pledges of solidarity by counterparts in Brooklyn and Newark. Consumers, too, were generally supportive. They dutifully turned to milk, eggs, and vegetables, paid a few cents a pound more for chicken, or patronized delicatessens, which did a brisk business in processed meats as the butchers, by and large, remained closed. That didn't mean there weren't outliers, though. A squad of butchers on the lookout for shops that attempted to do business prowled the streets and urged or forced several to close. Police had to be called in a few cases when rocks were thrown.

In the afternoon, a delegation of 350 butchers headed by Joseph Goldman met with representatives of the wholesalers at the Forty-Fourth Street offices of the United Dressed Beef Company. Frederick Joseph, son-in-law of founder Joseph Schwarzschild and a vice president of the company, appeared for Schwarzschild & Sulzberger; Isaac Blumenthal represented United Dressed Beef, of which he was president; and M. Meyer appeared for his own company, M. Meyer & Son. Officers of smaller slaughterhouses were present as well.

The executives insisted they were powerless to lower rates because these were governed by the price they had to pay for cattle from the West. They held firm to this line throughout the meeting. "It makes no difference to us whatever," Ferdinand Sulzberger told the *New York Times* later. "If the butchers do not require the meat then we will not be obliged to ship so many cattle. If they want to reduce the price they will have to go out West and try to do it. We cannot help them in any way."[4]

Sulzberger was lying about lacking power over setting the price, but the threat of simply ordering fewer cattle was real, and so as a practical matter, the boycott didn't hurt the local wholesalers as much as the butchers had hoped it would. But it was not true that calling a moratorium on beef purchases made *no* difference to the wholesalers. Lower volumes meant lower profits for them, too.

After the first day, the slaughterhouses simply bought fewer animals and sent most of the *shoychtim* home, saving the eighteen dollars a week they had to pay each of them. As they pointed out at the meeting, they could still do business with non-Jewish butchers, some of whom, they alleged, were already ordering kosher meat to sell to observant Jews.

14. East Side women dutifully turned to vegetables in support of their butchers, who had closed down temporarily to exert pressure on their wholesalers. Source: Library of Congress, Prints and Photographs Division, George Grantham Bain Collection, LC-DIG-ggbain-04487.

Their point was that consumers could still buy kosher meat if they wanted it; the only ones who would really suffer from continuing the boycott were the kosher butchers themselves.[5]

After initially refusing to attend, the wholesalers did agree to address an assembly of all of the butchers, and the next day Sulzberger, Blumenthal, and Joseph Stern courageously appeared at New Irving Hall before a crowd of somewhere between eight hundred and two thousand of them—press reports varied widely—in a meeting that began at 10:00 a.m. and didn't wind up until 4:00 p.m.

After Goldman presented the demands of the butchers, Blumenthal and Sulzberger both spoke. As they had the day before, they maintained it was impossible for them to reduce prices because the cost of cattle had risen. They insisted they were making hardly any profit.

To support their case, Sulzberger produced bills showing the price of cattle in both Chicago and New York and the freight rates his company was charged to ship it on the hoof, though it's a safe bet that these were the *published* rates, and that the substantial rebates his firm received from the railroads—off the books—did not appear. He denied that he and the other wholesalers were part of a beef trust, despite the fact that Schwarzschild & Sulzberger was the only New York slaughterhouse identified explicitly in the government's complaint as one of the Big Six.[6]

To placate the butchers, the wholesalers did offer them some modest concessions. If the butchers would resume their purchases, the wholesalers agreed that they would no longer sell kosher meat to speculators, the middlemen who bought up the choice cattle and resold it to the retailers at inflated prices. They would pledge to sell *only* directly to the butchers.

Second, they promised that they would repurchase "wurst" meat—unsold scraps of fat used for sausage-making—from Jewish butchers exclusively, and would raise the rate paid for it from two-and-a-half cents to three cents a pound. Third, the price of liver would decrease by a penny a pound. Fourth, they would send the butchers' association a list of Jewish butchers who purchased *treyf* meat that they then resold as kosher, presumably so these men could be exposed as frauds. And finally, they would support the butchers in their fight against forced Sunday closing.[7]

But they made it clear that this was as far as they were willing to go, so there was strong sentiment on the part of the butchers, who had by now gone several days without income, to pocket the concessions and reopen. By noon on Wednesday, May 14, most of them had done just that.[8]

In the grand scheme of things, however, the concessions were paltry, and no progress had been made on the central issue that had given rise to the boycott in the first place. As a matter of fact, when the butchers reopened, far from offering their customers any relief, they actually increased the prices they charged them for meat. Some were now asking as much as eighteen, twenty, and even twenty-five cents for better cuts. And even at these inflated prices, many were also now refusing to trim fat, selling meat and fat for the same price. Soup bones, once thrown in for free with a meat purchase, were now only available at six cents a pound. After four days of bologna and fish, the Lower East Side was ready to eat fresh meat again, and so there was pent up demand on Wednesday. But few would be able to afford the new prices for long.[9]

The *New York Press* claimed the butchers had "won their fight against the wholesalers." But nobody else thought so. Indeed, when all was announced and when the women of the Lower East Side discovered that retail prices had actually *risen* in the wake of the shutdown, they were outraged.

And nobody was more incensed than Sarah Edelson.

Wasting no time, she and two Russian-born neighbors— Paulina Wachs Finkel, a thirty-two-year-old mother of four, and Fanny Levy, a thirty-five-year-old mother of six, both of whom had been in America for about a decade—placed an announcement in the Yiddish papers inviting East Side Jewish women to meet that night to consider their options.

The gathering was to be held at 88 Monroe Street in the hall at the rear of Monroe Palace, Sarah's family's saloon.

Let the Women Make a Strike

Several butchers laughed derisively at the idea of a women's gathering, the *New York Post* reported later, and Sarah herself didn't expect more than fifty or so people to show up. But when the hour arrived, the five hundred–seat hall was filled to capacity. And many more who couldn't fit inside parked themselves outside on Monroe Street.[10]

"New York never saw such a huge gathering of Jewish women," the *Yidishes Tageblatt* proclaimed. Although they were all Jewish and principally of Russian or Eastern European origin, there was actually a fair amount of diversity in the room, both socially and ideologically. There were women from Poland, Romania, Hungary, and the Ukraine. There were Litvaks and Galitzianers. Those assembled almost certainly subscribed to different beliefs, as socialism, anarchism, Zionism, and other ideologies were all popular. Some had learned of them in the old country; others had been exposed only in New York. What united them was that they all considered themselves and their families bound by the dietary laws, and that they resented, and felt threatened by, the recent increase in the price of meat.

Now, however, the women's ire was directed not at the Beef Trust, but rather at their own East Side butchers. The concessions the butchers had obtained from the wholesalers may have been meager, but they should have resulted in *some* reduction in retail prices. Not only had they failed to make a dent in prices; rates had now *risen* as high as twenty-five cents a pound.[11]

Women who had stood by their local butchers the previous week now felt double-crossed by them. It appeared as if the butchers were taking advantage of the situation by laying on additional profits for themselves to make up for their losses of the previous week, even as they placed all the blame on the wholesalers. Some women even accused the butchers of establishing a "little Trust" of their own.[12]

"We will go to Jerome!" one of the speakers vowed, referring to William T. Jerome, the recently elected district attorney of New York County, although it is not clear what help

15. Monroe Palace, the saloon at 88 Monroe Street owned by Sarah
Edelson's family. Her son, "Big Jake," is second from the left; another son
is at the far right. It was at this location that the women's boycott
was planned. Courtesy of the Edelson Family.

he was in a position to offer them. "We will go to the mayor! We will see the wholesalers! But we will not allow the retail butchers to 'skin' us and give us bones and stones when we are paying for meat! If we can go without meat for four days to *help* the retail butchers, we can go without it for a month to *fight* them!"

Amid cries of "burn down their shops!" the women resolved to do to the butchers what the butchers had failed to do effectively to the slaughterhouses: boycott them.

In a passionate speech the *Tageblatt* described as throwing "oil on fire," Paulina Finkel, whom the New York *World* dubbed the "Napoleon of the East Side," vowed to make the butchers wish they had never been born. But the mood was perhaps best captured by Fanny Levy, who was particularly contemptuous of the butchers' strike and its miserable results.

"Look at the good it has brought," she noted sarcastically. "*This* is their strike? Let the *women* make a strike, *then* there will be a strike!"[13]

"Only a spark was needed to kindle a fierce flame among the excitable residents of that quarter," the *New York Press* observed later, and it was the meeting at 88 Monroe that provided the ignition. Each woman present was asked to pony up ten cents and a total of $28.85 was raised for the fight. A motion was passed to establish committees of five women to patrol each block on which there were kosher butcher shops the following day and dissuade customers from patronizing them.[14]

Paulina Finkel drafted a call to action in Yiddish, five thousand copies of which were quickly printed and distributed that evening in an effort to recruit women for the committees. It read:

Dear Sisters:

The time has arrived when we must take a hand in this meat fight. With our money, the butchers buy diamonds and wear diamonds. When meat costs only seven cents a pound wholesale, the butchers charge us 14, and now when they have to pay only one cent more, the butchers have raised a howl and have declared a strike.

Now, what shall we say, dear sisters, when they give us stone and bone and charge us five cents more?

We therefore ask and demand of all our dear sisters in Greater New York that they refuse to pay more than 12 cents a pound. If he refuses to give it to you at that price, do not buy meat at all. And if we work and act as one woman there will soon be found butchers who do not care for diamonds and who will open stores and sell meat to us at 12 cents a pound.

Buy no meat yourselves and let no one else buy!

Committee[15]

The *Forward*, the Yiddish socialist daily, did its best to cover the story from all angles. Its reporters met with Sarah Edelson and Fanny Levy, who confirmed the details of the planned boycott, and also with individual retail butchers. One of them gave voice to the deep resentment many of his colleagues felt against the men who ran the slaughterhouses. He made it clear that although these men were themselves Jews, he saw them as an entirely different species of Jew for whom he had nothing but contempt.

"I am pious and I am honorable," this retailer told the reporter, with tears in his eyes. "Why should these millionaire German Reform Jews—the wholesale butchers—squeeze us and draw so much blood in the name of our holy Torah on which they spit? Why should they force us to sell at a higher price when we want to sell more cheaply?" He accused them of a "swindle against poor workers, poor people and humanity as a whole" and derided them as capitalists "who had gotten fat from eating pork and *treyf.*"[16]

The women resolved to field squads on the streets first thing the following morning, which no doubt required a Herculean feat of overnight door-knocking. With an estimated six hundred kosher meat shops on the Lower East

Side, well over a thousand people would be required to execute the scheme.

The East Side housewives were aggrieved, and now they had a plan. What remained to be seen was whether they had the wherewithal and the stamina to pull it off.

8

If We Cry at Home, Nobody Will See Us

As early as three o'clock the next morning, Thursday, May 15, pickets began arranging themselves in front of the hundreds of kosher meat markets across the Lower East Side. By seven o'clock, some three thousand women had turned up, many with small children in tow. The plan, which had been hammered out the night before, did not envision or countenance violence, but nor was it entirely benign. The committees—five women per block—were to remonstrate with any patrons in hopes of persuading them not to buy anything from the butchers. But the instructions to "buy no meat yourselves and let no one else buy" implied that if potential customers were *not* cooperative, draconian measures would be necessary.

True to plan, when the markets opened and shoppers approached, demonstrators explained their cause and asked them not to patronize the stores. Most complied, but others, intent on making their purchases, filed past the pickets and entered anyway.[1]

And that's when things started to get out of hand.

The trouble began on Cherry Street, when Jacob Kalinsky, a butcher, sold a piece of chuck steak to a female customer. The team arrayed outside his shop chastised her all through the transaction, and when she emerged with her package, pounced on her. One woman grabbed the meat and threw it into the gutter, and the rest barged into the store and began doing the same to all of Kalinsky's stock as the terrified butcher and his family cowered in their living room behind the shop. The woman who had dared to make the purchase was chased down the block. She got separated from her *sheitl* in the process, but she managed to escape without harm.

When the police arrived, they arrested the instigators, Anna Rosen, Rose Baskin, and Rebecca Ablowitz, all Cherry Street residents, and eleven others. They were hauled off to Essex Market Police Court as a crowd of their compatriots followed, heckling the officers and pelting them with bits of Kalinsky's meat. One woman, a nursing baby in her arms, flung a plate at a policeman, knocking the helmet off his head. Patrol wagons ferried the accused to court, only to be dispatched again to pick up the next load of protesters.

On Essex Street, a woman who bought a pound of meat from Louis Glazman was also attacked when she exited his store. "I have a sick husband," she protested. "He *has* to eat meat." But the women in front of Glazman's shop were having none of it. "A sick individual can eat *treyf*," an elderly woman retorted. As a practical matter, the Talmud *did* allow for consumption of unkosher food in extreme cases, but the provision was generally invoked only when a life was in danger.[2]

A prominent thirty-nine-year-old Jewish collector for one of the wholesalers named Joseph Hantcharow was recognized as he drove his cart down Madison Street. Immediately, cries of "meat baron!" were heard. Samuel Weinstein caught hold of the horse's bridle and stopped the cart as its owner dismounted and fled. Weinstein was arrested and fined five dollars.[3]

Nor was all well on Monroe Street. A butcher from the same block as the Edelsons' Monroe Palace rushed into the Madison Street Station House bleeding from the back of his head. He explained in heavily accented English that a dozen women had massed in front of his shop. When they began interfering with his customers, he had scolded them and been knocked down and kicked. Captain William Thompson dispatched two officers to Monroe Street, where they

16. A squad of Lower East Side women remonstrating with a potential buyer outside a butcher shop. Source: Library of Congress, Prints and Photographs Division, George Grantham Bain Collection, LC-USZ62–55772.

found a crowd of angry protestors they were able to subdue only with billy clubs.[4]

When more wounded butchers showed up at his station, Thompson requested reinforcements. Eventually, men from eight other police stations and a squad of central office detectives were summoned, and as the day wore on they became more and more ruthless in the methods they used to suppress the demonstrators, who by now were roving from place to place and causing trouble all over the neighborhood.

"The police swung their clubs and many bruised heads and battered bodies resulted," the *World* noted. "Some of the policemen were rough to the point of brutality in enforcing the general order to 'move on.'" But the East Siders did not cower in fear. "A shower of bricks, china, utensils, flat irons and all sorts of missiles" rained down on the police, including several precinct captains. The barrage sent forty officers running for cover. And after this, the police were more merciless than ever. Whoever didn't obey an order to move was clubbed, whether man, woman, or child, and ambulances were kept busy ferrying the wounded to local hospitals.[5]

This was not the first time Jewish protesters had received such rough treatment from the police. Beatings had become almost standard operating procedure during the many garment industry strikes New York had seen over the previous decade, and had engendered a good deal of resentment toward law enforcement on the part of the Jewish community. During a protest by striking cloak makers in 1894, for example, police from the Madison Street Station "used their clubs freely and with vigor," to disperse the crowd, the *New York Times* reported at the time. Labor leaders decried them as "beasts" and "brutes" for the wounds they inflicted.[6]

But these were *women* being attacked, and that was different—and unseemly. At least one was beaten into semi-consciousness. Crowds took umbrage at the savagery and made things as difficult as possible for the police. "Had the rioters been men," the *New York Post* insisted, "a few well-directed prods with the clubs would have subdued them quickly, but with the women the officers were helpless. It took from three to five men to make an arrest. The women screamed and fought, each prisoner between a pair of stalwart men, with a third policeman pushing from behind, and two or three others driving back the crowd of would-be rescuers." Many women were injured; some were thrown to the pavement and trampled.[7]

It was bedlam on the East Side. The *Forward*, founded only five years earlier, was nonetheless sure that "in the 25–30 years since this area was settled by Polish, Russian, Hungarian, *Galitzianer* and Romanian Jews, there has never been a scene such as we have seen here today."[8]

The butcher shops weren't the only places visited. Some women and girls entered tenements on Pike and Madison Streets, seized meat from people's tables, and threw it into the street. Many were dragged off to jail, but the demonstrators weren't the only people arrested. A Norfolk Street butcher was also hauled in, as were the two boys he had hired to throw water on the crowds from his roof.[9]

Joseph Goldman, president of the butchers' association, insisted that the stories of butchers charging artificially high prices had been exaggerated, that no one had asked more than sixteen cents a pound and that the retailers had not even passed a half-cent rise by the wholesalers on to their customers. He maintained that the butchers were losing money, and attributed the disturbances not only to the desire of the women for cheap meat, but also to alleged underground activities of socialists and anarchists on the East Side.

Goldman also had unkind words for the speculators, the middlemen who bought up choice meat from the slaughterhouses and resold it to retail butchers at a profit. Five such concerns did business on the East Side, and Goldman's association had ostensibly put them out of the kosher business during its negotiations with the wholesalers the previous week. Two men hired by one of the speculators had come into his shop and threatened to put a knife through his heart, he told the press. Only with the help of several

WOMEN DRIVEN TO DESPERATION BY THE MEAT TRUST
MOB PURCHASERS OF BEEF AT EAST-SIDE MARKETS.

EAST SIDE WOMEN TRYING TO PREVENT THE SALE OF THE HIGH-PRICED TRUST MEAT.

17. A cartoon depiction of East Side women trying to prevent the sale of the high-priced Trust meat. Source: *New York World*, May 15, 1902.

friends was he able to eject them. He also blamed the speculators for getting the women agitated, though it was not a credible accusation.

Goldman predicted that if the trouble persisted, members of his association would meet on Sunday to consider their options, but that in any event, no more meat would be bought from wholesalers in the interim. He then shuttered his own shop, warning that the butchers could hold out for a month without business if necessary. He insisted that the fight had already cost his members sixty thousand dollars ($1.7 million today).[10]

The unenviable task of hearing the charges against the women brought in by the police fell on City Magistrate Robert C. Cornell, a Columbia-educated attorney who had been on the bench since 1895. When the Essex Market Police Court opened at 9:00 a.m. there were already thirty disorderly conduct cases on his docket, and dozens more followed as the day wore on. The *Tageblatt* was appalled that the women were processed "as if they had committed great crimes" and dealt with quite severely, especially since not a single butcher had filed a complaint against any of them. The cases were being brought solely on the say-so of the police.[11]

Certain their cause was just, the women were not in a mood to be cowed, even by a judge. Cornell demanded of Rose Baskin, who had been arrested on Cherry Street, whether it was true she had torn meat away from a shopper and thrown it into the street.

"Certainly!" she answered. "What then? Just stand there and look it in the teeth?"

"What did you have against this woman who bought the meat?" the Magistrate asked.

"We have nothing against her. But we don't want the butchers to get fat on our meat."

A murmur in court prompted the bailiff to call for order.

"I *am* in order," Rose insisted.

"You don't have the right to make riots," Cornell declared, "or to prevent anyone from buying meat."

"We want to strike against the Trust. We are poor people," she countered.

"What do *you* know about the Trust? It's not your business."

"So whose business *is* it?" Rose demanded. "Our pockets are empty. They are sucking our blood."[12]

She was fined three dollars. Then it was Russian-born Ablowitz's turn.

"We are on strike against the butchers," she explained to the Magistrate. "The kosher butchers charge us twenty-five cents a pound for meat, and we can get the same joints from Christian butchers for twelve cents a pound. We were pleading with the women not to buy meat!" she explained.

"It's none of your business whether they eat meat or fish," the impatient judge countered. "The trouble is that you women are ignorant of the meat business and do not understand the conditions," he declared condescendingly. But the women understood their own conditions all too well, and they were fighting back in the only way they thought they could be effective.

"Well, we feel it in our pocketbooks," Ablowitz retorted. "We see how skinny our children are. And our husbands have no strength to work because others want to get rich from their work."

"But you're not allowed to make riots in the streets," Cornell said, finally.

"We're not making riots," she answered. "But if we cry at home, nobody will see us. We have to help ourselves."

She, too, was fined three dollars. So was Anna Rosen, and so were Rebecca Weinberg and Ida Rubin, who had gotten into a hair-pulling match on Madison Street. As the day went on and Cornell heard more similar cases, he began to raise the fines to five dollars and, in some cases, ten. Friends and relatives of about two-thirds of those arrested were able to scrape up the money, but some of the women could not afford to pay and were locked up instead, many leaving unsupervised children at home.[13]

A Mrs. Golubkin told the judge that she and the other

women who had intercepted a purchase on Delancey Street had fully intended to repay the shopper for her loss, and this happened in more than one place. A woman stopped on her way out of a butcher shop at 98 Essex was scolded, "You're going to help the *bloodsuckers?*"

"I already paid for this meat with money that I have earned through hard work," she replied.

"Let's get together and pay her back," someone in the crowd cried out. "Let's not allow her to eat poison." The picketers dug into their purses and collected the money to reimburse her, and the meat was discarded.[14]

Sarah Edelson, who addressed crowds on Monroe Street several times during the day, was ultimately arrested and brought before Cornell. She was one of those who got a ten dollar fine. Cornell accused her of inciting the "wicked riots," and threatened that if she appeared before him again, he would not merely fine her again, but send her to the work-house, a prison on the East River's Blackwell's Island for people convicted of minor crimes.[15]

Sarah wasn't given a chance to defend herself in court; she simply paid her fine and was released. Then, undaunted, she called for a meeting at New Irving Hall that evening and invited several local luminaries to address what she now was sure would be a very large crowd. The speakers included Russian-born Rabbi Joseph Zeff, a charismatic Yiddish orator sent to America two years earlier by Theodore Herzl to agitate for Zionism, and local labor leader Joseph Barondess, a well-loved figure in the Jewish community. Sarah and her cohorts wisely decided to charge a nominal admission fee of ten cents, money they planned to use to defray the fines of the women who had been arrested.

She was not wrong to anticipate the popularity of the meeting. At 8:00 p.m. a mob of five thousand or more charged the doors. Many were trampled and one of the hall's doors was actually torn from its hinges in the rush. About two thousand people paid the fee; the rest—a crowd the *New York Herald* estimated at a whopping twenty thousand—remained outside and occupied the entire block of Broome Street between Norfolk and Essex and several nearby blocks. The mood was decidedly sour.[16]

Inside the hall, though, things were relatively calm. Those who had been arrested and released were invited to sit up front in a place of honor. All the speakers expressed support for the boycott, but all also preached against violence. Zeff, whom the *Forward* described as "an idealist who remains true to his ideals," told the crowd it was "better to go hungry than to give in." But it was Barondess who gave the most memorable address, evoking tears from the audience when he described the misery of poor people.

Born in Russia to a Hasidic family, he had received a traditional Jewish education but had rejected orthodoxy as a youth. He landed in New York in 1888, and after working as a peddler and a tailor became active in the nascent Jewish labor movement, organizing local cloak makers and leading them in a successful strike against the manufacturers. He was also a cofounder of the *Arbeiter Zeitung*—the "Workman's Paper," a Yiddish socialist weekly—and of the Social Democratic Party, whose motto was "pure socialism and no compromise." And in 1900 he had presided over the meeting at which the International Ladies' Garment Workers' Union was established. A tall, lanky, and handsome figure with dark hair and a sonorous voice, he had flirted with acting in his youth and was a brilliant speaker.[17]

Although not observant himself, Barondess was well regarded even in Orthodox circles and influential outside of them, and he sympathized with the women. He advocated doing without meat for a full month to bring the retailers to heel. If that failed, he suggested, "form a co-operative society. Buy your own cattle, slaughter them and sell the meat in your own shops." It was an idea that had been discussed before and would be again.[18]

Barondess put forward several proposals. He wanted an open-air meeting where people could air grievances and a protest march down Fifth Avenue. He supported sending a committee to the mayor to demand to know why the police had dealt so aggressively with peaceful demonstrators "who agitate in the friendliest manner," and a committee of three was promptly named. He exhorted people to go house to house to build support for the boycott and supported sending committees to every lodge and labor union to make the movement "greater and mightier."[19]

As the meeting wore on, the crowds outside got restless, and the police had to call for reinforcements. By now many men were home from work, and they had also come out in force to support the strikers. The police were determined to close Norfolk, Essex, Ludlow, and Suffolk Streets and part of Broome Street and to keep everyone in the neighborhood moving, something that proved quite impossible. The three hundred–odd patrolmen were no match for the throngs of angry people on the streets, and many responded violently, wielding their clubs indiscriminately.[20]

When four officers attempted to take fourteen-year-old Matilda Radinsky of Allen Street into custody for aiding a man who was disobeying a police order to move on, she, too, resisted. After she managed to cause one of the officers to lose his balance, he was pummeled by several demonstrators. Eventually Matilda was subdued, handled quite roughly, and dragged down the middle of Broome Street as her arresting officers swung nightsticks into the crowd for protection. But the clubs could not stop the bottles, stones, and bricks from the street and the water and other projectiles from the windows and roofs above. They finally managed to get her and two others into the patrol wagon, but it had been quite a struggle.

Smart butchers had already closed their shops, but several hundred people who invaded Orchard, Rivington, and Delancey Streets found some open, destroyed the "kosher" signs in their windows, and hurled their meat into the streets, where it was sometimes doused with kerosene—readily available, as it was used as a fuel for lamps—to render it inedible. A crowd entered several Broome Street tenements, seized all the meat they could find in people's apartments, and threw it out the windows. Three men were beaten and arrested at Allen and Rivington Streets when they hurled bricks at a police officer trying to disperse the crowd. Blood was everywhere.

"We did not come to fight with you," one woman in a crowd told a butcher on Essex Street. "We want you to strike with us." He said nothing, but retreated into his store, locked the door, went to the window, and proceeded to take off all his clothes—a nasty, calculated insult in an age of modesty. The women ran away, the result he had no doubt hoped for, but several hours later they returned. The one or two who wanted to break into the store were held back by the others. But one warned, "we will repay this lout of a butcher in another way." All swore to boycott his shop even after the strike was settled.[21]

The mere sight of the police enraged some protesters. They shrieked at them and called them murderers. Men cursed them. One officer who tried to rescue some meat buyers was slapped in the face with a moist piece of liver. More arrests were made and prisoners were locked up for the night at the Eldridge, Madison, and Delancey Street police stations. But demonstrators followed the police to Delancey Street and massed outside of the station. It took fire hoses to repel them. Although soaking wet, they did not go home, but simply withdrew until they were out of reach.[22]

Even innocents got caught up in the violence. Joseph Schipper of Ridge Street, who was not protesting but merely trying to get home from work, was set upon by three policemen, whose blows to his head sent him to Gouverneur Hospital. A doctor heading for a drugstore was beaten. And a young bookkeeper named George Seaman, outraged by the behavior of the police, rushed into a shop at Broome and Norfolk Streets and phoned the New York *World*. "The police are killing people down here," he said. "The *World* should have men here to see what is going on. The poor people need help, and they can't get it from the police, who are clubbing them brutally."[23]

18. Israel and Goldie Lustgarten ran a basement butcher shop on
Orchard Street between 1889 and 1902. Their window was smashed
during the protests and their business never recovered.
Source: Collection of the Tenement Museum.

No sooner did Seaman step back out onto Broome Street than he, too, was attacked. The police had no intention of brooking any interference from him. "Why, *that's* the man!" one officer cried out. "He'll breed a riot!" And at that, a policeman seized him by his throat and struck him forcefully with his stick several times. He was shunted into a patrol wagon and jailed.[24]

At about ten o'clock a group of women and children left New Irving Hall for District Attorney Jerome's house. The patrician Jerome had made a campaign promise to make his home among the people of the East Side if he and his reform ticket won the election, and he proved as good as his word. In early 1902, over the objections of his horrified wife, he leased a four-story brick building on Rutgers Street to use as both a home for his family and a branch of the District Attorney's office. His Jewish neighbors had watched open-mouthed as movers carried in all of his family's possessions, including chairs, mirrors, beds, tables and even a piano.[25]

After Jerome moved in, the *Forward* had asserted approvingly that although he had not promised to "make water come out of a stone" like Moses, he had nonetheless become "not just a neighbor, but a protector." And now his new Jewish neighbors were asking for his protection. He left a game of ping pong and allowed them to escort him to New Irving Hall. Outside the hall, Police Captain Richard Walsh told him he believed things were under control. But all was *not* under control. Shortly afterward, Walsh himself was struck in the back with a brick, followed by a shower of eggs from the upper stories of the tenements on Broome and Norfolk Streets.[26]

By several accounts, Jerome merely surveyed the scene and then disappeared. But the *New York Times* insisted that he had tried to persuade many demonstrators to go home, telling them that "they were proving themselves bad citizens" and warning that they would lose the sympathy of others. He also scolded many, lecturing them that they should be ashamed of themselves. The *Times* gave him credit as "a factor in quelling the riot," but nobody else did.[27]

If We Cry at Home

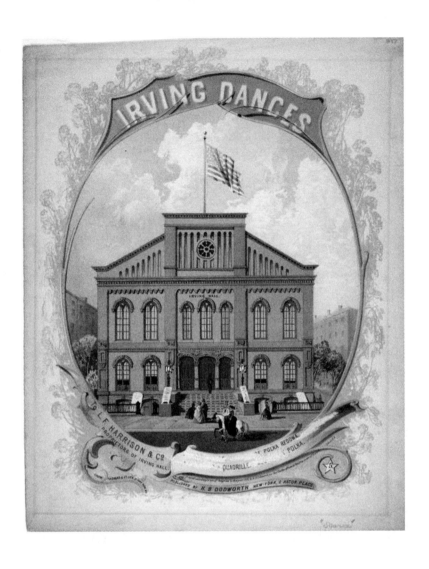

19. An early image of New Irving Hall.
Source: New York Public Library, Image ID: 1659151.

If there was any consensus on the pages of New York's newspapers about the disturbances, it was that although some of the women's tactics were disgraceful, their cause was just. In its news coverage, for example, the *Times* referred to the strikers as a mob, adding that "that is the only name that fits the sort of crowd this one was." And the *World* compared them to "a pack of wolves."

But on their editorial pages, the papers were more sympathetic. The *Times* suggested that the unrest, which it noted was the first instance of rioting directed at a trust, should give the Beef Trust "something to think about rather seriously." The paper was not about to prejudge the legal case against the Trust, but it added that "it cannot be denied that a half-dozen wealthy and powerful men have had it in their discretion to advance the prices of meat all over the United States." It suggested that purely as a matter of self-interest, "the public temper is something which such a body of men ought in reason and prudence to consider."[28]

The *World*, for its part, saw precedent for the strike in American history. In an editorial entitled, "It Will Not Do," the paper asserted that

> It is impossible not to feel a touch of patriotic sympathy for the East Side housewives who registered their protest against Beef Trust extortion by raiding the shops of the kosher butchers yesterday. Their method was censurable, but their motive was unselfish and even heroic. The tax levied on American tea by the arbitrary oppression of King George was less onerous than the tax levied on the East Side meat supply by the exactions of the Beef Trust, yet our school histories hold up to public approval the "Boston Tea Party," which raided the tea ships and dumped their cargo into the harbor.[29]

The *Forward* and both Brooklyn papers, the *Standard Union* and the *Eagle*, all remarked about the parallel to Boston in 1773. "No matter how much their indignation may have been misdirected when the women patrolled the entrances to the meat shops yesterday," the *Standard Union* wrote, "the spirit was the same which prevailed at the Boston Tea Party. They felt they were maintaining their rights as citizens." The *Eagle* saw it as a hopeful sign of Americanization on the part of newcomers who were "just about as far from the old world as were the Bostonese who dumped the stamped tea into the harbor." In an article later quoted in its entirety in translation in the *Forward*, it went on to note:

> They seem to have imbibed a fundamental principle of Americanism as quickly as any earlier emigrants did. They decided that they were unjustly taxed, or charged, which amounts to the same thing for the person who pays, and they went out to find a means to remedy the injustice. They found it. Their proceeding was not within the letter of the law, but neither was the Boston Tea Party.
>
> The Tea Party has become immortal because it embodied the principle of self-government. Precisely that spirit surged up and down the East Side ghetto yesterday. Whatever its temporary extravagances of expression may have been, the spirit promises a fine, sturdy, citizenship from the very newest seekers after American liberty.
>
> These people are notably peaceable and law-abiding when their rights are protected. And when the rights of any American are invaded, he has no business to be peaceable and if he temporarily defies the laws he is forgiven.[30]

The *World* did not miss the fact that the boycott of the local butchers did not reach "the really guilty criminals of the Beef Trust," however, and neither did the *Eagle*. As the latter pointed out, "the meat riot by the women of the East Side ghetto yesterday was not aimed at the Beef Trust. It was a fight between two conflicting interests in one race. . . . Their charge was not that the Beef Trust had cornered the supply, but that their own merchants, neighbors and countrymen . . . are 'wearing diamonds' as the result of unjust profits added to the price of their meat."[31]

Under the headline "Women's Revolution: A General Resistance against the Butchers," the Orthodox *Yidishes Tageblatt* described the events of the day in metaphors of war: "The whole Jewish quarter was transformed into a battlefield. The soldiers were women and they waged war against their female friends. The neighborhood looks like it was in revolution, but instead of shooting and guns, you heard women's voices. Instead of human flesh, over the streets there flew breast meat, knuckles and ribs from the carcasses of animals."[32]

The *Forward* was entirely supportive. The headline on its front page on May 15 read, "Brava, Brava, Jewish Women!" And the next day, Abraham Cahan, its founder and publisher, made it clear in an editorial that he believed that women were far better equipped for this particular struggle than men. True to his socialist orientation, he also managed to indict the entire capitalist system:

This protest movement of the women of the quarter is such that no Jew ever need be ashamed. Whether or not these women's fight succeeds, the Jewish people can be proud of it forever. We'll always be able to point to this fight in the quarter as evidence that despite centuries and thousands of years of Jewish subjugation under foreign despots, and despite generation after generation of Jews being yoked, enslaved and trampled under the feet of all types of tyrants and oppressors, despite all this, enough spirit and striving for freedom and justice remains, such that when injustice occurs, when cruelty is enacted against them or others, they are first to lead others in protest to fight against the injustice, against such cruelty.

It's good, very good, that the women were determined and that they decided to raise their voices against the Meat Trust leeches. No man's voice would resound with such an echo as do the women's voices that weep, yell out about their own lives, those of their young children on behalf of the poor slave, harnessed in support of his half-starved family. All of which is only half the battle. Yet, it's good to awaken and raise people's consciousness. It's good because it will open the eyes of everyone who is asleep and doesn't wish to see what is going on in the world.

When the people want to awaken and see the shame and misery throughout the community, then the work of the awakened will be completely different. Then, they'll see it's not the meat that needs to be soaked in kerosene, and not the puny butchers, who aren't responsible, but rather the huge Trust, the entire current capitalist system with its capitalist politics—from which the vampires, leeches and bloodsuckers of the people grow and prosper—all that has to be drenched in kerosene, lit on fire and then, on the pile of ashes of today's system, a community built of free and equal people.[33]

Like the *Forward*, several English-language newspapers took the opportunity to offer comments about the character of the Jewish people. In the case of the *Standard Union*, these were positive. "Among the most independent and most intensely patriotic of the foreign-born population are the Jews," the paper wrote, attributing this generalization to the persecution Jews had experienced in virtually every nation on Europe in which they had lived. By contrast, the *New York Herald* described the "wild scene of turmoil, especially in the evening, when all the pent up passions of the Hebrews—usually the meekest of mortals—were let loose."[34]

But if there was indignation that the women had allowed their demonstrations to get violent, there were also plenty of brickbats for the brutal behavior of the police. "Many of the men forgot they were facing women," the *Herald* noted critically. "Many of these were buffeted about and swept along the pavement as though there were no such thing as mercy." Robert Hunter of the University Settlement, which had been providing assistance to the immigrants on the East Side since 1886, agreed. He complained to the *New York Tribune*, about "unnecessary roughness the officers used," adding that he had personally witnessed outrageous examples of brutality.[35]

The *Tageblatt* was even angrier about it, calling the police "urban hoodlums," and asserting that "they could not get away with such *chutzpah*—audacity—in any other American city or any other quarter of New York City." No doubt with an eye to police brutality in past labor actions, the paper was accusing the force of antisemitism.[36]

Estimates of how many women took to the streets, how many police were called in, and how many demonstrators were actually arrested that day varied widely. The newspapers claimed variously that anywhere between three thousand and eight thousand people had participated, and that about three hundred police reserves had been summoned to control the situation. Arrests on May 15 had almost certainly numbered in excess of a hundred.

The crowds finally dispersed at midnight, just about the time that the meeting was adjourned, and calm returned to the streets. Most, if not all, of the kosher butcher shops were shuttered, and few Jewish people in the quarter enjoyed meat that night.

To that degree the strike had been a success.

But in no way had it accomplished its principal goal: meat hadn't gotten any cheaper. Nor was it over. When Captain Walsh predicted that trouble would break out anew the following morning, few on the East Side would have disagreed with him.

9

They Never Saw Such Assemblages
in Russia or Poland

The women who organized and carried out the meat boycott were not, by and large, educated people. Many had come from small towns or villages in Russia or Eastern Europe, and although they often spoke Russian or Polish in addition to Yiddish, they were unlikely to have been schooled except in the Jewish religion. Some had been in the United States for only a short period of time and could manage only rudimentary English. Many, if not most, were not yet citizens. Nor did many have much of an idea of the process by which the meat their families ate made it to their tables in America.

All they saw clearly was the *last* link in the distribution chain, the retail butchers with whom they did business every week. The factors that went into the price of meat, such as the cost of cattle feed, investments in stockyards and abattoirs, wages paid to slaughterhouse employees, and the cost of transportation and delivery, among others, could not have mattered less to them. All they knew, and all they cared about, was that their families required kosher meat, and that such meat had become unaffordable.

Few likely even understood much about the world of the meat wholesalers, just one link earlier in the chain, except to be told by their butchers that it was *they* who were responsible for the jump in prices. Just as the butchers deflected criticism by focusing their wrath on the local wholesalers—ignoring the Chicago conglomerates that supplied them, which were the true manipulators of prices—the women mostly did not look beyond their local butchers for enemies. They were told what wholesalers United Dressed Beef and Schwarzschild & Sulzberger were charging the butchers, but that was not their focus. It was what the retail butchers on Hester Street, Cherry Street, and the rest of the East Side were asking for meat that mattered. That is what had gotten them out into the streets.

Put another way, the Beef Trust was everyone's enemy, but to the slaughterhouses that term referred to the Midwestern packers. To the retail butchers, the Trust meant the New York slaughterhouses. To the women, it had come to mean their own local butchers. In the search for villains, nobody seemed able to see more than one step back in the process.

How did the *balebostes* of the East Side arrive at the idea of a boycott as a means of lowering meat prices? What experiences had they had, or what knowledge did they possess, that led them to the idea?

In the old country, some of these women had worked in factories or as home-based skilled or unskilled laborers, and some had gone into similar trades or into shopkeeping in America. Many had a firm grasp of the basics of running a profitable business. The concept of supply and demand and their relationship to price was not unfamiliar to them. It was not hard to understand that dialing back demand—in this case, by persuasion and, if necessary, by force—was likely to exert strong downward pressure on price.

Nor was there anything extraordinary or abstract about the concept of a boycott. Europeans had been using that weapon to victimize Jews for as long as anyone could remember. In Russia, Hungary, Austria, Romania, and just about every other country in which Jews dwelled, they were often singled out for unfavorable treatment. Sometimes they were excluded from membership in guilds or societies; at other times they were prohibited from purchasing land. Quotas limited their access to education. And it was not unusual for their businesses to be targeted, whether the goal was to extort money from them, to put them out of business, or to drive them out entirely. No Jews who were paying attention would have found anything unfamiliar about boycotts, although they had usually been on the receiving end of them. Indeed, for many, boycotts were probably among the reasons for their emigration to America.

Strikes, to which their boycott was constantly compared, were also nothing new. As socialism grew in popularity in Russia in the late nineteenth century, partly as a result of appalling labor conditions, labor societies choreographed work stoppages to press for higher wages and better working hours. In 1897 the League of Jewish Workingmen was organized in Vilnius. Better known as the Bund, it was essentially a secular Jewish socialist labor party that sought to unite all Jews in Lithuania, Poland, and Russia under its banner. Many zealous Bundists made the journey to America, where they found like-minded people among non-Jews. Their socialist ideology remained popular among Jewish immigrants, spawned a number of fraternal organizations, and was a frequent topic of conversation among secular and observant Jews alike.

Nor did the women necessarily need to hark back to the old country to appreciate what strikes could accomplish. Even those who didn't have such memories had only to look around New York to discover how to band together and organize to put pressure on an adversary. Labor stoppages were commonplace and the newspapers, Yiddish and English alike, covered them extensively.

The advent of labor unions in New York preceded the coming of Russian Jews, and although their arrival in great numbers coincided with explosive development in the ready-made clothing industry, most early immigrants, including large numbers of women, worked in small sweatshops and were not candidates to join them. But as the industry grew and the locus of activity shifted from sweatshops to factories, many of those who became skilled tradespeople eventually joined unions. Jews also set up unions of their own; these often came and went, depending on working conditions, and sometimes did not outlast the strike that had been the impetus for their formation.

As Jews established themselves as tailors, garment cutters, cigar makers, bakers, typographers, and other skilled workers, low wages and unsafe working conditions made them ripe for the message of organizers—often radical socialist or anarchist agitators—who called meetings and preached that strength could be found in unity. Joseph Barondess himself, who worked in the garment industry after he emigrated to America, led the first cloak makers' strike in 1890.

During the years immediately preceding the meat protests, there were always people walking off their jobs *somewhere* on the East Side. In January 1900 four thousand pants makers laid down their scissors, refusing to resume work until they were granted a ten-hour workday. Later that year, six hundred Jewish bakers in 120 shops shut off their ovens, also in pursuit of a ten-hour day. The following year, some fifty to sixty thousand tailors called a "strike for fresh air" to force manufacturers to assume responsibility for sanitation in contractors' shops and to stop withholding wages. Nor was there any hesitation about going after Jewish employers. In early 1900, at Barondess's instigation, actors and actresses struck three Yiddish theaters for a fixed scale of wages and better hours.[1]

And in no way was striking just a local phenomenon. At precisely the same time the Jewish women of New York began their march, teamsters in Chicago struck the meat packing houses there for better pay and overtime, and more than a hundred thousand anthracite coal miners in Eastern Pennsylvania walked out, seeking higher wages, shorter workdays, and recognition of their union. That bitter strike posed a serious threat to the nation's coal supply, but the mine operators were determined to break it and refused to negotiate. Amid reports of violent confrontations, President Theodore Roosevelt sent in the National Guard to protect the mines and attempted to mediate, although he had no legal authority to do so. He was eventually successful. The Yiddish-language press was full of news of the five-month strike as it progressed.

They Never Saw Such Assemblages

The tactics used by union organizers were well understood in the Jewish quarter. Bernard Weinstein, a longtime labor agitator, gave a taste of some of them. "We did our principal work of organizing unions by calling meetings, which we called 'mass assemblies', but first we had to lay the groundwork by sending volunteers to the factories and sweatshops to distribute handbills to the workers," he recalled in a 1929 memoir. "We also gave handbills out in restaurants, dancing schools, cigar stores, and on the bridges where the workers in some trades used to congregate." In addition, the activists delivered motivational speeches, held outdoor demonstrations, spoke with the press, solicited funds for war chests, and picketed employers.[2]

That the female protesters saw their meat boycott as of a kind with the labor strikes was evident in the vocabulary they chose. The boycott was often referred to as a "strike." A person who crossed picket lines to buy meat was a "scab"—that is, when not being derided as a "Christian" or a "*ganef*," the latter a Yiddish term for a thief or a scoundrel.[3]

Yet another influence was surely the then-current agitation for women's suffrage. Women pushing for the vote had not yet begun their annual parades, but they were quietly using a variety of tactics to build support for their movement, including knocking on doors, speaking from soap boxes to crowds in the streets, printing circulars and distributing them to passers-by, and lobbying men with whom they came into contact.[4]

But there were significant differences between the ways Jews and other New Yorkers conducted strikes. In 1896, while a tailors' work stoppage was going on, the *New York Sun* observed "several peculiar features" of strikes in the trades that were largely Jewish: "The men, however greatly excited, hardly ever resort to violence, and never use lethal weapons. The few disturbances during the present strike have been but slight. There have been some scuffling, some pushing, some whisker pulling and some body blows, along with much scowling, much threatening and much Yiddish bombilation; but nothing more than the appearance of a policeman has yet been needed for the restoration of peace and order." Only in America, the *Sun* was certain, could Jews enjoy such freedoms as the freedom to strike: "Meetings of the kind are novelties to most of the people who attend them. They never saw such assemblages in Russia or Poland, the countries from which they came; never till they got to New York did they know of such a thing as freedom of speech; never in their native places did they enjoy the great and glorious American right to go on strike."

The paper probably overstated the case, since strikes had not been unknown in Russia. But it marveled at the lack of conflict among the leadership. "In most strikes," it wrote, "the leaders find it hard to retain their power for weeks, and are pretty sure to have bad times, with plenty of quarrels." The *Sun* believed that Jews were different in this respect. But, as would soon be seen, the women who led the meat boycott were not immune to internecine struggles.[5]

Common tactics notwithstanding, the meat boycott was not entirely like the earlier labor strikes. Here was a movement initiated and organized by *women*, something that had not happened before. And those being mobilized were not fellow tradesmen or union members, but an entire community—in fact, the largest and most densely populated Jewish community in the world. The goal was to help them act in their common interest and find their common voice—this much was similar to strikes—but then to wield their collective power not as laborers, but as consumers, something none of them had ever done before.

10

Hebrews with Shaved Beards

On Friday morning, May 16, 1902, the Jewish quarter looked as though it had been bombed. The *Forward* compared its appearance to the aftermath of a Russian pogrom. For several blocks there was not a butcher shop with an intact storefront in sight; some markets had been completely demolished.

And there was no reason to believe the boycott was anywhere near over.[1]

A few shops displayed signs offering kosher meat for sale at twelve cents a pound, which, for some butchers, was better than not selling any at all, since the seventy-two-hour window between slaughter and *kashering* was fast closing, and the meat would soon no longer be able to be rendered kosher. But when their fellow butchers heard about the discount, they pressured them to close. They could still sell the meat to sausage-makers, and many did.[2]

Beyond this, there was little evidence of any change in the price of meat in the shops that dared open their doors. Charges for eggs, chicken, vegetables, and even coal had also risen dramatically, as had the cost of sausage, pressed beef, and other wurst meat sold at the delicatessens, which had been in high demand in recent days. The *New York Tribune* noted that where fifty cents a day would have been sufficient for a typical East Side housewife to meet her family's food needs, it would now buy only two-thirds of what it had a few months ago. Spending seventy-five cents a day for what had cost fifty meant expenditure of an additional $1.75 a week, a sizeable chunk of the ten or twelve dollars the average East Side husband brought home.[3]

Sarah Edelson managed to find some time on Thursday to meet with a reporter from the New York *World*. Her interview took place in the rear of Monroe Palace as she gutted a fish. "I had no idea of starting such a big movement," she told the reporter. "but all that was needed was a word or two. Then everybody jumped in and said, 'No, we won't be robbed anymore! Let's boycott the butchers!'"

She gave a somewhat disingenuous account of how the strike got started, making it all sound quite spontaneous, and making no mention of the meeting she had called on Wednesday during which the activity had been planned. She also took pains to refute Joseph Goldman's claim that anarchists were behind the strike.

"Anarchists? The butchers who call us anarchists are crazy," she asserted. "You never saw a woman with a husband and half a dozen children who was an anarchist. No, no; we're just human beings who are sick of being robbed."

"We won't quit," she continued. "We will go without meat for six months, if necessary, to bring the price down. Two years ago it was 12 cents a pound. Then it was 14, then 16, and now it's 18 and going to be 20, the butcher says. We're going to be cut off from eating meat anyhow, and it might as well be now."

"I was arrested yesterday. I didn't mind. I did nothing. I was out in the street coaxing women to go home when I saw they were trying to break things. You don't have to break butchers' windows to win a strike. I was on my way home when a man pointed me out and says, 'She's a leader'. The policeman took me to court. The judge didn't give me a chance to say a word. He says, 'What do you know about trusts? Ten dollars fine.' We will win this strike. We want meat for 12 cents a pound, and we'll get it."[4]

The police anticipated another day of unrest. Commissioner John Nelson Partridge ordered five hundred men to report for duty on the East Side. Surely in response to the

Hebrews with Shaved Beards

widespread criticism of police brutality the day before, Partridge also issued orders to deal gently with the protesters, and officers were issued four-foot lengths of rubber hose and rattan canes to use instead of their billy clubs.[5]

By 6:00 a.m. small squads of women had already gathered, armed, as the *New York Tribune* put it, "with sticks, vocabularies and well-sharpened nails." As fast as the police dispersed them, they regrouped elsewhere. They paraded up and down the streets scolding butchers and breaking windows. It was still not safe for anyone on the street to carry a package that looked as if it might contain meat.[6]

If things were less violent than they had been the day before, the *New York Times* speculated, it was because the women had been cowed by the brutal behavior of the police. Another thought was that it was the steep fines assessed by Magistrate Cornell. It may also have been the fact that so many butcher shops had closed, though some had shut only their front doors and secretly let customers in through side or back entrances.

In any event, there were many more arrests on Friday. Some protesters were taken into custody but never made it to court if they were liberated from their police captors en route by angry demonstrators armed with eggs, stones, and garbage, or by water bags and rotten vegetables dropped from tenement windows above.

Magistrate Cornell began his day by clearing his backlog. He heard the cases of forty women and ten men arrested outside New Irving Hall the night before, and then turned his attention to new defendants. Most were demonstrators, but some were butchers. Now in a decidedly irritable mood, Cornell was more than willing to hand out ten-dollar fines with impunity. He ordered the courtroom cleared, and even insisted that police clear the street outside the courthouse, where nearly a thousand had taken up positions. This was easier said than done, because in the course of the day sympathizers and relatives of prisoners unable to make bail kept coming; many denounced Cornell and the police in impromptu speeches. Officers made valiant efforts to repel the crowd, which swelled to about three thousand at one point, but at times it seemed a futile endeavor.[7]

Cornell found Minnie Ostlander of Orchard Street guilty of terrorizing the family of Abraham Schwartz. She and others had chased Mrs. Schwartz up the stairs of the tenement at 82 Norfolk in which she lived, demanding that she hand over a chicken they had seen her buy. Mrs. Schwartz was determined to stand her ground, but when the women threatened to wreck her flat, her husband handed the bird to Ostlander, who held her quarry high above her head and screamed with delight as she carried it down to the street, where she was promptly arrested. Schwartz swore to the judge that he had thought he was going to be killed. Ostlander was fined ten dollars.[8]

Twenty-seven-year-old Annie Sonnenschein, twenty-four-year-old Anna Karpf, and thirty-six-year-old Rosa Edelman were all assessed ten dollars for throwing kerosene on the floor and fixtures of Matthias Burnett's butcher shop at 103 Rivington. Someone had then thrown a match and a small fire had broken out.

The widespread use of kerosene concerned the police and fire departments greatly. The meat shops, which were saturated with fat and grease, were located mostly on the ground floors of large, densely populated tenement buildings, where fire could threaten many lives. According to the *Forward*, within a half hour of the start of a fire on Monroe Street, it had spread among the tenement houses until ten o'clock, "when the entire Jewish quarter, from Cherry Street to Houston and from Grand Street Ferry to the Bowery was lit up by the brave striking *balebostes*." Captain Walsh later called it one of the worst days of his police career.[9]

Some people received especially severe treatment from the judge, whose "ten dollar fine" refrain was compared by the *Forward* with tongue in cheek to a *nigin*—an improvised, repetitive Jewish religious melody. Ida Basucky of Forsyth Street, a large, muscular woman, was sentenced to three

Hebrews with Shaved Beards

months in the workhouse for beating up Officer James J. Devine, a policeman trying to clear a path through a crowd in front of the Essex Market Court. The *World* described her as a "giantess" who "put a neck lock on Devine, back-heeled him, threw him down and fell on him." Elsewhere, the *Tribune* made a reference to "Amazonian warfare."[10]

Two important meetings took place on Friday afternoon. The first, called by Sarah Edelson and held at Monroe Palace, was to decide how to deal with kosher delicatessens. Their business had thrived over the past several days, and they had raised prices as butcher shops had closed down. Reasoning that, preserved or not, meat was meat, the women assembled voted to extend the boycott to the delicatessens. And sure enough, later in the day a mob of five hundred attacked Herman's Restaurant on Allen Street. They enjoined a man who had ordered cured meat to send it back, and when he refused, someone snatched it from his table and several men pulled him out onto the sidewalk and beat him.[11]

Like the butchers, the delicatessen owners felt ill-used. The proprietor of an East Broadway café gave voice to what many were surely feeling:

> Who is there looking after *our* interests? The Mayor doesn't care; he rides home in his automobile. Jerome takes a vacation, the police beat our women and drag them to jail. Even in Russia we were not so badly treated. In my own province I have known the governor to compel the bakers to sell bread so the poor could buy. But here we have no one. Why, the price of meat and provisions has risen so that it makes the difference of $20 a week to me in this café. The people here lay it to the Low government. They will have to pay the piper.[12]

The second meeting that day involved Paulina Finkel, Clara Korn, and Caroline Schatzberg, the trio appointed at the New Irving Hall meeting the night before to call on Mayor Low. Although they were not permitted to see the mayor, they were granted an audience with his secretary, James B. Reynolds, that afternoon.

„מיר ווילען כשר'ע פלייש!" שרייען פרומע ארעמע אידען, „אבער א דאַ-
פעלטער טראַסט פאַר וואָס קומט אונז!"

20. "'We want kosher meat', scream pious, poor Jews" begins the caption for an illustration from the front page of the May 17, 1902, edition of the *Forward.* The drawing depicts a Jewish man being crushed by a joint effort of the Meat Trust, represented by a large steer, and the "Kosher Meat Trust," symbolized by a *shoychet.*

"The Christian butchers are buying and selling their meat at about the same price as formerly, and we do not see why the kosher butchers should try to raise their prices six and eight cents a pound," forty-three-year-old Romanian-born Clara Korn asserted. "They say they have to pay 16 to 20 cents a pound for their meat. But we hear that the retailers are making a profit of four or five cents a pound, and we do not see why the poor should have to pay that."[13]

"I think the blame rests with the shopkeepers, and too much censure cannot be given them," Reynolds observed. "At the same time, when attempts are made to burn stores and officers are assaulted there can be no two ways of acting," he warned.

The women had also come seeking a permit for a mass outdoor meeting and to ask the mayor to order the police not to molest them while it was going on. Reynolds referred them to police headquarters for both requests. When they were told there that no permit would be granted, they headed for Rutgers Street to call on District Attorney Jerome, but he was not at home.[14]

By the end of the day, Magistrate Cornell had fined ninety people, seventy of them women. Twenty-five of them, like Sarah Wasserman and Sarah Reich, convicted of assault, had no money to pay and were kept in jail. This left many small children with no one to care for them and, as a result, about two hundred husbands, brothers, and other male relatives of the women gathered outside the Essex Market Court to protest.

"Release the women!" several shouted as they attempted more than once to storm the jail's gate, but under the direction of Captain Walsh, police from the Eldridge Street Station, nightsticks at the ready, managed to drive them away. One man, Isaac Weisberger, refused to move, asserting that as an American citizen he had the right to stay right where he was. The police had a different view of his rights, however, and he was taken into custody himself and charged with disorderly conduct.[15]

Some of the newspapers were getting impatient with the rioting. "The East Side demonstrations against the kosher butchers have gone too far," the *World* asserted on its editorial page. "It is time cooler counsels prevailed. Public sympathy undoubtedly is with the poor who have been deprived of meat by the cruelly unfair advantage taken by these retail butchers of the Beef Trust's extortion. They have made the situation much harder for the East Side people than there was any need of its being. But the public peace requires that such disturbances as have been taking place shall be stopped."

Long on platitudes, however, the paper was short on practical recommendations. "The proper remedy lies with the more intelligent citizens in the communities affected," the editorial went on. "The *World* urges them, as the leaders of the people, to give calm counsel, to point out that there is nothing to be gained and much to be lost by rioting, and so persuade these unfortunate people out of the passionate mood which, though they are under great provocation, they must restrain."[16]

The *New York Sun* expressed sympathy for the butchers. "The kosher butchers against whom the mob rose are poor men, whose characteristic industry gains but a scanty living for them," the paper opined. "Because they did not carry on their business precisely as their neighbors liked, the latter broke into their stores, destroyed their stock and defied the police."

"The butchers are entitled to the full protection of the law, and insofar as they need that, the undivided sympathy of the entire city," it continued. "And the rioters should be taught as impressively as possible that one of the first rules of law is that people mustn't interfere with other people's business."[17]

To the extent that both papers were criticizing the lawlessness of the past two days, they certainly made a valid point. The violence wasn't doing the women's cause any good. But how did the *World* propose "the more intelligent citizens" solve the problem of unaffordable meat? What did the *Sun* suggest the women who were destroying butchers' stock do instead? Neither paper offered any practical suggestions likely to break the impasse.

The *Forward*, by contrast, made no mention of rioting in its coverage, and placed no blame on the women, whose struggle it found heroic. It depicted their picketing as friendly and well organized. The *Forward* saw only women speaking pleasantly to butchers and asking them to be true to the great strike, and, the paper assured readers, when they remonstrated with would-be meat purchasers, "99 out of 100 stopped and obeyed with enthusiasm and stood with the strike." In the *Forward*'s world, there were apparently no broken windows.[18]

The paper, however, saw a bigger enemy than the local butchers. In a May 17 opinion piece, editor Abraham Cahan reminded readers that the enemy was not so much their retail butchers as the "Hebrews with shaved beards." By this he meant the German "millionaire Jews" who "themselves eat *treyf*," and he demanded to know why "they are so pious at the expense of poor tailors' pockets."

But Cahan went even further. He suggested that the *shoychtim* and *mashgichim* appointed by Rabbi Jacob Joseph—the ones who were supposed to bring order and integrity to the kosher meat market—were in fact working corruptly in cahoots with the German-Jewish slaughterhouse operators to profiteer off the sale of kosher meat. He didn't blame Rabbi Joseph for this; a truly pious man, the good rabbi had suffered a series of strokes, the last of which, two years earlier, had rendered him an invalid. He could barely move and could no longer work. It was, rather, the people operating in his name who were to blame.

Cahan accused them of affixing "all kinds of crooked *karobkes*" to their meat, and noted that Rabbi Joseph's son, parading around town in a carriage, continued to collect fees in his father's name. He implied it was all a conspiracy to skim money by selling unkosher meat as kosher and driving good Jews to eat *treyf* unknowingly, "all in the name of their true enslavement to the Trust." He did not, however, present evidence for his case.

21. Abraham Cahan. Source: Wikipedia.

"One thing we know," Cahan concluded, "is that the poor people who want true kosher meat can and should do away with this harmful union of the Trust and the rabbis who serve it so faithfully." And they should take aim at the rabbis. "Against these true servants of the Trust, one must strike," he wrote.[19]

The unrest wound down quickly that Friday after sundown, which occurred just after seven. It was the onset of the Jewish Sabbath, widely observed among the East Side's Orthodox Jews. But what would come next? If the butchers reopened on Saturday night or Monday morning and maintained their high prices, more trouble was a foregone conclusion. Many of those whose shops had *not* been raided were now sitting on surplus stock with which they would have been happy to part at discounted prices. But more than seventy-two hours would have passed since the meat was slaughtered, which would mean it could no longer be kosher.

The arrival of the Sabbath brought peace of a sort to the East Side. But, as the *New York Press* warned readers, "neither the police nor the people themselves looked on the interlude as more than a brief truce."[20]

11

And He Shall Rule over Thee

The streets were quiet on the morning of Saturday, May 17, when many Orthodox Jews of the Lower East Side were at worship. But though it was the Sabbath, the women behind the meat boycott were not idle. They planned to make the rounds of the synagogues and *shtieblach*. It was an excellent opportunity to spread their message to a captive audience of Jewish men, who made up the bulk of the worshipers but who worked during the week when the picketing was going on. It was also a radical and impertinent move.[1]

In most places, things went smoothly. A pair of women would ask the synagogue president for an opportunity to speak and, if granted, would spend a few minutes explaining their movement. Worshipers, in turn, would generally pledge their support. Two women particularly successful at these congregational visits we know today only as Mrs. Kiseloff and Mrs. Silver; their given names, unfortunately, are lost to history, as are their biographies. But it is clear they were effective, articulate speakers committed to their cause.

The pair began with four *shtieblach* on Broome Street. Mrs. Silver, who had a Jewish education and understood Hebrew, made a clever appeal to the male worshipers in one hall by quoting from Genesis 3:16, in which God, speaking to Eve about Adam in the Garden of Eden, tells her that "he shall rule over thee." With tears in her eyes, she implored the men to use this God-given power they wielded over their wives to ensure that they bought no meat. The *Forward* asserted that "all the men and women who found themselves in this synagogue joyfully promised to uphold the boycott." The ladies secured similar promises from congregants at the Beis Hamidrash HaGadol on Norfolk Street, where Rabbi Jacob Joseph had given his first address to the Jews of New York in 1888.[2]

They arrived at the imposing Eldridge Street Synagogue during morning prayers and asked to speak from the *bimah*, the platform at the center of the sanctuary from which the Torah was read and lectures and sermons delivered. It was usually off-limits to females, who, by custom, were relegated to an upstairs gallery. The synagogue president dismissed them. But one mounted the platform anyway, availing herself of a seldom-invoked Jewish tradition dating from the Middle Ages that permits the interruption of prayers, and even of a Torah reading, to seek redress of a grievance.

She asked the rabbi to "lay a *cheyrem*" on meat, using a potent Yiddish term for a boycott that suggested a religious ban. He declined to go that far, admitting quite candidly that he feared the kosher butchers might lynch him if he did so. But he did request that congregants support the women and give up meat.

At the Forsyth Street shul, Mrs. Silver was heckled by a large-bellied man who said he objected to speeches from the *bimah*, calling it chutzpah and an insult to the Torah.

"The Torah will forgive me," she assured him without missing a beat. "We ask only that you forbid your women to buy meat." Unmollified, the man then proceeded to mount the *bimah* and make a speech of his own, suggesting that maybe it was just *women* speaking from the platform that had disturbed him.

"Jews!" he proclaimed. "Do not make a *cheyrem*. Just see to it that your women buy *less* meat. We can't manage without meat. Buy *half* of what you need and don't go to the theater so you'll have more money for meat."

This caused a ruckus, and someone brought in a policeman. Told to arrest Mrs. Silver, the officer began dragging her from the platform. But then someone else spoke up.

"Jews! Remember the prophet Zechariah. He was killed on the *bimah* of the Holy Temple because he did harm to the truth and justice of his people. Don't let anyone get arrested." That point of view apparently carried the day, because Mrs. Silver was released and she and Mrs. Kiseloff continued on to other shuls, one of them muttering on the way out, "woe to us, *such* a synagogue!"

Women from the ladies' galley at the Madison Street Synagogue who insisted on addressing the congregation were blocked by male members. They then asked one of the men to speak instead, but he refused, citing fear of the slaughterhouse bosses. So they waited until the Torah reading was finished and tried again, at which point the synagogue president sent for the police. There was a huge brouhaha, but, as on Forsyth Street, no one was arrested.[3]

The women received their worst treatment at the People's Synagogue of the Educational Alliance, a settlement house on Jefferson Street founded by German Jews in 1889 to help "Americanize" Eastern European immigrants with English lessons, citizenship classes, and the like. Rabbi Adolph Radin, who had emigrated from Prussia in 1886, was in the middle of a sermon when Caroline Schatzberg, Paulina Finkel, and others entered the hall. Mrs. Schatzberg waited politely until he finished to ask him to allow her to speak.

The rabbi bluntly refused. He insisted that women were ignorant of the facts and not competent to manage a boycott. "If you are unable to pay 25 cents a pound for meat, don't eat it!" he asserted dismissively. Then he called Mrs. Schatzberg a "beast," which infuriated her and the others who had come in with her. It was a very nasty insult.[4]

Such difficulties were the exception, although they make clear that there was opposition to the boycott within the Orthodox community, and to female activism in general. In most of the houses of worship the women visited, their message was well received. Half a million of the city's Jews, according to the *New York Herald*, pledged that day not to purchase kosher beef or other meat products until the butchers reduced prices. But there were holdouts among the Orthodox, who found the entire subject of a women's boycott unseemly.[5]

The streets were mostly quiet while services were underway, but there were a few incidents reported in the *Yidishes Tageblatt.* Annie Goldstein was arrested on Christie Street, ostensibly for doing nothing more than "expressing herself strongly" about the horrible behavior of the police and of Justice Cornell. Israel Weinberg of Ludlow Street was detained for "making a scandal" at a delicatessen at Orchard and Rivington Streets, though what sort of scandal was not disclosed.

And at Forsyth and Henry Streets, the *balebostes* conducted a reconnaissance mission at several bakeries where, the previous night, women of the neighborhood, as was their custom, had brought their *cholent* pots to slow cook in the ovens. They systematically lifted the lids of each pot to determine whether the stew contained meat. Where it did, it was discarded. "A *cheyrem* should remain a *cheyrem*," one of them insisted at the time. "If *we* can't eat meat, *nobody* should eat meat."[6]

Joseph Barondess, assuming a more central role in the movement, asked Police Commissioner Partridge to grant the women's request for a demonstration permit. Partridge took the request under advisement, and when the team that had unsuccessfully sought a permit from the Mayor's office called on him, he promised to consider their request. But it came out later that another member of the Jewish community had approached him to request that he *not* approve a permit. It was none other than Rabbi Radin of the Educational Alliance, the boycott opponent who had publicly cursed Caroline Schatzberg and her cohorts.[7]

"I have decided not to issue this permit," Partridge eventually announced. "Joseph Barondess gave me his personal guarantee there would be no trouble, but I doubt he could control the situation. We have been sending police reserves to the East Side to maintain order, and I do not think a mass meeting would be wise at this time. I have so advised the committee of women."

22. Joseph Barondess. Source: Wikipedia.

On Partridge's orders, the police dispersed a crowd of several thousand that had spontaneously assembled in Seward Park. But a meeting already scheduled for Central Hall at 1915 Third Avenue took place as planned, despite efforts by a couple of butchers to disrupt it. About two thousand people, mostly women, attended, and Caroline Schatzberg, Paulina Finkel, and Barondess all spoke. Money was collected to pay the fines of those who had been arrested.

In his remarks, Barondess expressed only opprobrium for Partridge and for District Attorney Jerome, who happened to be his next door neighbor on Rutgers Street:

> Ever since this agitation began, the authorities have shown themselves incapable of appreciating its importance or realizing what it means to thousands of orthodox Jewish women who would starve or eat poison before they would eat meat not prepared according to the Mosaic law. They have been patient and long-suffering, and now they have revolted.
>
> Police Commissioner Partridge and Deputy Commissioner [Nathaniel] Thurston have practiced the most dangerous sort of deceit. Neither has risen to the occasion or seems to understand it. District Attorney Jerome, who has made his home in this district, has not opened his mouth and has not stirred hand or foot to relieve an intolerable condition, which in all speeches before election he pledged himself to correct.
>
> I am not a religious man myself, but I believe in even justice. It does not matter that the persons now suffering are of the Jewish faith. I would be as insistent on fair play if the complaint came from Catholics or Protestants or any other denomination.
>
> There will be a day of reckoning. The East Side, which looked to the reform administration for support, has been betrayed. The police on Friday night were permitted to club defenseless women whose only crime was that they demanded food at fair prices. The reformers have not kept faith with the people, and I promise now to use every effort to retire them from office at the next election.[8]

And He Shall Rule over Thee

Of course, not all of what he said was entirely fair. Demanding food at fair prices was not criminal, but seizing meat, destroying property, attacking the police, and resisting arrest certainly were. The police had been overly brutal, but the women had been anything but defenseless. Several officers had the wounds to prove it.

The members of the Hebrew Retail Butchers' Kosher Guarantee and Benevolent Association were decidedly uncomfortable at the situation in which they found themselves. When they saw police brutality and heavy fines being assessed against their customers, they regretted being the targets of what the *Forward* called the "righteous scorn of the Jewish masses." Association president Joseph Goldman sent word to the women that if they would send a committee of *male* representatives to a meeting, he would be glad to discuss the situation with them. There was no immediate response, but the proposal can hardly have sat well with Edelson and company. The women had given the entire city reason to take them deadly seriously; suggesting that only men were worthy of negotiating on their behalf must have appeared a calculated insult.[9]

News of the denial of the demonstration permit hit the streets at about the time the synagogues were emptying out. The proprietors of New Irving Hall, where Sarah Edelson and her cohorts had called a second meeting for 8:00 p.m., had also been ordered by police not to open the hall for the women. It was an ill-advised decision, because when people arrived and were denied entry, they simply massed on the street, which is just what Commissioner Partridge had hoped to avoid.

"Not even *this*?" someone yelled out. "Isn't it *enough* that they have beaten us with clubs for nothing? Not even letting us have a *meeting*?"[10]

The situation was tense. When the *Forward* noticed police reserves entering the Jewish quarter in large numbers, it, too, anticipated trouble after sundown, when the Sabbath would officially be over, and so it published a special 4:00 p.m. edition with advice for both the women and the butchers:

> Women: Don't buy meat, but stay calm. Don't give the Trust or the police an excuse to break heads. If you behave lawfully and calmly but firmly, you can accomplish more. Be friendly; be watchful on the streets and in your houses. All honorable families are with you. Don't forget that the Trust is praying to God that you should be unruly and start fights; that way you would lose the sympathy of the public and they would win. The best you can do against them is to remain calm and stay off the street.

> Butchers: Don't forget that you live off the sweat of the workers. Lock up your shops! Don't let them break heads and arrest brave, innocent women in your name.[11]

Most of the neighborhood's butchers had indeed decided to stay closed on Saturday night; there was no need to remain open for deliveries, because few of them had ordered any meat since the previous Thursday, which also meant that few had anything to sell. But not everyone heeded the call to stay home. Crowds once again fell on those few shops that opened, and Essex Street, Hester Street, and a half dozen other locations saw more arrests. Police were called to quell a riot at a Pearl Street poultry market where women had broken in and thrown the chickens into the gutter. If there was any good news, it was that Saturday night was not nearly as violent as Thursday and Friday had been.

The *Tageblatt* compared the Saturday scene to "Purim back home." It was a reference to the Festival of Lots, which celebrates the saving of the Jewish people in ancient Persia, and which was often celebrated in the old country by going house to house in costume, performing skits and collecting for charity. In this case, donations would help defray the fines of those who had been arrested.[12]

But the Lower East Side wasn't the only locale that saw protest that night. In Brooklyn, a crowd of several hundred appeared at Graham and Seigel Streets; some said women had come from Manhattan to Williamsburg to organize them. Their first target was a corner butcher shop run by Russian-born Joseph Serinsky. Rioters threw stones at his window and then stormed his premises, overturning tables of meat and seizing his knives. Fearing for his life, he abandoned the store to the crowd and fled.

Raphael Bernstein's store on Manhattan Avenue was the next target, but news of the coming mob had reached him and he, too, bolted as people cleaned out his store. Simon Brothers on Seigel Street came next; they initially refused to close, but were persuaded when pelted with rotten eggs and vegetables.

When the crowd reached Julius Goldberg's shop on Moore Street, however, he met them at the door brandishing a meat cleaver in one hand and an axe in the other. He announced that he was a working man who meant to defend his livelihood. He maintained he had been compelled to raise his prices by the action of the Beef Trust, and that he would kill the first person who attempted to prevent him from earning money to feed his family. By one account he was cheered for his stance; by another, he received a full complement of rotten vegetables. And by a third he got away with only broken windows.

Police from three stations dispersed the mob, but they reassembled on Manhattan Avenue, where some women who had already bought meat were heading home. They were followed, and a number of private homes were invaded, their meat seized and discarded. What happened next was a brawl between demonstrators and police, with its attendant stone-throwing, meat-throwing, and clubbing. At least fifty people were trampled in the melee. Police didn't regain control of the streets until 10:00 p.m., having quelled the most serious disturbance among the borough's Jews any of them could recall.[13]

Similar scenes played out on a smaller scale in the Bronx that night, principally on Third Avenue between 170th and

23. A Mrs. Perlmutter and others outside a Brooklyn butcher shop discussing the price of meat. Source: Library of Congress, Prints and Photographs Division, George Grantham Bain Collection, LC-DIG-ggbain-01489.

172nd Streets, where a half-dozen kosher butcher shops were located. Here a couple of dozen women, all dressed alike in white blouses and black skirts, begged would-be meat purchasers not to buy from butchers charging "extortionate rates." When they were ignored, like their downtown sisters, they stopped the customers and seized their quarry. Even a little girl was intercepted on her way out of a Third Avenue shop, to cries of "We'll have our rights!" and "Down with the butchers!"

Police warned the protesters, but they were jeered. As one of them grabbed Bertha Siegel, a large, thirty-two-year-old woman, she brazenly ordered him to mind his own business and not to interfere.

"That's right, stick up for yourself," said a voice from the crowd. "You're all right, Mrs. Siegel." But she and four others were eventually arrested. They and four more were held by police in a Chinese laundry as a crowd threw stones and tried to break in and free them. But the police prevailed, and finally the patrol wagon arrived to cart them away. Bail, set at $500 for each woman, was posted for them by a Jewish alderman.[14]

The most violent altercation of the night took place in Harlem, where a hundred women led by thirty-five-year-old Yetta Hirschberg set on a man coming out of Abraham Lippman's 106th Street butcher shop. They shoved him against a wall and continued to rain blows on him until he ran away. They also stopped other meat buyers and destroyed several neighborhood establishments until the police stopped them. It was a standoff: the police didn't want to club the women, but the latter stood their ground. Finally, they placed Hirschberg under arrest.[15]

Brooklyn, the Bronx, and Harlem were now all in turmoil, and within a day or two Boston and Newark would join the list. It was no longer just a Lower East Side phenomenon.

The kosher meat strike had metastasized.

12

No Industry in the Country Is More Free from Single Control

As U.S. Attorney Solomon H. Bethea prepared to argue the federal case for a temporary injunction against the Big Six packers in Chicago, several states also got into the act. Missouri instituted its own investigation. The Ohio legislature passed a new antitrust measure aimed at the Beef Trust. And New York Attorney General John C. Davies launched an investigation of the Trust for possible violation of state antitrust legislation.[1]

By mid-May, Davies was ready to move ahead, and to increase his chances of success, he bifurcated his effort. He requested the New York State Supreme Court in Albany to appoint a referee—a retired judge—to determine whether prosecution to revoke these corporations' business certificates was warranted. And he instituted a formal action against the Trust that would be heard by a sitting state supreme court justice.

In the first instance, ex-Justice Judson H. Landon was chosen to hear witnesses, all of whom would be testifying for the state. And Justice Alden Chester would hear from both sides in the formal case.[2]

On the morning of May 15—the very day the protests in New York City began—Justice Landon heard testimony from Andrew W. Gerlach, a New York City retail butcher who had done business for twenty-seven years with all the companies of the Trust. Gerlach asserted that when the wholesale price of beef began to rise on January 1, *all* the companies raised it simultaneously, in lock step. He also described a dispute in which a Swift & Company agent told him he had been placed on a credit blacklist. Thereafter, no Trust member would do business with him except on a cash basis.[3]

While the hearing was adjourned for lunch, however, Davies received a telegram from U.S. Attorney General Philander C. Knox asking that testimony of Daniel W. Meredith, a Jersey City–based former employee of both Swift & Company and Armour & Company and one of Davies' key witnesses, be postponed. The Justice Department intended to argue the federal case before the Seventh Circuit Court in Chicago on Tuesday, May 20, and Knox didn't want Meredith to tip his hand before that. In light of the request, Davies asked Justice Landon to adjourn until May 22.[4]

But there was no bar to continuing the case before Justice Chester. Davies hadn't made his witness list public, but it was widely rumored that the star witness under subpoena would be Arthur Colby, allegedly the Trust's New York City–based "arbitrator," the point person who set the prices Trust members were required to charge for beef in the Eastern region. Colby, it was believed, had the authority not only to fix prices, but also to impose fines on constituent companies that violated the packers' agreement.

Also on Davies' witness list were the New York representatives of the Big Six—Armour, Swift, Cudahy, Hammond, Schwarzschild & Sulzberger, and Morris. And on May 13 he had dispatched a representative from Albany to New York City to serve subpoenas on all of them.[5]

There was just one problem. The men were nowhere to be found.

Despite repeated visits to their homes and places of business over two consecutive days, the server could neither locate them nor learn their whereabouts. Nobody would say where they had gone. Davies had been assured that they would welcome his investigation as a means of clearing themselves of allegations of wrongdoing, but their disappearance suggested otherwise.[6]

No Industry in the Country Is More Free

"The developments of the last few days have convinced me that the companies are afraid of a judicial inquiry, and their representatives have placed themselves outside the jurisdiction of the court," he told Justice Chester. Under the circumstances, there was no immediate way to proceed, so Chester, too, was forced to postpone his hearing. He set Monday, May 26, as the date to reconvene.[7]

As all of this was happening, news came out of Chicago that beef prices had broken all previous records. "This advance," the New York *World* insisted, "is plainly an arbitrary decree of the Trust, as the supply of cattle in the stockyards is as large as usual." And the paper published the numbers to prove it.[8]

On Sunday, May 18, the day before the federal case was to be presented in Chicago, both the *Chicago Tribune* and the *New York Herald*, in cooperation, published a blockbuster story. The papers had somehow gotten hold of internal Armour & Company correspondence. The *Herald* promised the letters would be turned over to the Attorney General for use in the federal case.

But not before the papers gave their readers a taste of what was in them.

The file included thirty letters to and from Armour executives in several eastern and midwestern cities. Code names were used for each Trust member, but it wasn't hard to figure out who was who. They told a tale in black and white of a conspiracy among the so-called competitors to control the price of meat, parcel out territory, act in unison against "outsiders," and be sanctioned for any violations of their agreement.[9]

Attorneys at the Justice Department were jubilant when they learned of the scoop, which essentially made most of their case against the Trust. Assistant Attorney General William A. Day, who was to help argue the case for the government, declared that the new evidence proved the existence of an agreement to raise and maintain prices in violation of the Sherman Antitrust Law. "It shows the existence of a hard and fast combination between the six great packing houses not only to regulate prices, but to divide territory," he said. "I consider this a very important contribution to the campaign." After reading the coverage, Solicitor General John K. Richards took off for Chicago to help Day and U.S. Attorney Bethea make the case.[10]

The next day, the papers reported that when Colby and the six Trust companies' New York managers disappeared from the city, they had taken with them all of the books and papers they had been ordered to produce as evidence by Justice Chester in Albany. The men had not gone far, however. They had simply moved their headquarters, lock, stock, and barrel, across the river to Jersey City and Hoboken, conveniently out of reach of the New York judicial system.

As for the office of the arbitrator, its "complicated network of special telephone, telegraph and ticker wires" that connected Colby with more than sixty Trust branch offices in New York, Brooklyn, and Jersey City was impossible to pack up and move overnight. But all of the books and papers—including records of fines imposed under the Trust agreement—had been removed to Jersey City, and Colby himself, it was reported, had left on a long vacation, destination unknown.[11]

The *Herald* explained that the reason for the exodus was that the Trust members feared that information revealed at the hearing before Justice Chester in Albany would prejudice their federal case in Chicago. As far as the New York *World* was concerned, however, the move was an admission of guilt. "Removal is confession," it declared on its editorial page. "The Beef Trust is on the run."[12]

The publication of the Armour correspondence blew a huge hole in the strategy the Trust's lead counsel, John S. Miller, had intended to use in court. The packers had vowed to fight a temporary injunction by denying that any cooperation agreement existed. Now, in the face of incontrovertible evidence to the contrary, they changed their tune. They would now *admit* the allegations, but argue that their activities did not violate the Sherman Antitrust Act.[13]

No Industry in the Country Is More Free

On Tuesday, May 20, in an unusually crowded courtroom, Judge Peter S. Grosscup called the case of *United States v. Swift & Co. et al.* U.S. Attorney Solomon H. Bethea laid out the government's evidence against the defendants, claiming they controlled 60 percent of the nation's fresh meat trade. He filed twenty-odd affidavits from people formerly employed by Trust companies, the most damning of which was from Daniel W. Meredith, the witness whose testimony the Justice Department had asked New York to defer. Meredith's statement revealed that the six New York–based general managers of the defendant companies had met weekly since 1893 to set prices for the week to come. Whenever they felt it was advantageous to raise prices, they agreed to curtail meat shipments from Chicago and points west to reduce supply.[14]

Other affidavits were from two former Nelson Morris employees. One claimed to have transcribed an 1888 agreement between three Trust companies binding them to meet regularly with an arbitrator to maintain prices, pay fines for violations, and share information about discharged employees. The other had had the duty of translating coded telegrams from other Trust members.[15]

Taken together, they were an extremely damning set of documents.

Bethea asked the judge to bar the Trust companies from further collusion. Attorney Miller did not object to the issuance of an injunction, though he did assert brazenly and disingenuously that "no industry in the country is more free from single control." He claimed that because he had not been afforded the opportunity to examine the government's affidavits in advance, he was not prepared to refute them. But he objected to the government's assertion that the defendant companies controlled 60 percent of the nation's packing business—he insisted the figure was closer to 40 percent.[16]

So at 3:00 p.m. Judge Grosscup issued a temporary order enjoining the companies and their agents from "entering

24. A sketch of the courtroom scene in the Beef Trust case.
Source: *Chicago Tribune*, May 21, 1902.

25. Judge Peter S. Grosscup. Source: Library of Congress,
Prints and Photographs Division, George Grantham
Bain Collection, LC-DIG-ggbain-06248.

into, taking part in or performing any contract, combination and commerce in fresh meats" by:

> instructing their agents not to bid against one another in the purchase of livestock;

> arbitrarily raising or lowering prices or fixing uniform prices;

> arbitrarily curtailing the supply of meat shipped;

> posing penalties for deviations from agreements;

> establishing uniform rules for credit;

> imposing uniform charges for delivery; or

> obtaining rebates or special rates from the railroads.[17]

It was a total victory for the government. Day, the Justice Department's special counsel, gave the press his interpretation of the Trust's languid defense. "It means that the government's case is more than the counsel for the packers cares to tackle."[18]

Attorneys for the packers did not tip their hand about their next move, which in any event would not have to be revealed for several months, since the companies had been given until August 4 to reply to the basic complaint.[19]

Whether they would comply with the terms of the injunction was an open question, but they would be subjecting themselves to substantial penalties if they failed to do so. They would be subject to being held in contempt of court, and the burden of proof that they had *not* violated the order would be on them rather than on the government.

Nothing about their history, however, suggested that they were the sort of companies to simply roll over and play dead.[20]

13

Essentially It Is a Fight among Ourselves

On Sunday, May 18, the day the papers printed the purloined documents that exposed the inner workings of the Beef Trust to the world, the kosher butchers of New York voted to keep their shops closed, and the Jewish women of the Lower East Side formalized their alliance.

Police reserves stood at the ready to quell any violence, but apart from a disturbance in the Brownsville section of Brooklyn that morning that involved some hair-pulling and shattered windows, things were quiet. The butcher shops were closed, if not out of fear of marauding women, then because state law forbade them from opening on a Sunday. The only movement of meat took place before daylight, as uncounted pounds of it, no longer salable as kosher, were carted away, bound for out-of-town sausage factories.[1]

But if it was not a day for protest, it was one for organization and planning. When the East Side Hebrew Retail Butchers' Kosher Guarantee and Benevolent Association convened on Attorney Street, members voted to keep their shops closed. And five hundred people, mostly women, attended a day-long meeting at New Windsor Hall on Grand Street to establish a permanent advocacy association and develop a plan of action. There were many scathing denunciations of the magistrates who had fined them and of Commissioner Partridge, who had denied them a demonstration permit and whose policemen had abused them. Then they voted to establish what they dubbed the "Ladies' Anti-Beef Trust Association" and proceeded to elect officers.[2]

To the surprise and dismay of her many supporters, Sarah Edelson was not chosen to lead the group she had founded. In fact, she wasn't chosen for *any* office. Caroline Schatzberg was named president; Paulina Finkel was elected treasurer; Maurice Blumenthal, a representative of the Garment Workers' Union, which had sent a contingent to the meeting, was named vice chairman; and Jacob Kirschberg, also from the union, was tapped as secretary.

The establishment of the new organization, despite its title, marked the end of the completely female-led movement. Mrs. Schatzberg would be advised by an executive committee of nine women and eight men. The group would be headquartered at 412 Grand Street, a building associated with several labor unions, and staffed day and night.

The *Forward* hailed the meeting for taking the next logical step in the struggle. It was now time for "a well thought-out plan," it opined, and to carry it out "in a calm, peaceful manner and not rest until the price of meat returns to that of a year ago."[3]

A six-member committee was charged with appointing sub-committees to distribute circulars in the tenements to build support for the boycott. Its members were cautioned not to create disturbances or clash with the police. If they happened on others who were breaking the strike and buying meat, they were to ask them to discard it. If they refused, they were to offer to buy it from them and dispose of it themselves. And they were to attempt to recruit them to join the association.[4]

An auxiliary committee of nine men, several of them husbands of female members, was also named. They were to visit the Bronx, Brooklyn, Harlem, and Long Island City to help organize boycott committees in those locations, and even to recruit non-Jews where possible, although few of them would presumably have had much of a stake in the price of kosher meat. Other committees were tasked with contacting the various benevolent societies and lodges in the Jewish quarter.[5]

It Is a Fight among Ourselves

26. Outside a kosher butcher shop in Brownsville, ca. 1918.
Source: Old NYC Photos.

The new officers announced that all who had been fined in connection with the previous week's meat riots would be made whole, and $500 collected earlier was used to reimburse those women for fines paid or bail posted. They also launched a new collection to replenish the association's coffers; some $200 more was taken in that very evening, most of it in small contributions. In a few cases someone would toss in a crisp five-dollar bill, but more often it was a few coins extracted from a pocketbook or a crumpled handkerchief.

"We will go on collecting for this purpose as long as there is one person who has suffered through coming into conflict with the police," Secretary Kirschberg vowed dramatically.[6]

"It will be a question of endurance between us," Caroline Schatzberg predicted. "If the retailers can afford to pay rent and do no business, I guess we can afford to do without meat. Fish and vegetables are pretty good food at this time of year, and we can stand it as long as they can." She didn't mention the fact that the prices of poultry, milk, and eggs had also risen precipitously because people had switched to other sources of protein, or that even demand for vegetables and cereals had more or less doubled.[7]

Schatzberg also announced another initiative. "We have had letters from independent slaughterhouses in Boston and Philadelphia, and we expect to start about 200 butcher shops of our own. The meat we get from these cities will be tagged and marked to show that it is kosher." Kirschberg suggested that new shops might be located on every fifth block on the East Side. "Each customer will be a stockholder in proportion to the amount of his purchases. That means a share of the business and a share of the profits. The price of meat will be ten cents per pound and the profits on it will be divided among the buyers."[8]

It was an admirable, if somewhat unrealistic, aspiration.

Behind closed doors, the leaders of the new association also decided to settle a score with Rabbi Radin, who had so viciously insulted Mrs. Schatzberg, Mrs. Finkel, and the other ladies at the Educational Alliance on Saturday. "While still wearing the vestments of his holy office, and in the presence of more than one hundred men," Mrs. Schatzberg reported, he had used "a term that should be resented by every woman of Hebrew origin."

The women he had insulted signed a formal denunciation of him that was published in the Jewish newspapers the following day. They made sure to mention his Prussian origins, branding him a "half-German." Pointing out that he moonlighted as chaplain for Jewish prisoners in the city jail, they wondered "what kind of sympathy such a German can have with our unfortunate people who fall into prison. He called us beasts and insulted us so coarsely in public. How must he behave behind those iron bars?"

Finally, they called him out for his perfidy in lobbying Police Commissioner Partridge to oppose their demonstration permit. "He is the only Jew who wants to thwart us, and he should be damned by every respectable person who wishes us success," the statement concluded.[9]

On top of the participation of Barondess, the appointment of Blumenthal and Kirschberg and the issuance of an explicit invitation to representatives of the Garment Workers' Union to attend future association meetings signaled not only the infiltration of males into the movement, but also a deepening alliance with the labor unions. The Children's Jacket Makers' Union had already sent a message of support, and Sunday saw Barondess address a meeting of New York's Central Federated Union. His speech resulted in a proposal from a member of the Amalgamated Sheet Metal Workers that *all* the unions abstain from meat for a month in solidarity.

The resolution, however, was opposed by a delegate from the Cigar Makers' Union, who argued that it would be outrageous to ask working men to give up meat entirely, and it failed to pass. But a motion to appoint a committee to draw up resolutions of sympathy with the Jewish women carried, as did another that offered the Settlement Building Hall, where the Central Federated Union met, for use by the Ladies' Association if the police continued to block them from meeting on the East Side.[10]

It is not difficult to see why the women sought out the labor unions for support, or why the unions offered it. The unions were well established and well organized, and endorsement from them brought in hundreds of supporters at a time. And the Jewish union movement, while not entirely a socialist phenomenon, was nonetheless born of a deep suspicion of capitalism. Although it was the petty capitalism of their local butchers that the women had in their crosshairs, it was certainly increasingly apparent to many that the principal villains in the drama were the large packing houses that made up the Beef Trust. And finally, the unions were experienced in organizing and winning strikes, to which the boycott was constantly compared, and the boycotters had borrowed many of their tactics.

The New York *World*, which had interviewed Sarah Edelson a couple of days earlier, now gave its readers a picture of the new titular head of the movement, Caroline Schatzberg. It described her as "a humanitarian of natural eloquence."

"I was born a Jew, but my religion is humanity," she told the paper rather pretentiously in an interview. "I will have been here 19 years on the coming Fourth of July. In that time, I have tried to help the poor people, for the rich can help themselves. I am interested in this appeal for meat at a proper price because it affects the poor. We have been compelled to pay very high prices for very poor meat. But what has incensed me most is that the gentiles could buy their fine meat in their better shops at a lower price than we could get [for] our miserable lot. It has not been right. We have been imposed upon by our own people and essentially it is a fight among ourselves.

"I do not believe in fighting or violence and I have counseled against it. But our people are ignorant and they recognize power only in physical strength. We hope to show them, however, that more can be won by a good argument and a consistent stand."[11]

It was inevitable that someone would discern Machiavellian motives in the unrest. The *New York Herald* reported that the authorities suspected that the Beef Trust was actually behind it.

> It is the opinion of the police that the representatives of the Beef Trust, far from being opposed to the rioting that has been going on, are engaged in fomenting the trouble. They are believed to see in the action of the dwellers of the East Side something that will in the end result to their benefit. There are indications that agents employed by the packers are among the agitators who are persuading the poor classes to outbreaks. Believing this, the police expect a resumption of the troubles of last week, and plans are being made to meet any mob that may be formed.

Proof, the paper continued, could be found in the fact that prices had recently been raised *only* on the cheaper cuts of meat favored by the poor, and on the forequarters, the source of all kosher beef.

"This shows clear discrimination," the *World* noted, "for one part of the beef costs the packer the same as the other parts, and if there is an increase in the price of cattle, it would affect the whole beef, and not just the forequarters." The *Herald* agreed. "Excuses of short supply cannot affect only one part of a steer. It is believed by conservative dealers that the unfair squeeze is made for the purpose of showing the East Side butchers who have dared to defy the Trust that they still must pay anything the combination chooses to ask or go without. It is the most barefaced case of deliberate extortion ever perpetrated at one blow by the Beef Trust." It was an implausible theory, and the only evidence for it was the price rise. No proof was offered that any agitators had been sent in by the packers.[12]

For its part, the *Forward* put forth a somewhat different conspiracy theory. In a May 18 editorial entitled, "The *Karobke* in Russia and Here," it pointed out that in Russia, the tax on kosher meat had been about seven cents a pound. In America the sum was similar: about five or six cents. But in Russia, the *karobke* supported *all* of the communal activities of the *kohol*, whereas in America, the differential went only to the Trust, the *mashgichim* and the *shoychtim.*

The paper's solution? "Rabbis should be rabbis and slaughterers slaughterers. They should not serve the Trust at the expense of the poor people," the *Forward* opined. It was nothing more nor less than a restatement of the very problem Rabbi Jacob Joseph had been brought over to address fourteen years earlier and had failed to solve—that those responsible for kosher slaughter were in the pocket of the meat industry.

In the same article, the paper reported that some of the workers at the retail kosher butcher shops discerned a plot by the larger retailers to destroy the smaller ones. Speaking of the earlier butchers' strike, the paper wrote, "they say the whole settlement of the strike was collusion of the rich retail butchers with the Trust against the smaller butchers and the poor people."[13]

A local butcher agreed in a letter to the *Tageblatt.* "I would ask you to tell your readers what kind of a swindle the large butchers are perpetrating with this strike. It is no more than a trick by the large butchers to make money and ruin the small butchers. What have they accomplished here? They have driven 150 small butchers out of business." He went on to explain that the agreement the butchers had struck with the Trust to put the speculators out of business had been the real prize, since the speculators had been willing to extend credit to the small butchers, something the Trust had stopped doing. Withdrawal of credit hurt the smaller butchers far more than the larger ones.[14]

Although the conflict was pitting the Jews against one another, it was far from clear how much of the blame actually rested with Jews. The women were struggling against the retail kosher butchers, the smaller of whom were blaming the larger ones. And all were pointing fingers at the German Jewish-run slaughterhouses. The *Forward* was blaming corrupt slaughterers and supervisors ostensibly in bed with the Trust. But at the end of the day, as the government was asserting in Chicago, it was the Big Six that had quietly been setting the prices.

Monday, May 19, saw its share of unrest. Shortly after Joseph Solomon opened his uptown Madison Avenue store, he was set upon by a group of women. The police arrived in time to forestall damage to his premises, but he closed up quickly after the altercation. Later that day, police at the 104th Street Station dispersed a mob that had massed on Second Avenue when Morris Wigdorowitz left his store with a large parcel of unsold meat he intended to unload elsewhere. When women tried to seize it, he managed to retrace his steps and return to his shop. He then sent his daughter for the police, who escorted him and his meat to the elevated train station.[15]

Brooklyn also saw trouble, but nothing of the magnitude of the previous Saturday night. A policeman was badly beaten in Brownsville in an effort to disperse a crowd of three hundred who attempted to interfere with a butcher shop that had opened. In Williamsburg, too, there were minor outbreaks. And on the East Side, a patrolman broke up an open-air meeting on Hester Street by taking Samuel Smaller, the ringleader, into custody.[16]

But the real chaos on Monday did not take place in the streets. Rather, it was a gathering of the new Ladies' Association that evening at New Windsor Hall that degenerated into pandemonium. Six hundred people attended the meeting, which Caroline Schatzberg called to order. But she had not spoken more than a dozen words before she was interrupted by shouts.

It was Sarah Edelson, smarting from her ouster the night before and determined to reverse what she considered a grave injustice. She made a grand entrance, escorted by her burly son and followed by a dozen "determined looking" women, according to the New York *World*. Mrs. Edelson herself had a large frame, and so, apparently, did several of her companions. Shouting that the election had been a fraud, she led her procession to the stage where Carolyn Schatzberg, Sarah Finkel, and others were seated.

Here's how the *World* described the melee that ensued:

> Mrs. Edelson placed herself at the head of her women, with her 400-pound son as a rear guard. Then the party moved forward, cutting a path through the mass of humanity as they went. The platform people nerved themselves for the conflict, and when Mrs. Edelson essayed to climb the first step, they moved against her *en masse* and tried to push her back. The fat women behind Mrs. Edelson and the giant son braced themselves, and their great weight moved onward and upward as relentlessly as fate, Mrs. Edelson and all of her party finally landing on the platform, breathless but triumphant.
>
> All this time about 20 men and women were making speeches, the audience was howling hysterically, epithets were being hurled about and a few were shrieking at the top of their voices, "Beware! Beware the newspaper reporters! Beware the disgrace!"
>
> Mrs. Schatzberg, in widow's weeds, with a wild shriek made a jump at her rival, but a dozen men grabbed her and held her back. Mrs. Edelson stood as motionless as a statue, staring at her rival. Speeches were made by advocates of the rivals and finally a man proposed that both women be elected president with equal powers. The meeting adopted this with a roar.[17]

But sharing the office didn't appeal to Mrs. Edelson, who insisted that it was she who had launched the movement, and reminded everyone that unlike Mrs. Schatzberg, *she* had actually been arrested. Since the assembly was not prepared to overthrow Mrs. Schatzberg, who had been duly elected, Mrs. Edelson eventually left the hall in a huff, declaring that she would start an independent movement and that she intended to hold on to the money she had collected rather than hand it over to the Ladies' Association.[18]

When the meeting finally got down to business, a committee of twenty-five was appointed to patrol the East Side and report any kosher butchers caught selling meat so they might be "blacklisted and boycotted for all time." The leaders also showed circulars printed in Yiddish for distribution—clearly primarily to men—in the Jewish quarter. One, decorated with a skull and crossbones, read, "Boycott! Boycott! Don't Eat Meat. They are Eating the Flesh of Our Women." Another read, "Eat No Meat While the Trust is Taking the Meat from the Bones of Your Women and Children."[19]

The plan for cooperative butcher shops came up again, and it was announced that a committee of Boston-based wholesalers independent of the Beef Trust would arrive the next day for discussions about supplying beef to the shops. And a representative of the Butcher Workers' Union expressed the wish to cooperate with the Ladies' Association in the establishment of such shops.[20]

The Trust had thrown down the gauntlet; it remained to be seen whether the Ladies' Anti-Beef Trust Association was ready to go to the mat. The *Chicago Tribune* was pretty sure they were. "What gives the present movement strength," the paper noted admiringly in an editorial, "is the character of the people engaged in it. The Jews have a genius for resistance. They showed that at the siege of Jerusalem. They have shown it many times since. As the writer of the Book of Kings says, they can 'harden their necks like to the necks of their forefathers'. The stubbornness of the Teuton is sweet reasonableness compared with the stubbornness of the Hebrew."[21]

"In this case, stubbornness is not unnecessary," it went on. "He who fights the Beef Trust must be prepared to contemplate the last ditch. It will be interesting to see what the women's Anti-Beef Trust Association can accomplish. It will be hoped that it may accomplish a great deal."[22]

14

Vein Him as He Veins His Meat

Although the Ladies' Anti-Beef Trust Association had not yet achieved its ultimate objective of lowering the price of meat, it *had* accomplished a great deal. Through a variety of tactics, women who had never organized anything remotely like it in the past had managed to mobilize the East Side Jewish community, not to mention Jews in surrounding areas, in pursuit of a common cause. And they had shut down the butcher shops, which they saw as a prerequisite to attaining their goal.

With so much bad blood among factions within the Jewish community, however, and now with a public split within the association itself and no solution in sight, it was probably only a question of time before men would attempt not only to participate, but to assume some leadership over the movement. In an age when women were expected to be homemakers rather than participate in public life, many men felt *their* assistance was vital to the cause.

They didn't relish the spectacle of their wives and daughters being beaten with nightsticks by the police in the streets, and they knew the clashes weren't doing anything to generate sympathy for the boycotters. Then, too, most of the association's potential allies in the struggle were institutions that were better organized and better positioned to undertake the fight—all of them run by males.

The first of the efforts by men to assert some control occurred on Tuesday, May 20, when the United Hebrew Community of New York (UHC) appealed to the newly established Ladies' Association to join them in negotiating first with the retail butchers, and then with the slaughterhouses. The UHC had been formed only a year before on a model somewhat different from that of most of the *landsmanshaftn*—the Jewish mutual aid societies. The latter had been founded by and for people who originated in a specific region or town in Russia or Eastern Europe. The UHC offered similar services, but without regard to a person's place of origin, and provided free religious services as well. In that sense, it served the entire Jewish community.

A meeting between the officers of the Ladies' Association and those of the UHC was held at the latter's headquarters at 215 E. Broadway. Carolyn Schatzberg and a few other women spent several hours there. Afterward, the UHC Secretary, a Mr. M. Malkowitz, spoke with the *Daily People*, the official organ of the Socialist Labor Party.

> Our plan is to get the butcher shops open the first thing, without regard to the price of meat. The Hebrew people cannot live long without meat, and we are already tired of fish, eggs, milk and vegetables. I want meat and so do they all. This rioting does no good whatever and must be stopped. If we can get the women to permit the butchers to sell meat, then our committee and the women's committee will go together to the wholesale butchers and try to secure a reduction in prices, or a compromise of some kind. Of course it will be hard to keep the women quiet when the shops open, but the thing's got to be done some way.[1]

The problem, of course, was that to permit the butchers to reopen without any stipulation as to price would have been to fly in the face of everything the women had stood for since the movement had begun. Then, too, however much the women blamed their butchers for the price rises, the retailers were, at best, responsible for only a portion of them. There was no particular reason to believe that the UHC and the Ladies' Association, even if they joined forces with the

Vein Him as He Veins His Meat

retailers, would be any more persuasive with the wholesalers—who still insisted that the problem stemmed from the limited supply of cattle—than the butchers alone had been. And it made little sense to give up the leverage a boycott afforded them in *advance* of such negotiations.

The upshot of the gathering was ultimately no upshot at all. A committee of ten headed by Dr. Henry Pereira Mendes, the well-regarded rabbi of the Spanish and Portuguese Congregation Shearith Israel, was charged with meeting with the wholesalers to determine whether the retail butchers were charging fairly for their meat. But nothing ever came of his initiative.[2]

That night, as fifty police officers looked on, several thousand people, mostly women, assembled in Rutgers Park and loudly cheered a dozen or so socialist speakers who denounced not only the Beef Trust, but "all corporations, capitalists and oppressors of the working classes and the poor." The meeting had been organized by the Social Democratic Club, headquartered on East Fourth Street. The enthusiasm worried the police captain, who summoned another hundred reserves, but there was no rioting.[3]

The next morning, however, the *New York Sun* reported that an unnamed socialist newspaper had announced that the Ladies' Association had "joined hands with the socialists," undoubtedly a reference to the Rutgers Park meeting. But there is no evidence that suggests any formal involvement by the Ladies' Association; it was likely no more than an opportunistic effort by the Social Democratic Club to use the meat boycott to build support for its anticapitalist cause.

Caroline Schatzberg smelled a rat. "The Beef Trust has had this printed so that people will imagine we are the same as socialists and will withdraw their support," she told the *Sun*.

An editorial from the socialist *Daily People* does survive for that day, but it suggests nothing about cooperation with the Ladies' Association. On the contrary; its portrayal of the group was quite contemptuous:

The anti-open-Kosher-shopites on the east side have taken to fighting among themselves over the leadership of the Amazonian band that has chased those who defied their mandate, and have recklessly thrown liver to the four quarters of the globe, and have scattered mutton chops about as though they were mere gold. Mrs. Sarah Edelson started the riots, and decided that she should be queen of the Society for the Making of Hamburger Steak out of Any Kosher Butcher that Refused to Shut Up. Her ambition was defeated, so Mrs. Edelson, who weighs 250 pounds, and her little son, Isaac Edelson, who weighs 400 pounds, tried to enforce their demands.

The result was a fight, but right, backed up by 650 pounds of Edelson, was on the point of winning when the police interfered. No arrests were made and finally the matter was compromised by making Mrs. Edelson joint president of the lengthy society above mentioned.[4]

For the record, the author of this satirical piece got several of the details quite wrong. Sarah Edelson had pointedly *rejected* the role of joint president. The son in question was known not as Isaac, but as "Big Jake," and the police never interfered with the meeting.

The *Sun* got something else wrong. It asserted that the Ladies' Association had denounced Joseph Barondess for passing himself off as a leader of their movement and voted to refuse him and his followers admittance to future meetings. There is no evidence for this. On the contrary; Barondess was instrumental in securing police permission for a conference of social, fraternal, mutual aid, and religious society leaders, two per organization, to meet with the Ladies' Association and seek a way to end the trouble, and he remained quite active in the effort. Whoever was lying to the *Sun* was no friend of the Ladies' Association or their boycott.[5]

Harlem saw disturbances on May 20, while the East Side remained relatively calm. Riots also broke out in Newark, New Jersey. Three butcher shops along Prince Street, the

Vein Him as He Veins His Meat

major Jewish marketplace, were raided and damaged by Jewish women; one was completely stripped of its inventory. The impetus appears to have been two mass meetings attended by about a thousand people the night before. A committee of forty women was appointed to continue agitating for lower meat prices, and the Newark police assigned a special detail to Prince Street.[6]

But it was Boston that boiled over.

At first, the conflict was just among the kosher retail butchers. For eight hours that afternoon and evening, a mob of about a hundred who had formed an alliance against Samuel Solomont & Son, the city's principal kosher meat wholesaler, besieged the stores of several noncooperating butchers, pelting them with eggs, vegetables, and stones. A few gunshots were also fired in the air. Solomont had recently jacked up prices, and the alliance was intent on bypassing the firm entirely and buying directly from its supplier, the New England Dressed Meat Company.

But the New England Company, which was in fact an arm of the Beef Trust, refused to sell directly, prompting the butchers to shut down to apply pressure, and the Jewish community supported them. When three butchers, including Julius Levine of Morton Street in the North End and Mendel Egyes of Spring Street in the West End, refused to agree and went on selling Solomont meat, the other butchers attempted to shut them down, and pretty soon an army of Jewish women joined the fray.

"Vein him as he veins his meat," one of them cried as meat was thrown into the street and Levine was assaulted. But the police intervened and he agreed to close down. Egyes, however, did not, and his store was attacked three times. On one occasion, he and his son brandished knives, but the shop was largely destroyed. Two men were injured, and an agent of the New England Dressed Meat Company was bombarded with eggs, as were Samuel Solomont and his family. Things did not calm down until 10:00 p.m., and disturbances resumed the following day.[7]

SCENE ON MORTON STREET WHEN THE RIOTING WAS AT ITS HEIGHT. IN THE FOREGROUND IS THE STORE OF JULIUS LEVINE, WHICH WAS PELTED WITH MISSILES. JULIUS HIMSELF, WHO IS SEEN IN THE PICTURE, WAS ROUGHLY HANDLED.

27. A sketch of the sacking of Julius Levine's Morton Street kosher meat market in Boston. Source: *Boston Post*, May 21, 1902.

Back in Manhattan, committees from the East Side Butchers' Association and a newly formed Uptown Butchers' Association called on the United Dressed Beef Company, the largest of the kosher slaughterhouses, on Wednesday, May 21, as several hundred of their members waited outside, hoping for some sort of breakthrough. No details of the discussions were released, but no agreement was reached.[8]

In the meantime, Sarah Edelson, who had vowed to work apart from the Ladies' Association, had booked a hall on Grand Street for a meeting of her rump group. She was, however, prohibited from entering it by police who insisted it was not big enough for the gathering. The conference of community groups Barondess organized, however, did take place that night. It was held at the Educational Alliance in the same hall in which the women had been cursed by Rabbi Radin on Saturday.

Dr. David Blaustein, superintendent of the Alliance, was asked to chair the meeting. Born near Vilna, Blaustein had received a Jewish education and trained as a rabbi in Russia and Prussia before emigrating to America in 1886. He initially settled in Boston and studied at Harvard and Brown Universities before accepting an offer from the Educational Alliance to come to New York. His was a life dedicated to public service, and as an immigrant himself, he had tremendous empathy for the struggles of the East Side Jews and often took up their mantle.[9]

Admission was by ticket only, which meant that six hundred people representing three hundred organizations were permitted in, but several hundred others who showed up were not. The latter group loitered in front of the Alliance building all evening as fifty policemen kept order. There was a brief disturbance when a butcher entered the hall; had it not been for the police, he might have been injured, but he was escorted safely out of the auditorium.[10]

If Blaustein's assumption of the chairmanship of the meeting was not, in itself, strong enough indication that the women were no longer in full charge of the movement they had

28. The Educational Alliance building, early 1900s.
Source: New York Public Library, Image ID: 801461.

launched, he made that fact crystal clear in his remarks. After threatening to withdraw his delegates unless the women who were present stopped "chattering," he warned that they should henceforth let the men do the fighting for them, lest they be blamed in the event of defeat.[11]

Convening a forum of such a wide range of organizations with their divergent perspectives was not without its own problems, but Blaustein was equal to the task of running such a meeting. To avoid chaos, he announced that in addition to Barondess and Caroline Schatzberg, he would limit speeches to delegates from the Jewish newspapers, since they were fairly representative of the various currents within the Jewish community. It took until about 11:00 p.m. for all to be heard.

At that point, it was agreed that Blaustein would appoint a committee of ten—three from the Ladies' Association, six from other organizations, and, presumably, himself—and that they, in turn, would elect forty more. All would work together as a Committee of Fifty that would effect "a consolidation of forces." These would be delegates to a general convention of a brand-new, permanent organization to be known as the Allied Conference for Cheap Kosher Meat. Blaustein would lead the new organization, at least temporarily, and Carolyn Schatzberg, a Mrs. Breckstein, and Sarah Edelson were all named vice presidents.[12]

One of the most important tasks facing the new group was to get control of money. The Ladies' Association, by all accounts, had been quite responsible about using the funds it collected to pay bail and fines for those who had been arrested, and to compensate many whose meat had been confiscated. But Sarah Edelson had refused to hand over the cash in her possession once she split with the Ladies' Association. To make matters worse, other individuals had been out on the streets collecting for the boycott, and it wasn't at all clear where that money was going. The Allied Conference aimed henceforth to represent *all* the Jewish people, and would put the word out that the Jewish newspapers would serve as its only official channels for donations.

29. Dr. David Blaustein. Source: *Memoirs of David Blaustein, Educator and Communal Worker* (New York: McBride, Nast & Company, 1913).

Both the *Yidishes Tageblatt* and the *Forward* saw the meeting, which lasted past midnight, as a watershed. The *Tageblatt* praised the women for taking the movement as far as they had, but saw "dark intent" on the part of "wheeler-dealers" who had begun to manipulate it for their own purposes. Without specifying exactly who it was talking about, the paper decried people who, "like lizards out of the mud" had attempted to negotiate directly with the wholesalers for resolution that would accrue to their own benefit. Insisting that there be no more "*kunkel munkel biznes*"—that is, monkey business—the paper was confident that the meat strike would best be handled by "a mighty organization" that would serve as "one official power for the whole city, with representation by all classes and all people."

The *Tageblatt* asserted that the movement was being taken over by the established Jewish organizations with the assent and even enthusiastic support of the Ladies' Anti-Beef Trust Association. It quoted someone in the association as saying that the organization had decided that "we should not take the whole responsibility onto ourselves." Indeed, if the women had resentments or reservations about their struggle being appropriated by men, there is no evidence of it. They likely accepted it without protest, since women taking the lead was something quite novel, and since men ran everything *else* on the East Side. And it probably appeared to them the best way of building a coalition to address meat prices.[13]

The *Forward* hailed the meeting as the "most important day in the great war between the Jewish Trust and the Jewish people." It marveled at the diversity of the gathering—Orthodox Jews, freethinkers, socialists, and democrats—all united in a common cause.

In an editorial, publisher Abraham Cahan argued that it was in the interest of the labor unions to support the strike even though they included many non-Jews and Jews who did not keep kosher homes. "The question is whether we should allow a Trust to suck the blood of the workers," he wrote. The payoff might come later. "If someday you fight a big battle for better wages or shorter hours in your trade, you can hope for the support of the women," he wrote.

He exhorted freethinkers, who also did not keep kosher homes, to play their part in helping those who did "not to get fleeced," adding that "everybody who has a warm corner in his soul and is ready to be called when there are struggles against bloodsuckers must heed the call of these brave women." Here he was referring not only to the kosher butchers, but to religious authorities who had not supported the strike, often out of interested motives. "When it comes to the question of kosher meat," he pointed out, freethinkers "are much more honorable than God's thieves."

Those religious authorities were probably the same people whose *kunkel munkel biznes* the *Tageblatt* was complaining about. Cahan was likely referring to the *shoychtim* and *mashgichim* on the payrolls of the Trust companies. Their fortunes rose and fell not with the welfare of the common people, but with that of the slaughterhouses.

The joining together in a common effort was something to be celebrated. The individual congregations, unions, and fraternal organizations had been "making *Shabbos* for themselves," Cahan wrote, using a Yiddish expression connoting not celebration of the Sabbath per se, but rather an unfortunate and wasteful lack of cooperation and unity.

Making *Shabbos* for themselves had been a success, but it had gotten the women only so far. Perhaps making it together with others would advance them to their goal.[14]

15

Patience Will Win the Battle

Despite nascent efforts at mediation, the violence continued unabated on Thursday, May 22.

Barnett Azwolonsky braved the fury of his neighbors and opened his Norfolk Street butcher shop in the early evening. When a mob of seven hundred massed in front of his store and ordered him to close, he resisted, unleashing an assault on his property. One woman threw a can of ashes into the shop as others hurled objects through his windows. A poor fish peddler perched nearby watched in horror as his wagon was looted of its stock for use as projectiles. Police were pelted with fish, ash, stones, and garbage and responded with their billy clubs. As Azwolonsky cowered in fear, several boys and girls who had been egged on by the rioters were injured. In the end, police arrested four people.[1]

That same day, a female-led mob of one thousand marched through the Williamsburg section of Brooklyn, destroyed half a dozen butcher shops, and attacked several of their customers. Confiscated meat was carried aloft in triumph at the ends of sharpened sticks. Some was not only doused in kerosene, but also set aflame. The crowd set fires in some of the stores they raided, though these were rapidly extinguished by their owners.[2]

Williamsburg was also the setting for what might have been the most barbarous police attack of the entire protest. It occurred on the corner of Moore Street and Manhattan Avenue, where Abram Krieger had set up his pushcart. Nearby, a gathering of Jews were ruminating about the meat strike but not bothering anyone. Several policemen arrived on the scene and, without warning, fell on the Jews and beat them with billy clubs. The crowd quickly dispersed in all directions, but Krieger did not. He refused to abandon his pushcart and was struck on the head until he bled. His pregnant wife, who was nearby, screamed. But when she approached her wounded husband to aid him, a policeman beat *her* unconscious. She was finally taken by ambulance to St. Catherine's Hospital, her little children running after the vehicle, screaming and crying.

The *Yidishes Tageblatt* was scandalized. "Even a stone would be moved" by such a story, it asserted. "Brooklyn Jews will not be silent about those 'thugs in blue jackets,'" it predicted, and it demanded the arrest of the officer involved.[3]

In Boston, the struggle moved from the North End to the West End. In the morning, about three hundred people attacked Isaac Leibman's Brighton Street meat store, pelting it with rotten fruit, breaking his windows, and assaulting one of his customers. Later, a mob went after Samuel Solomont & Son, the major kosher meat wholesaler, which had brazenly and opportunistically opened three retail stores of its own that morning. Here, however, it was marauding butchers, furious at this new competition organized by their former supplier, who led the charge. A mob of several hundred tried to prevent customers from patronizing the stores, and there was much yelling and smashing of windows. Showers of bricks and eggs greeted the police as they attempted to intervene. Several officers were injured: two lost teeth in the fracas, and one had his thumb badly bitten. Fifteen arrests were made in the course of the day.

Samuel Solomont then went to court seeking an injunction enjoining a list of forty-four butchers—presumably his ex-clients—against threatening or intimidating his customers. He alleged that the butchers were conspiring to destroy his business, which amounted to somewhere between $150,000 and $175,000 ($4.4 million to $5.1 million today) annually. He

דיא מאכט פון פרויען.

30. *The Power of Women,* an illustration by M. Mendelson from the
front page of the May 24, 1902, edition of the *Forward* shows a woman
with a key standing in front of a gate labeled "Kosher Meat Trust" whose
gateposts are decorated with steer heads. The word on the lock,
barely visible, is "boycott."

managed to secure a police guard for his premises, and continued to do business with those who dared buy from him.[4]

Hyman Pike, president of the Boston Hebrew Butchers' Association, laid out his colleagues' grievances in a statement to the *Boston Globe*. He maintained that his association was amenable to appointing a committee to confer with local rabbis and a delegation of wholesalers *other* than Solomont & Son. He added that the retailers hoped to resume business on Saturday night, selling kosher beef from a different supplier.[5]

And that is exactly what happened on Saturday, May 24. The kosher butcher shops opened that evening. Prices were all over the map; depending on where they went, customers could buy beef at twelve, sixteen, or seventeen cents a pound. Solomont & Son, determined to win back business, charged only fourteen cents for chuck steak, a middle-grade cut. Although there was a general understanding that the battle was not yet over, meat-starved Bostonian Jews rushed to make their purchases, grateful to enjoy the rewards of the truce as long as it lasted.[6]

Back in Brooklyn, not even the arrival of the Sabbath stopped the rioting. A wholesale butcher in Brownsville named George Davis, the only kosher meat dealer in the borough who remained open, was injured, as were two policemen who were escorting him to shul. The *Brooklyn Daily Eagle* counted fifteen hundred people involved in the incident, which resulted from a meeting the night before in which Davis was criticized for refusing to close. He was saved from more serious injury by police reserves wielding clubs, but one officer was hit in the head with a brick and had his uniform torn off of him.[7]

The uptown Jews were getting fed up with the constant stream of embarrassing news, which they felt reflected badly on them. That day, the *New York Times*, under the editorial control of Adolph Ochs, of German-Jewish extraction, ran a vicious and condescending editorial critical of the events in Williamsburg. In it, the paper justifiably decried the recent violence, but it also made clear exactly what it thought of the Russian Jewish rabble in its city:

> The class of people, especially the women, who are engaged in this matter have many elements of a dangerous class. They are very ignorant. They mostly speak a foreign language. They do not understand the duties or the rights of Americans. They have no inbred or acquired respect for law and order as the basis of the life of the society into which they have come. They have known authority mainly as wielded despotically, and as something to be submitted to only under compulsion, not as the source of their own safety. Resistance to authority does not seem to them necessarily wrong, only risky, and if it ceases to be risky, the restraint it can have on their passions is very small; practically it disappears.
>
> The more easy it is to explain or even to excuse their lawlessness on account of their utter ignorance, the more important it is to make them feel the immediate and severe imposition of the proper consequences of their lawlessness. The instant they take the law into their own hands, the instant they begin the destruction of property and assail peaceable citizens and the police, they should be handled in a way that they can understand and cannot forget.
>
> It will not do to have a swarm of ignorant and infuriated women going about any part of the city with petroleum destroying goods and trying to set fire to the shops of those against whom they are angry. The attempted incendiarism could not happen in an American crowd at all. These rioters were plainly desperate. They meant to defy the police and were ready for severe treatment. They did not get treatment nearly severe enough, and they are therefore far more dangerous than they were before.[8]

The *Times* couldn't have been more wrong, or more prejudiced, in suggesting that "an American crowd" would not behave in this way. Food riots had occurred in New York before, notably in 1837 when prices were high. Merchants were denounced and two hundred barrels of flour and a thousand bushels of wheat were dumped in the streets, stones were thrown, and windows were broken. Although the paper was within its rights to call the women to account for illegal and violent actions, there was no mistaking the disdain it felt across the board for the immigrant matrons. Nor was there any sign of empathy for the desperation that had driven these otherwise peaceable and law-abiding people to violence.[9]

But at least the *Times* was willing to tolerate their *presence* in Manhattan. In an editorial that purported to be sympathetic to the East Side Jews, the *Jewish Messenger* more or less suggested exiling them:

> The agitation in certain sections of New York, Brooklyn, Newark, and Boston against the local kosher butchers has quieted down. Much sympathy has been felt for the thousands of working people who, in their frantic excitement at the rising prices for meat, came in conflict with the police, and had in some cases to pay the penalty of the law. The incident is unpleasant to chronicle, and illustrates rather painfully the difficult problem which must be solved in overcrowded sections of New York and elsewhere.
>
> There should be no delay in applying the policy of dispersion and distribution which has already been adopted by the Hirsch Fund. There is a danger in local congestion with its hysterical manifestations from time to time, and of this our leaders are well aware.[10]

"Dispersion and distribution" was a reference to plans that had been discussed for two decades by establishment Jews who felt their own status in America threatened by the antics of their unenlightened and seemingly unassimilable Eastern European kin. The paternalistic schemes aimed at relocating them elsewhere in the country, where their presence might not be so obvious and embarrassing. The "Hirsch Fund" was a foundation established in 1891 by the Baron Maurice de Hirsch, a German Jewish financier and philanthropist, to fund agricultural colonies, such as those in southern

New Jersey, and trade schools aimed at making farmers and craftsmen of the new immigrants.[11]

The *Messenger*, of course, never made clear how relocating the East Siders to farms in New Jersey or making plumbers and carpenters of them would lower the price of kosher meat. It just wanted them banished.

On the East Side, the end of *Shabbos* shepherded a renewal of the unrest. At precisely sunset, when the rest day was over, crowds began to assemble in front of three shops on Orchard and Rivington Streets owned by the United Beef Company, one of the larger retail concerns, that had stubbornly attempted to open. This appears to have been a targeted effort. They immediately began to drive away customers, but then they attacked the shops. Windows were broken and managers threatened, but the effort was isolated and short-lived, as police were able to move in quickly and scatter the crowds.[12]

Also on Saturday night, at a closed-door meeting that included Carolyn Schatzberg, Paulina Finkel, Sarah Edelson, and some fifty retail butchers who were not Butchers' Association members, an effort at mediation was made by Dr. Blaustein. A proposal was floated by the butchers to permit *rabbis* to decide whom to permit to resume business. The meeting lasted until midnight and apparently led to an important change in policy. The next day, the Allied Conference for Cheap Kosher Meat issued a circular. It read:

> Women! Victory is near! Order and persistence will win the struggle against the butchers. Do not buy any meat. All the organizations fighting against the Jewish Meat Trust have now united under the name of the Allied Conference for Cheap Kosher Meat. Brave and honest men are now aiding the women. The conference has decided to help those butchers who will sell cheap kosher meat under the supervision of the rabbis and the conference. The Trust must be downed. For the present, do not buy any meat. Patience will win the battle. Seek the sympathy for your cause of old and young.[13]

The announcement was signed by Dr. Blaustein, Mrs. Schatzberg, two rabbis, and the Committee of Fifty. The Allied Conference would permit *independent* butchers—that is, not members of the Butchers' Association—to reopen if they agreed to sell meat at a reduced price, and rabbis would furnish them with a certificate to hang in their windows that would signal customers that the boycott did not apply to them. Appealing to rabbis to adjudicate the issue was a throwback to the old world, when the chief rabbi of a given community had the final word over matters affecting the *kohol*.[14]

That, of course, did not mean the end of the strike, which was still active against most of the butchers. The next day, the Allied Conference released a longer statement. It was, in the main, a response to critics:

> The spontaneity of this movement for cheaper meat is the best proof that the grievances of the poorer classes on the East Side against the Jewish Kosher Beef Trust are very real and serious. Prices have been raised six and seven cents a pound. It is conservatively estimated that 50,000 Jewish families have been abstaining from the use of meat for over two weeks. The people feel very justly that they are being ground down, not only by the Beef Trust of the country, but also by the Jewish Beef Trust of the city.
>
> The conference wishes to state most emphatically that the leaders of the movement do not countenance any violence, but it desires to state also that the sensational reports of violence committed on the East Side are a libel upon the good name of a peaceful, honest and industrious section of the city.
>
> The conference further calls the attention of the general public to the fact that the Jewish press has from the very beginning and continuously headed the news columns of the strike with injunctions to maintain order. The people of the East Side feel that the unwarranted summary action of the police in refusing to allow the people to assemble peaceably under police protection is tantamount to an attack on the right of free speech. It is to be admitted, however, that such

Patience Will Win the Battle

unprecedented action was due to the sensational reports of the newspapers. The conference wishes to enlist the sympathy of the public at large in this cause.[15]

The statement was unlike earlier declarations by the Ladies' Association, probably reflecting the addition of men of affairs to the movement's leadership. It was notable, first of all, in that it drew a clear distinction between the *national* Beef Trust and the *local* merchants, whom it branded the "Jewish Beef Trust." It renounced violence and maintained that responsible voices in the Jewish community had always done this, and it blamed the press—but not the Jewish press—for portraying them in an unfavorable light. It also revisited the disapproval of the demonstration permit, framing it as a denial of free speech, a criticism that had not been articulated in the past.[16]

On Monday morning, May 26, about fifty kosher butchers on the Lower East Side reopened for business. These, however, were *not* independent butchers who had agreed to roll back prices. Rather, they were members Joseph Goldman's East Side Hebrew Retail Butchers' Kosher Guarantee and Benevolent Association who had opened in a pre-emptive move to forestall competition from independent butchers who, they feared, would soon have certificates from the Allied Conference for Cheap Kosher Meat. They had taken delivery of meat from wholesalers the night before and obtained promises of police protection from Commissioner Partridge. True to the stated principles of the Allied Conference, there was almost no violence against them.[17]

But that didn't mean they sold much meat.

Instead of throwing rocks, members of the Ladies' Association, which continued to exist as a constituent organization of the Allied Conference, tried a new tactic. Their women went from shop to shop and asked at each one to examine the various grades of beef offered for sale. After it was brought out of the ice box, they would handle it as much as possible and expose it to air in an effort to spoil its fresh appearance. This accomplished, they left each store without making any purchases.

The decision by the Allied Conference to appeal to rabbis to decide whom to permit to resume business brought Orthodox congregations, some of which had kept their distance until now, squarely into the alliance, and gave them considerable latitude within it. Control by socialists and unions of an organization whose goal they saw as essentially a religious one had never sat well with them. And the quality problem—that of butchers selling nonkosher meat as kosher—which was a huge issue, had never been adequately addressed. Now, at a meeting at 412 Grand Street on May 27 attended by more than two hundred Orthodox Jews representing dozens of congregations, the boycott "took on a new character," according to the *Tageblatt*, which now jubilantly declared it a "truly kosher movement" led by genuinely pious Jews.

In something of an overstatement, the *Tageblatt* also crowed that "all honorable Jews have now aligned themselves with the struggle," and insisted that "socialists, anarchists and plain free thinkers had agreed to transfer the whole movement into the hands of the pious Jews, because the great mass of Jews who want kosher meat should not be able to have any excuse that non-pious Jews are leading the movement."

If the socialists were actually happy with the ascendance of the Orthodox, however, nobody told the *Arbeiter Zeitung*, their newspaper. The paper didn't see why the issue had suddenly become the "kosherness" of the meat when it had always been its cost, and it believed the struggle had been co-opted. It served socialist purposes far more when it was portrayed as a battle between common people and nefarious capitalist enterprises, and, like Abraham Cahan, it believed some of the "holy rabbis" to be tied up with corporate interests and lax in their enforcement of the rules of kashrus. In short, the socialist paper was deeply skeptical of the new arrangement.

"It will be no surprise if the whole agitation is used in the interest of certain businesses or companies, if not the Meat Trust itself," it wrote acidly.[18]

But even with the Orthodox now in the driver's seat, there were apparently no defections on the part of the other organizations, socialists included. Dr. Blaustein gave the gavel to Austrian-born Rabbi Adolph Spiegel, the widely respected head of Congregation Shaare Zedek, who was elected chairman, though Blaustein said he intended to remain active.

The *Tageblatt* revealed that more butchers were poised to negotiate with the Allied Conference with the goal of selling cheaper meat. The *New York Sun* reported that about 150 of them, some of them defectors from Goldman's association, had signed an agreement to sell meat at thirteen cents a pound, and had applied to the Allied Conference for certificates. And the *Daily People* proclaimed, in a headline, that "Butchers Resume. Kosher Meat War Appears To Be Over."[19]

But it was not quite that simple.

16

Disregard All Verbal or Written Agreements

Federal Judge Peter S. Grosscup had issued a temporary injunction against the Big Six of the Beef Trust on May 20, enjoining them from colluding, and the Trust companies had dutifully distributed thousands of copies of the order throughout their national networks. Although they pledged to follow the injunction to the letter, they refused to admit wrongdoing. In the text of an internal memorandum distributed within Armour & Company, however, they practically did. In the letter, J. Ogden Armour himself directed subordinates to "disregard all verbal or written agreements" that may have been struck with other corporations, and to "do business entirely as an independent company."[1]

It was nothing if not a tacit admission of guilt.

Judge Grosscup had spoken in the federal case, but New York State had yet to act. Since the New York City–based representatives of the Beef Trust companies had all stolen off to New Jersey, and as long as they remained there could not be served with subpoenas, Justice Chester's hearing had to be postponed. Ex-Justice Landon, however, who had been asked to evaluate whether sufficient evidence existed for the state to revoke the corporations' business licenses, was free to proceed.[2]

State Attorney General John C. Davies was certain the Trust operated in more or less the same way throughout the state, and that even without any New York City witnesses he could shine a spotlight on their anticompetitive activities with testimony from upstate. So on May 27, he put up witnesses from Troy and Albany. The subject, however, was not price-fixing, but blacklisting.[3]

The Troy-based arbitrator for the Trust packing houses, who had been given his walking papers immediately after Judge Grosscup's ruling, asserted that while in the Trust's employ he had received weekly reports from each constituent company tattling on retail dealers who had failed to settle their accounts promptly. His job was to compile a blacklist to ensure that if one Trust member experienced payment problems with a customer, the latter would be refused credit by all other members. He also testified that he had overseen an account funded by deposits from each company and had been empowered to deduct one hundred dollars for each violation of the Trust agreement, a copy of which was entered into evidence.[4]

The Schwarzschild & Sulzberger manager from Troy also took the stand. It had been his responsibility to submit his company's weekly list of delinquents. He told Justice Landon that the agreement to do so had been abrogated the previous week on instructions from Ferdinand Sulzberger. Similar testimony was heard from local Nelson Morris & Company and Hammond & Company employees, and from two former Albany arbitrators.[5]

What did the extension or denial of credit have to do with price-fixing? U.S. Solicitor General John K. Richards explained the relationship this way: "Men who are selling dressed meat for consumption may compete not solely by price, but by the character of the credit extended. One man may be induced to purchase dressed meat at a slightly lower price per pound, another by an extension of credit. Therefore any combination to be effective must not only establish and maintain uniform prices, but must establish and maintain a uniform rule of credit, and so too with that arrangement which governs the transportation and delivery of the dressed meat."[6]

In other words, it was not just price-fixing by the Trust that accounted for the rise in retail prices. It was also the credit policy of the wholesalers.

Disregard All Agreements

It appeared that the Trust companies had now abandoned their blacklist, at least in New York, though local butchers could be forgiven for being skeptical. "In the minds of men who do business with the Beef Trust . . . there is not an implicit faith in the unsupported promises of the packers," the *New York Herald* reported. Any confidence that the list was really a thing of the past came not from their words, but from the fact that it would be impossible for them to continue the practice without being detected. Putting it a little less delicately, the paper wrote, "No consideration of business policy or symptoms of tenderheartedness inspires the greedy packers in burying the weapons with which they have beaten dealers into submission. It is the cold order of a federal judge . . . which was so overwhelming that they did not dare to oppose it."[7]

As long as the injunction remained in force, the blacklist was history. And in another indication that the companies intended to comply, news came on May 28 that they had ordered the tickers removed from their branch offices in New York, Brooklyn, and Jersey City. This was an elaborate and costly electronic network that had been set up for the sole purpose of collusion. But the wire connections that powered the tickers were not ripped out, meaning that the system could easily be reinstalled and put back to work should the government lose its case.[8]

It took until June 4 for New York to act, and the key testimony that undergirded its decision was that of Daniel W. Meredith, the former employee of Swift and Armour whose deposition had also been introduced in the federal proceedings in Chicago. Reprinted verbatim in the *New York Sun*, it contained a detailed and damning description of the mechanisms employed by the Big Six to manipulate prices.

Meredith testified that when he had first gone to work for Armour in 1883, there had been normal competition among all the packing houses, but that after 1893 agreements were signed and regular meetings held "to arrange prices at which the products could be sold." He explained that the six New

York City–based general managers had control over the local affairs of their respective companies, "subject to the principal officers in Chicago."

The managers had met once a week, and sometimes more frequently, at the St. James Building at Twenty-Sixth Street and Broadway to set prices for the coming week. Considering the amount of inventory on hand and the quantity of cattle already in transit, they would also sometimes agree to curtail shipments from the West to prop up prices. Decisions were reached by majority vote.

The six packing houses, Meredith asserted, had also agreed not to compete against one another in smaller towns. If one house had a branch office in a given town, the others would avoid setting up there. And sometime around 1901 a second accord was reached concerning the blacklist, whereby credit customers who defaulted on their obligations to one house would be denied credit at all of the others.

Meredith reported also that Arthur Colby, the Manhattan-based arbitrator, extracted fines from each company for violations of the agreement, and that any employee found cheating would be fired and unable to secure employment with any other wholesaler. In other words, there had been an employee blacklist as well.[9]

Once Attorney General Davies brought Meredith's incriminating affidavit to the attention of Justice Chester, the latter issued an injunction along the same lines as Judge Grosscup's order of two weeks earlier. It enjoined the "managers, agents, attorneys and servants and all persons acting or assuming to act" under the authority of the defendants from colluding on the price of meat, the supply of meat brought into the state, the price of labor, or competition in the labor force. Copies of the Judge's order were served on all of the defendants.[10]

But, as the *New York Press* pointed out, the injunction didn't really settle anything. It functioned as a stay as far as collusion was concerned. But the real test would be when the state got around to *prosecuting* the Big Six. To make the injunction permanent, it would be necessary to prove that they were

Disregard All Agreements

acting in restraint of trade. But Samuel Weil, second vice president of Schwarzschild & Sulzberger, indicated that the companies intended to take the case to the U.S. Supreme Court. He insisted his firm had done no wrong and had never entered into any combination to set prices, and therefore there would be no change in its methods of doing business. What the newspapers had printed, he declared, had been "rot and lies."

A representative of Swift & Company agreed. "How can the courts settle the price?" he asked rhetorically. "When there are 2,000,000 cattle less than in former years, and the population is ever on the increase, there should be no decrease in prices, and there cannot be any lower prices unless the price of cattle on the hoof is lower at the stockyards."

Despite the mountain of evidence in both the federal and state proceedings that exposed them for blatant price-fixing, the Trust firms still had the temerity to cling to the fiction that high beef prices were solely a function of a diminished supply of cattle. Through its *National Provisioner* organ, the Trust continued to propagandize against the retail butchers.

"The 'kosher' butchers of Greater New York have been the first to reap the bad fruits of the present regrettable agitation about high beef prices," the paper wrote. "The badly informed butchers have filled the daily papers and their customers' ears with a lot of senseless rot about 'Trust' prices when they must have known that beef cannot be sold cheaper than it now is while all grades of cattle are dear."

It went so far as to blame the kosher butchers for the boycott, not because they were gouging their customers, as the women had alleged, but because they had failed to manage their customers' expectations. "The *National Provisioner* has been telling the butchers all along that cattle and beef would be high," it wrote. "The paper has been advising the butchers to gradually get their prices up and explain to their customers that cattle were scarce and high and therefore beef was way up. If this advice had been heeded, the disgraceful meat riots and destruction of butcher shop stock and property witnessed in New York City during the last ten days would not have taken place."

It was an entirely specious argument based on a lie; nor did it deal at all with the fact that kosher meat had become unaffordable to its customers, which was the basic reason for the unrest.[11]

Despite their unwillingness to admit fault, the Trust companies seemed intent on complying with the injunctions. It remained to be seen what effect, if any, their doing so would have on the price of kosher meat.

17

This Cooperative Shop Is Here to Stay

By the end of May, the Butchers' Association finally decided to stop resisting. With both independent butchers and defectors from its own ranks seeking to cut deals with the Allied Conference for Cheap Kosher Meat, its remaining members risked being left out. Accordingly, Joseph Goldman announced that his butchers were "ready to close their stores and align themselves with the people to oppose the Trust." He provided the Allied Conference with a list of six hundred butchers, all members of his association, who had agreed to shut their doors and work together with the conference.

It was a stunning victory for all who had supported the boycott.

But the butchers weren't the only ones to come around. Dr. Blaustein and Rabbi Adolph Spiegel had been talking directly with the wholesalers. At a meeting of the Allied Conference's Committee of Fifty at Blaustein's office on June 3, Spiegel announced that they had been assured by them that thereafter meat would be sold to kosher butchers at nine or nine-and-a-half cents a pound. This was a drop of two cents a pound, a level that would enable retailers to sell it as cheaply as fourteen cents and still make a small profit.

This was enough for the *Tageblatt*. On June 5, the Orthodox paper proclaimed that "the great struggle ends with great victory." Amidst lavish praise for Blaustein and Spiegel, it declared that "today ended the three tumultuous weeks in New York."

That, however, was an overstatement. Although the whole-salers had agreed to lower prices, it was not clear for how long. They refused to bind themselves for any length of time. They insisted that selling at nine cents a pound amounted to a loss for them, which, if true, meant that doing so would not be sustainable over time.

If the wholesalers could not commit to a time frame, the retailers could not do so, either. So before it would agree to call off the boycott, the committee sought to exact a pledge from the retailers to sell meat at fourteen cents *as long as* the wholesalers kept their price to nine or nine-and-a-half cents. It seemed a reasonable condition, but no one knew how many would be willing to make the promise.[1]

Shops began to reopen the next day, leading many to assume a final agreement had been reached. This forced Blaustein to issue a clarifying statement: "Tempted by the temporary reduction in the price of meat, many of the butchers have, in violation of their promise, opened their shops. A part of the public, on the other hand, weary of the struggle, is buying meat. Under the circumstances, the Committee refers the matter back to its constituents and asks them what steps are to be taken."[2] Reading between the lines, the statement suggested that Blaustein and Spiegel, on behalf of the Committee of Fifty, believed that they had gotten all they could from the wholesalers. They intended to buck the decision on whether to carry things any further back to the entire membership of the Allied Conference for Cheap Kosher Meat at a meeting scheduled for the following Saturday, June 7.[3]

Not everybody was happy with this turn of events. The socialist *Arbeiter Zeitung*, which had fretted from the start when rabbis were invited to adjudicate the problem and the conversation had been diverted from price to purity, declared that the meat boycott had disintegrated into "a gelatinous state." Butchers had reopened, but it was unclear which had agreed to offer lower prices on a sustained basis and which had not. "The Allied Conference for Cheap Kosher Meat has not accomplished anything," it declared. The masses were

This Cooperative Shop Is Here to Stay

still in the dark, and "charlatans" were using that darkness for their own wicked purposes.[4]

Carolyn Schatzberg, for her part, was also deeply troubled. She felt that Blaustein and Spiegel had betrayed the committee. On the morning of June 4, she visited the *Forward*'s offices, hoping to use the paper as a megaphone. With clasped hands and tears in her eyes, she requested the *Forward* to join her in asking Jewish workers and labor unions to step in and reassert control over the situation.

Apart from the lack of an accord on sustained prices, Mrs. Schatzberg fretted about the quality of the meat being sold. She told the *Forward* she knew for sure it was not good meat. "It is a trick from the Trust to confuse people," she asserted. "They are providing the cheapest meat for sale now. And when things quiet down, they think they will again be able to sell it at high prices like before."[5]

But she was no longer in charge, and her words were for naught. The delegates who attended the Saturday conference did address the question of how to secure affordable meat on a constant basis, but they had no appetite for sustaining the boycott. One alternate suggestion was to require a guarantee of $500 from each butcher in exchange for certification by the conference; another was to require that each dealer adhere to a regulated scale of profits. The meeting went on past midnight. It was reported that sixty butchers had declared themselves willing to sell meat at a fixed price for at least six months if the conference issued them certificates.[6]

The rest of the discussion centered on the idea of cooperative butcher shops, which finally seemed poised to become a reality. A Prince Street cloak manufacturer named Nathan Schlessel pledged $3,000 ($88,000 in today's currency) toward such an effort. The hope was to raise $15,000 ($440,000 today) for a plan that envisioned selling ownership as cheaply as two or three dollars per share. Accordingly, the assembly designated a Committee of Fifteen to explore where cattle might best be obtained apart from the Trust companies. Philadelphia and Canada were named as the most likely sources.

The committee thought co-ops would be the only way to guarantee price stability. The wholesale price, after all, was not something they could control, and who was to say it would remain low? History suggested otherwise. "The figures collected by the Committee show that, for about three weeks, 50,000 families in greater New York abstained from all meat and that 1,500 butcher stores had remained closed. No movement ever took such a hold on the people in my experience," Dr. Blaustein told the *New York Sun*, "and they deserve to have some permanent beneficial results. The only way that any permanent low price can be obtained would be, it would seem, through the plan we are considering."[7]

That plan, of course, made the Beef Trust nervous. The Big Six were wary of cooperatives, and especially threatened by the possibility of co-ops sponsored by the Butchers' Association buying cattle elsewhere or establishing their own slaughterhouse. In the *National Provisioner*, the Trust companies asserted of Canadian beef that "kosher meat cannot be got here quick enough for consumption according to the Hebrew law," a misleading argument that would have been true only if the cattle had been slaughtered in Canada before shipment. If it came in on the hoof and was killed locally, it would be no different from cattle from the Midwest.[8]

The *Prosivioner* also argued that a kosher abattoir would have difficulty disposing of the nonkosher hindquarters of its beef. "It is hard to send the forequarters into one channel of trade under one set of conditions and the hinds into a different channel under different conditions and to do it cheaply," it opined. But that is essentially what the wholesale houses in New York had been doing for years to no discernible ill effect.[9]

The Ladies' Anti-Beef Association was not dissuaded and didn't feel like waiting any longer. On June 10 the group opened its first cooperative kosher butcher shop and announced plans for five more. The proprietress of the store, located at 245 Stanton Street, was Sarah Cohn, née Zucker, who lived down the street and who had long been a proponent of co-ops.

Thirty-one year-old Sarah was a woman of boundless energy. Tall, blue-eyed, and fair-haired, she had emigrated to the United States from her native Austria at the age of nineteen and married her husband, Tobias, a locksmith who was also Austrian-born, in New York in 1894. By 1902 she had borne two boys and three girls. Despite having a house full of children, the eldest eight and the youngest less than two months old, she was now also running a butcher shop.

Sarah had printed circulars in Yiddish announcing the venture, and as a result, when she opened her doors just opposite Hamilton Fish Park at 6:00 a.m. on June 10, the eve of the Jewish holiday of Shavuos, customers were already lined up. The *New York Tribune* painted a vivid picture of that block of Stanton Street that morning:

> The scenes there during the last week beggar description. Traffic was stopped in front of the shop, teams being unable to ride down the dense throng. Housewives with their baskets stood in line a block away. Men left their work and waited for hours to get the first meat the family had tasted for weeks. People rose before daylight to be the first at the door. The policeman on that beat gazed with astonishment at the scene when the shop opened its doors on Monday morning. When he attempted to manage the crowd, he was lost in the shuffle. Two of his colleagues likewise disappeared from view.
>
> Behind the blocks stood seven stout fellows, chopping and sawing for dear life, while the perspiration poured down in blinding streams. Behind the desk sat a big man with a Panama hat and a cigarette making change with silent and imperturbable coolness. He is a well-known and wealthy restaurant keeper of the East Side who has consented to act as treasurer of the association.[10]

By 11:00 a.m. the shop ran out of meat and several hundred people had to be turned away. Mrs. Cohn told a *World* reporter,

This cooperative shop is here to stay. How did I do it? It was very easy. First I went to the landlord and hired the store for $35 a month. Then I went to the place where they sell fixtures and purchased a complete outfit for $40. I then went to the slaughterhouse and purchased 2,000 pounds of chuck meat. I bought only chuck because people on the East Side like it the best. They make soup of it and still have the meat. We do not care much for roasts. After I got the beef, I hired men to work in the shop. I am sorry that I had to close up so early today, but I have no more meat to sell. There will be enough meat tomorrow for everybody. We sold the beef at 14 cents a pound, while the butchers sold at 15 cents a pound. . . .

Thirty-six dollars of the money spent I collected myself. The other thirty-odd dollars I needed to open the shop with I received in $1 installments from persons who agreed to start this shop.

Temporary receipts are given to the subscribers until the shop can be incorporated under the name of the East Side Ladies' Anti-Beef Trust Association of the Sixteenth Assembly District. After that, we will give out regular shares. We did such a rushing business today that I believe we will be able to pay profits within a month. The public is with us and we are bound to succeed.

There were already a hundred shareholders, most holding only a single share.[11]

No arrangements had yet been made for an independent beef supplier, but that didn't faze Sarah Cohn. She was perfectly willing to deal with local wholesalers and sell Beef Trust meat. Her competitive advantage against the retail butchers was twofold. First, the co-op would sell the meat at a price that just met expenses. And second, its ability to place a large order guaranteed a good price from the slaughterhouses. The wholesalers charged the retailers nine-and-a-half cents per pound; Mrs. Cohn paid only nine-and-a-quarter for her first order because it was so large.

But the Stanton Street shop was not the only cooperative shop to debut on June 10. Another one at 57 Monroe Street opened that same day under the management of none other than Sarah Edelson and several of her friends. There was clearly some competition between the women, as there generally was when Sarah Edelson was involved. Sarah Cohn dismissed her counterpart's effort as an imitation, insisting that *her* store had opened first.[12]

Both shops were successful, but it was Sarah Cohn who was the darling of the press that week. The *Tribune* gave a capsule history of the involvement in the movement of the "young Austrian Jewess," children clustered at her feet as she "stood like a figure of personified order in the midst of chaos." The paper reported that she had led the boycott in the sixteenth district from the very beginning, that she had been an early supporter of cooperative shops, and that she had waited in vain for others to come up with a plan before seizing the moment and taking on the project herself.

In its first two days of operation, the Stanton Street shop sold forty-nine chucks, each weighing 120 to 140 pounds, leaving its butchers—three of whom had been forced to close their own shops—panting. Few East Side butchers went through that many chucks in a month. Sarah Cohn's success was causing panic among them; some were selling little or nothing.

"The women are having fun with the butchers in the Sixteenth Assembly District," the *Tribune* observed. "That is, the women are having fun and the butchers are not. Now the butchers are standing in the doors of their empty shops and gazing with horror at the packed, jammed, wedged mass of humanity that blocks the street in front of the co-operative butcher shop at 245 Stanton Street."

A mass meeting of the Ladies' Association held on Thursday, June 12, was all about plans for future shops. Sarah Cohn stood on a high table to address what the *Tribune* called a "solid, packed mass of humanity." The paper went on to describe "the straight folds of the long blue wrapper falling about her, her face flushed, her shapely arms and hands eloquent in the impassioned earnestness of their gestures," adding, "she brought to the inner eye a fleeting picture of those old German women who used to go to war fighting by their husbands' side."

"Do you people want cooperative shops or not?" Sarah demanded of the crowd.

"Yes!"

"Well, then, you have to understand, you must put up the money for them. If you don't, we'll have to give certificates to the shareholders and serve them alone. It is not fair that some should put up the money to open the shop and get no meat, and those who put up no money get all the meat. We can't give meat to the whole East Side in that little shop. We'll be having women knocked down and trampled to death there."

"If you want shops, you'll have to come down with the money to open them. We sold 50 chucks there in two days, and the Sixteenth District didn't get a taste. Why, the police even made us take down our sign because it drew a crowd that blocked the street, even when the shop was closed. If you want to pay 14 cents for meat instead of 18 or 25, you'll have to give the money to open another shop."

"Yes, and I'll be the one to do it," came a voice from the crowd. It was Annie Wurtzel, a diminutive Delancey Street cook in a pink blouse. She raised her hand and declared, "I'll buy 200 shares in the Ladies Anti-Trust Association, so as to give $200 to open another shop."

"Does the lady want to be a boss?" Sarah asked.

"No sir," she answered. "I don't want to be no boss. I don't want no rights that the woman that puts in a dollar don't have." At this, there was tumultuous applause, and by the end of the evening, an additional $140 had been pledged by others.

It was also announced that five or six retail butchers had agreed to turn their shops and fixtures over to the Ladies' Association if they could be hired at a wage of ten dollars a week. This brought a mixed reaction from those assembled. On the one hand, it was proof that their boycott had been

This Cooperative Shop Is Here to Stay

successful, and a ringing endorsement of the cooperative model. But there was also lingering resentment against the very men at whom the strike had been aimed. "When I said I couldn't pay 18 cents, these butchers told me to get out of the shop," said one voice from the audience. "Now they come and ask for a job!"

On her way home after the meeting, Sarah Cohn waxed eloquent to a *Tribune* reporter, evincing a clear understanding of the supply chain and the economics of the kosher meat business that had eluded many others on the East Side during the height of the boycott. She asked rhetorically,

> What has the strike done? We thought we could hurt the Beef Trust. We couldn't touch them. We thought we could reach the Wholesalers' Trust. We couldn't reach them. But we got back at the Kosher Trust, and brought meat down from 18 to 14 cents. Every kosher shop has got to meet our price. We can sell at 14 and make expenses.
>
> More than that, we *know* we are getting kosher meat, and that is more than we have been sure of for a good while. We believe now that for years the Jewish people have been getting meat that was too old to be kosher. We are buying meat that has never been frozen through. If this shop continues successful, we can put in chickens and other things that the people use the most. Everything is going up. It is not only meat. If we can run a cooperative meat shop, we can run all kinds of cooperative shops. We need one to every block. When we are taking 80 chucks a day from the wholesalers, we can have anything we want of them.

"It has been a woman's strike throughout," the *Tribune* observed approvingly, "and its efficiency shows what power lies in the hands of the administrator of the family funds. These rotund mothers of many, these Jewish matrons, with their queer old wigs and their keen black eyes and their kosher principles, goaded to desperation as they saw themselves unable to feed their families with the money at their command, made a combination which it was impossible to break."[13]

18

There Was Never Such an Outrage on Our Race

The cooperative shops' success put more pressure on the retail butchers to agree to lower their prices, but it did not seal the deal. There was still an impasse, as many members of the East Side Hebrew Retail Butchers' Kosher Guarantee and Benevolent Association were loath to be tied down to a fixed price agreement. And this meant that as late as mid-June, the boycott remained officially in effect.

There were even minor skirmishes at several of their shops when they offered beef for sale at anywhere between eighteen and twenty-three cents a pound. Three men were arrested for rioting in front of Louis Cohen's store in the Bronx on June 18. Lena Lipis of East Eighteenth Street was fined ten dollars for seizing meat a neighbor had purchased from a First Avenue butcher. And a hundred pounds of meat and sixty chickens were destroyed by boycotters at a Suffolk Street shop.[1]

Members of the Butchers' Association held an inconclusive meeting in Eagle Hall at Forty-Third Street and First Avenue that same day to discuss the situation. Three days later, at a meeting of the Ladies' Association, Zionist leader Joseph Zeff, who presided, reminded those assembled that unless the butchers agreed not to charge more than fourteen cents a pound for kosher meat, their shops were supposed to remain closed.

But most of the talk was about cooperatives, four of which had already opened. Zeff announced plans for the Ladies' Association to enter into partnership with the United Hebrew

Community, or the UHC, to expand the number of such shops. The debates centered on what rules should govern the organization's participation, what limitations should be placed on ownership of the enterprises, and how to guarantee the purity of the meat.

Now that the Ladies' Association was in the meat business and its cooperatives were employing their own butchers, the question of how to guarantee the sanctity of their product had to be addressed. One proposal was for the Committee of Fifteen of the Allied Conference for Cheap Kosher Meat to appoint rabbis—that is, *mashgichim*— paid by the Ladies' Association as inspectors in the shops. "At the present time, the rabbis are not in our employ," Dr. Zeff pointed out. "Now they can't very well help us under these conditions. It is our scheme to pay the rabbis from the funds of the Association and thus secure their help."

"One might infer from this," the *National Provisioner* remarked snarkily, "that the rabbi is an untrustworthy individual or that the new co-operators desire to do a little business not quite straight. It looks that way."[2]

Whether anyone realized it or not, this was an echo of the same debate the New York Jewish community had been having, on and off, since the 1870s, and the same discussion that had led to the appointment of Jacob Joseph as chief rabbi in 1887 and that also, in part, spelled his downfall. It was already clear to many that *mashgichim* paid by the meat industry could not be trusted. Rabbi Zeff apparently believed things would be different if they were employed by the Ladies' Association, but he gave no reason for this view. The association was now running butcher shops of its own, with all the attendant financial incentives.

Rabbi Joseph himself had largely been out of the picture since he lost his position and was reduced to functioning as an ordinary *mashgiach*, and he ceased to be a force at all after he was incapacitated by a series of strokes in the mid-1890s and finally bedridden, as he had been for the previous two years. As fate would have it, at the very end of July 1902, just as new life had been breathed into the debate about who should pay the *mashgichim*, the rabbi himself drew his last breath.[3]

When his death at the age of sixty-two was announced on Monday, July 28, men and women gathered on the street outside his home to pray. His body was brought downstairs and many filed inside to pay their respects; some even brought children for a glimpse of the great talmudic scholar. By the next morning, the sidewalk on Henry Street was impassible; nearly a thousand people had assembled there.[4]

Meanwhile, several of the congregations that had brought the rabbi to America fought about where he should be buried. Congregation Rodeph Sholom's Union Field Cemetery near Cypress Hill in East New York finally got the nod, likely because of a payment to his widow. No one could have predicted, however, that there would be bloodshed before the rabbi's remains arrived there.

Orthodox Jewish custom forbids embalming and mandates burial as soon after death as possible, but since the rabbi had perished late on Monday, arrangements for what everyone expected would be a huge funeral could not be made in time for a Tuesday burial. So his interment was set for Wednesday morning, July 30. The night before, a representative of the funeral committee applied at police headquarters for a permit for a cortege he estimated would attract some twenty thousand people. The authorization was granted, together with the assurance that twenty-five policemen would be on hand to keep order over the three-mile route. Later that night, however, a reporter from one of the Yiddish newspapers phoned the police sergeant who had issued the permit and suggested that many more officers than that would be necessary.

Tradition called for the rabbi's body to be ritually washed by members of the *chevra kadisha*—the religious society tasked with preparing corpses for burial—dressed in a *kittel*, or shroud, and draped in his *tallis*, or prayer shawl. Members of the society would then place it in a simple, unpainted pine coffin. Not for the Orthodox were elaborate caskets; the lack of adornment signified the equality of all in death.

After prayers at the rabbi's home, a procession would carry his casket to six Orthodox congregations on the East Side for brief prayers by their respective rabbis. Plans for a lengthier service and a eulogy at the Beis Hamidrash HaGadol, the rabbi's home synagogue, had to be scrapped because of the sheer numbers of people expected. The cortege was to traverse Madison, Pike, Eldridge, Forsyth, and Norfolk Streets and then, at the end of Grand Street, the rabbi's remains were to be placed aboard a ferry for East New York.

Despite his rousing welcome in 1888, Rabbi Joseph had been humiliated during his later years in New York, and perhaps out of a collective sense of guilt, Jewish New Yorkers seemed intent on according him in death the honor they had denied him in life. Merchants along the funeral route closed their shops and mourners lined the streets. There was real pathos in the reaction of the crowds as his procession passed by; in more than one location, bystanders rushed up to the hearse in tearful attempts just to touch his casket. Estimates of crowd size varied widely, but the police said later that fifty thousand would not have been far from wrong.

The procession, led by a thousand yeshiva boys chanting psalms, encompassed some two hundred carriages. Several dozen officers were added to the police detail, bringing the total to nearly a hundred, but this was still far short of the number needed to provide security for such a large event. All went smoothly until about 1:00 p.m., when the cortege made its final turn from Norfolk Street onto Grand Street and passed R. Hoe & Company, a printing press factory on the north side of the street between Sheriff and Columbia Streets.

There, without provocation, factory employees on an upper floor, who were just returning from their lunch break, ran to the windows and jeered at the crowd. Workers, many of whom were Jew-haters, maliciously emptied pails of water on the mourners massed on the sidewalk, who were packed so tightly that there was no escaping the drenching. Oil-soaked rags followed, as did tools, scraps of iron, blocks of wood, and even a dead cat. One missile narrowly missed the hearse.

Naturally, this infuriated the people on the street, some of whom retrieved the missiles and flung them back at the factory, together with rocks and anything else they could find on the street. Before long, there wasn't a window in the building that hadn't been shattered.

New York City marshal Albert Levine and a few other Jewish men in the crowd hurriedly made their way into the factory office on the ground floor to demand that the managers stop the assault. They were received courteously, but when a second group attempted to enter the building to stop the attacks, those in charge insulted them and called the police. One even drew a gun and ordered them to leave. The managers insisted later they were only trying to protect their property from a disorderly mob. At that point, several factory workers turned fire hoses on the mourners as many denunciations of Jews were shouted and objects continued to rain down on them. A few returned fire and gave back as good as they got.

Two hundred reinforcements, under the leadership of Inspector Adam A. Cross, were called in from all the downtown police stations. When they arrived, however, they attacked *not* the workers who had started the brawl, but the *mourners*. They took possession of the street by brandishing clubs, shoving, and shouting. Some of the factory workers brazenly joined the police in their efforts to subdue the crowd.

As many as a hundred people were injured. Some bled from the metal shards thrown at them; others from the billy clubs. Still others were hurt when carriage drivers in the procession hurried their horses to get out of harm's way. There were wounded hands and sprained ankles, but there were also cracked skulls and internal injuries. When an ambulance arrived from Gouverneur Hospital, its doctors worked feverishly for a full hour treating flesh wounds on-site. Those with more serious injuries were spirited away.

It was the worst outbreak of antisemitic violence the city had ever seen. Neighbors reported that it was not the first time Hoe factory employees had tussled with local Jews. When company President Robert Hoe issued a statement, he blamed everything on the Jews. But he did acknowledge that among his eighteen hundred employees and three hundred apprentices there were many antisemites.

Anticipating trouble in Williamsburg on the other end of the ferry ride, Captain Thompson phoned ahead to warn his Brooklyn counterpart. Fully seventy-five thousand people were there to greet the cortege, but many missed it entirely when the procession was rerouted from Broadway at the last minute. When it passed an axle foundry on South Sixth Street, someone threw a piece of wood and several mourners tried to storm the factory, but the police were able to keep the peace, albeit with difficulty.

Another fifteen thousand people waited at the cemetery, where sixty-two rabbis disembarked and assembled behind Rabbi Joseph's family at the gravesite. All waited while the grave was dug, the casket was lowered into it, and more prayers were recited. It was nearly nightfall when the last of the mourners left Rabbi Joseph to the ages.

Back in Manhattan, a police spokesperson told the *New York Times* that not even the kosher meat riots of the previous two months, which were quite fresh in memory, could compare with the violence on Grand Street that day. Many Jews and workers were taken to Essex Market Police Court to be arraigned. Some were let off, others were fined, and still others were held over for trial.[5]

The Jewish community, still seething over the brutality of the police toward their women during the meat riots, was up in arms about the treatment the mourners had received at the hands of the police department. That night, at a meeting of Jewish doctors, lawyers, and businessmen at the East Broadway residence of Dr. Julius Halpern, a labor leader, socialist, and well-known physician, a committee was designated to investigate and formulate charges against the officers.

"Instead of protecting the Jews," Halpern complained, "the police attacked them. There was never such an outrage on our race as that which happened this afternoon. The action of the police in attacking and brutally beating with their sticks our women and children in the performance of one of their most sacred religious rites—that of mourning for their greatest rabbi—is an outrage of which no barbaric country of the Middle Ages was ever guilty."

"We will thoroughly investigate the matter," vowed attorney Abraham Sarasohn, "and our evidence will be placed before Police Commissioner Partridge. If he fails to act, we will call upon Mayor Low and District Attorney Jerome." It was no idle threat; Mayor Seth Low had been elected on a reform platform with substantial Jewish support, and one of the areas most in need of reform was the notoriously corrupt police department.

The mayor didn't need much persuading. That same day, he wrote Commissioner Partridge demanding a full report of the incident, calling it a disgrace to the city and threatening punishment for the guilty. The Board of Aldermen, too, called for retribution against the instigators.[6]

The next afternoon, at an impromptu meeting of several hundred Jews at the Educational Alliance chaired by Halpern, a nine-person East Side Vigilance Committee was named with the goal of conducting a fair investigation of the incident. Their task was to collect evidence and turn it over to a group of five attorneys who would decide what legal remedies to seek. They also vowed to do what they could to keep Inspector Cross, who they believed was part of the problem, *out* of the investigation. While the meeting was going on, Mayor Low telephoned and pledged his hearty cooperation.[7]

At a mass meeting at Cooper Union on August 1, three thousand men and women heard denunciations of the police as stonefaced police officers, ironically, kept order outside and in. The speakers focused on what they saw as bald-faced antisemitism and on the need for reform in the city administration. Louis Miller, a Russian-born political activist and cofounder of the socialist *Arbeiter Zeitung*, chaired the meeting. He asserted that "there is no politics in this. All we want is to maintain our rights as free Americans. We came here tonight to serve on all bigots and toughs that, if the fathers of our country did not shed enough blood, we Jews are ready to shed ours for this principle."

He was followed by Abraham Cahan of the *Forward*. "In the case of a funeral in Russia, the most miserable beggar will take off his hat, whether the dead be a rabbi or a Christian clergyman," he asserted. "If this thing of last Wednesday is repeated, if we cannot be protected by the duly constituted lawful authority, we Russian Jews want to tell the policemen that we shall protect ourselves in the future." This last line engendered prolonged applause. And finally, Joseph Barondess took the stage with choice words for the mayor, District Attorney Jerome, and for Commissioner Partridge, the latter of whom was still resented for having denied the Ladies' Association a demonstration permit the previous May.[8]

At that meeting and others, $7,000 (just over $200,000 in today's dollars) was raised to retain legal counsel. Organizers told the press they anticipated no trouble raising an additional $30,000 ($880,000 today). Five hundred dollars was to be paid out in rewards for information leading to the arrest and conviction of anyone who threw a missile or sprayed water on the mourners. And a small group was appointed to seek a meeting with the mayor the following Monday.

Commissioner Partridge asked for a report from Inspector Cross despite the fact that the Jewish community had made it clear that they had no faith in Cross's objectivity. And they were right to be concerned. Cross's report contained the preposterous assertion that the violence had been premeditated on the part of the Jews.

> At the time the procession was passing there were no stones or bricks, or anything else in the street that could be used for breaking the windows of Hoe & Co. As a matter of fact, there were sixty-four missiles found in R. Hoe & Co.'s building after the crowds had been dispersed . . . showing conclusively, to my mind, that those who broke the windows and

There Was Never Such an Outrage

destroyed the property of Hoe & Co. came there prepared to do what they did do, showing at the same time that the attack on Hoe & Co. was premeditated.[9]

Not coincidentally, Inspector Cross's transfer from the East Side was announced the next day. Partridge insisted that it had been in the works for a while and denied that it was related to his report. It's not clear if anyone believed him.

Dissatisfied with the report from Partridge, which had been based in part on Cross's account, the mayor lost little time in appointing an independent, blue-ribbon citizens' committee of five to investigate the circumstances of the disturbance. The committee held public sessions and took testimony over a six-week period. It also examined police records and affidavits obtained by District Attorney Jerome. Its report, submitted to the mayor on September 15, placed blame for the altercation squarely on the employees of H. Hoe & Company and also found the police negligent and culpable. It exonerated the mourners and completely discredited Cross's report.

The committee also found "undisputed testimony that the attitude of some of the Hoe employees toward the Jewish residents of that vicinity had been for a long time hostile." They also criticized the "great roughness of language and violence of manner" of the police reserves.

"Many complaints have also been laid before us that the police have for a long time been insulting and brutal in their treatment of the Jews of the Lower East Side," the report continued. "We find that instances of uncivil and even rough treatment toward the people of this district by individual policemen are inexcusably common." This, of course, gave credence to the complaints of brutality during the recent meat protests. Finally, the committee complained that the police involved were only reprimanded or fined a few days' pay. Not a single officer was discharged from the force.[10]

Most of Rabbi Joseph's obituaries emphasized his scholarship and kindness, barely touching on his aborted efforts to rationalize New York's kosher meat industry. Only the Social-ist Labor Party's *Weekly People* recalled how he had "fallen a victim of the heartless and contemptible Jewish bourgeoi-sie in this country, which has turned religion into a busi-ness institution."

Recalling the rabbi's kosher slaughter initiatives, the paper dripped venom on the businessmen who had brought him to New York and ostensibly used him as a tool for their own disreputable purposes:

> The first, last and only "improvement" he made in Judaism here was a so-called strict observance of the kosher meat rites. High prices on kosher meat were imposed. Kosher meat signs and tags were issued in the rabbi's name, and they proved to be an inexhaustible source of profits, monopolized by the Jewish Meat Trust. Large sums of money have been extorted from the kosher butchers, and these, in return, have thrown the burden upon the consumers, who are principally poor workingmen. . . . The kosher meat capitalists who themselves often found pork chops more to their taste than kosher beef, have reaped a rich harvest.
>
> The money spent on the rabbi was considered an invest-ment, which was bound to yield large profits, and there was no mistake made in that. . . . A few years elapsed, everything was in good working order, and the rabbi was found to be no more an urgent necessity for the business purposes of the God-fearing cut-throats. They forsook their rabbi, and left him to his fate.[11]

It was not a fair characterization, but it served the Party's anticapitalist purposes handily.

Prague-born rabbi Max Heller, a pioneer Zionist in the Reform movement, saw strong parallels in the outrages that occurred at Rabbi Joseph's funeral and those of the meat protests, and drew an important object lesson. In a column in the *American Israelite*, he admonished his fellow "uptown" Jews for their failure to support their coreligionists during the boycott and expressed the hope that the Grand Street disgrace would open their eyes to their responsibilities toward their East Side brethren.

The events surrounding the rabbi's funeral, he wrote, "should act as an awakening to the consciences of the 'better' class of New York Jews. Not so long ago, at the time of the meat riots, there was ample occasion for energetic interference on the part of influential New York Jews. When Jewish wives and mothers were clubbed and dragged by a brutal police and decent journals treated the matter as a humorous episode," he scolded, "it was high time for those in exalted places of wealth and political standing to call a halt to the tragic farce, and to vindicate the justice of their outraged brethren."

But the "better class of New York Jews" had failed to take a strong stand.

The troubles would grow and spread, Rabbi Heller concluded, unless they were stopped by "emphatic and united protests," adding that "the wrong which the American Jew permits to be visited upon his Russian brother will find him out in due course of time. Let New York Judaism stand idly by these outrages, and the moral rottenness of such cowardice will draw upon itself the contempt it will merit."[12]

19

We Don't Feel Like Paying Fifth Avenue Prices

No press reports chronicle how many kosher butchers ultimately signed the pledge to sell meat at fourteen cents a pound as long as the wholesale price permitted it, or how many certificates were issued by the Allied Conference. Indeed, there is no record of any formal announcement by the organization that the protest was officially over. If the movement had begun in mid-May with a bang, it had ended by mid-June with a decided whimper. But there could be no arguing with the fact that its overarching goal had been achieved, at least in the short run.

The wholesalers had come to terms, and kosher meat was affordable once again.

But *why* had wholesale prices come down? Certainly a key factor was the relentless pressure of the boycott, which did a remarkably effective job of suppressing demand. This, in turn, meant that wholesalers weren't doing much kosher business in New York, and that their profits were down, as were those of the Midwestern houses from which they bought cattle. Since the whole point of raising prices had been to *increase* profits, that plan was clearly no longer working for the Trust companies, and abandoning it, at least for the moment, made good economic sense.

But all this occurred within the larger context of the dismantling of the mechanisms they had used to fix prices that was mandated by the injunctions against them. Without the ability to coordinate and set artificial prices, the Trust companies once again found themselves at the mercy of market forces. Those that offered retailers the best prices would be the ones that did business. Put another way, to the extent that the mechanisms the Trust companies had dreamed up to foil the laws of supply and demand were no longer operative and had not been replaced by winks and nods, those laws once again governed the market.

And market forces were the boycotters' best friend.

As long as this was the situation and regular retail butchers sold meat at affordable prices, there was no longer any pressing need for organizations to fight price hikes or, for that matter, much of a need for cooperative shops. And indeed, within a month or two there were no further references in the press to the Ladies' Anti-Beef Trust Association or the Allied Conference for Cheap Kosher Meat. Not even the new cooperative butcher shops appear to have had much staying power. The city directories list a meat shop at 245 Stanton Street through 1905 and one at 57 Monroe through 1906, but not afterward.[1]

Anyone who expected the Beef Trust to roll over and play dead in response to temporary restraining orders, however, wasn't reckoning with the greed and guile of the men who had built it up in the first place. Although the Big Six were technically complying with the orders of the federal and state courts, that didn't mean their bosses weren't huddled with their lawyers plotting ways around them.

The question of whether the federal injunction against them would become permanent remained before Judge Peter S. Grosscup for the balance of 1902. Finally, in February 1903 he rendered his decision. Taking a broad view of interstate commerce, he concluded that the Trust companies were, indeed, acting in restraint of trade as envisioned under the Sherman Act. Accordingly, he granted the government's motion for a preliminary injunction against them. In May, he made it permanent.[2]

But the Trust's men had another tactic up their sleeves. If it was unlawful for independent firms to collude, why remain

We Don't Feel Like Paying

independent? A new structure in which the companies consolidated and were commonly owned could solve the problem handily. And as a first step, three of the Big Six—Swift, Armour, and Morris—decided to form a holding company. They incorporated it quietly in New Jersey in mid-March 1903, and named it the National Packing Company.

All but two of the new company's directors were officers of Armour, Swift, and Morris. In fact, four of the eleven directors were *named* Armour, Swift, or Morris. Capitalized at $15 million dollars ($400 million in 2019 dollars), the corporation began by merging small meat companies in Chicago and Omaha the three had purchased earlier. It was a first step in a slow but measured strategy designed eventually to bring everything under one umbrella. At its formation, seven companies were placed under its aegis, G. H. Hammond Company of Chicago and the United Dressed Beef Company of New York among them. Everyone assumed the new arrangement would be the forerunner of a bigger merger to follow. The *New York Tribune* even ran the news under the headline "Start of Beef Trust."[3]

A reporter from the *Tribune* asked Frederick Joseph, vice president of Schwarzschild & Sulzberger, for a comment on the merger.

"We feel satisfied with our present business," he replied evasively.

"Was an offer made for your company?" the journalist asked.

"Well, I would rather not talk about *that*," Joseph replied.[4]

There had indeed been discussions with Schwarzschild & Sulzberger and with Cudahy, but these companies ultimately remained independent. Four of the "Big Six," however, had now joined forces.

Their effort to combine assets notwithstanding, the Trust companies still wished the injunction against them to be lifted. Accordingly, on July 18, 1903, they appealed Judge Grosscup's decision to the Supreme Court of the United States. Throughout 1904, while the appeal was in process, the

Justice Department—now under the leadership of Attorney General William Henry Moody, Philander C. Knox having resigned to accept an appointment to the Senate—was watching carefully for any further violations of the antitrust laws.[5]

Whatever the cause of the return to reasonable meat prices—whether it was the strike, the appearance of co-ops, or the injunction, or, most likely, a combination of all three—they continued to prevail for several years. But the financial pressures on East Side families did not abate, and in early 1904 a new threat emerged when rents began to rise abruptly.

Landlords had begun demanding ten dollars a month ($280 in today's dollars) for flats that had formerly let for $7.50; apartments that had cost $5.50 had risen to $7.50. Leases were rare, so landlords could raise rates at will. And with shelter being most families' greatest expense, rent rises averaging 25 percent posed even more of a threat to the lives of East Side families than had the increase in butchers' charges two years earlier. There were nearly eight thousand evictions on the East Side alone in 1903, and 1904 threatened far more.[6]

It was market forces, however, rather than some unseen corporate trust, that were primarily responsible for the rise in rents. New York's growing population of immigrants was chasing too few flats. More than 600,000 aliens, mostly immigrants, arrived at Ellis Island in 1904 alone. The city's population had expanded by more than 14 percent just since the turn of the century, even as tenements on the East Side were being torn down to make way for parks, schools, and the new Williamsburg Bridge.

In addition, the government had added to building owners' financial burdens with the passage in 1901 of the Tenement House Act, which not only introduced specifications for new buildings, but also required significant upgrades to existing structures, including installation of indoor toilets, windows, fire escapes, hall lights, and waterproof cellars. And because builders and contractors had been on strike since 1903, the pace of new construction had slowed.

We Don't Feel Like Paying

The first of the month was when rent was generally due, and so it was also normally the time that suits were filed against tenants, and marshals posted eviction notices on their doors. It was often not the building owners themselves who took legal action, but rather speculators who signed leases with them for entire tenement blocks and decided on their own how much to charge for the flats. As far as the renters were concerned, the speculators were the ostensible landlords, and many of them were fellow Jews, widely disliked and derided on the East Side as "cockroaches." Positioned between the owners—some of whom were also Jewish—and the tenants, it was they who had the strongest incentive to squeeze the renters.

The tenants sensed a conspiracy. They believed the lessee landlords were exploiting the situation, just as the retail butchers before them had victimized the meat strikers. As a Mrs. Wexelman put it at a meeting organized to consider a rent strike, "the East Side landlords and agents have a secret organization and a blacklist. Their plan is to make it so uncomfortable for anyone who refuses to pay the increased rents that it will be impossible for him to live on the East Side. Many of us *must* live down here, but we don't feel like paying Fifth Avenue prices," she added.[7]

No one who had lived on the East Side for more than two years could fail to grasp the striking parallels between meat in 1902 and rents in 1904. And as the drama played out over the next month, the similarities became even more evident. Once again, the people of the Lower East Side perceived a grave threat to their welfare, and once again they rose up to fight. Once again they felt exploited and saw other Jews as their enemies. Once again socialist agitators would attempt to use the movement for their own ends. Once again the organizers would be denied the right to hold rallies, but would be remarkably successful in building support by going door to door. Once again cooperatives would be prescribed as a solution to the problem. And once again a previously obscure woman would take center stage to mobilize her community, but ultimately be sidelined by better-connected men.[8]

This time they had a model from which to work. The successes—and the blunders—of the meat boycott were still fresh in memory, and much of the violence that had marred the earlier movement could be avoided. During the meat boycott, it had taken several days of riotous demonstrations before the established organizations came together to address the issue; this time the community was largely able to short-circuit trouble in the streets. On April 6, delegates from several East Side organizations assembled. Several were Jewish groups; others were unions with large Jewish memberships.

The *Forward* made the parallel explicit and encouraged the protest. "This strike can be as great as the meat strike," it asserted, urging the women to "take the rent question into their hands as they did the meat question."[9]

In the same way that the Allied Conference for Cheap Kosher Meat had been established in 1902, the delegates voted to establish the New York Rent Protective Association to act on their behalf. They also decided to ask for a permit for a large protest parade and an open air anti-landlord rally to be held in Seward Park on the following Monday, April 11.

Samuel Katz, an East Third Street machinist, was named president, and a young woman named Bertha E. Liebson was elected treasurer. Only seventeen years old and Russian-born, Liebson, the daughter of a cloak maker, possessed boundless energy. She had immigrated in 1900 and her day job was as secretary of the New York Protective Association, a labor union advocacy group. But she became a local folk hero for all of the time and effort she had invested raising funds to hire counsel to defend tenants whose eviction hearings were scheduled for the week after Passover. Just as the New York *World* had given Paulina Finkel the sobriquet "the Napoleon of the East Side" in 1902, papers now dubbed Bertha Liebson "the East Side Joan of Arc."

"I am going to devote everything a girl can to the poor tenant and to defeat the landlords," she vowed during the meeting, "and I mean to win!" She also pledged to recruit more females into the association. To that end, she helped canvas the quarter and distribute thousands of flyers in English and Yiddish, reminiscent of those produced by the Ladies' Association to ask fellow Jews to boycott the meat shops. The *New York Sun* printed an example: "Tenants, keep away from this house. In the name of your children we ask you not to hire any rooms in that house, as the house is on strike because the rent is raised every month, and we want to put a stop to it once and for all. Keep away!—The Committee."

An unnamed rabbi told the *Sun* that "we are advocating arbitration because unless there is an amicable and fair settlement by some such method, there is likely to be serious trouble in the East Side within a week. We had violence here during the so-called kosher meat riots two years ago," he continued, "when butchers were beaten in the street and their stores wrecked. The present increase in rents is a much greater hardship than was the increase in meat prices. But the causes are similar." He went on:

> Many of the landlords are Jews who began buying East Side property ten and twelve years ago, when it was much cheaper. The landlords have exaggerated the increase in their own expenses and tried to throw dust in the eyes of the people. An increase of five percent might have been justified. They ask twenty percent. The people . . . are organizing, which is a good thing if the organizations don't fall into the hands of the agitators and become incited to violence. That is what we will strive to prevent. We hope to convince the landlords that public opinion will be too much for them and that they will hurt their own pockets in the end by driving the people away.[10]

The next day, Samuel Katz outlined the Protective Association's plans. The group would encourage people to organize individual tenants' associations to fight their landlords. And it would establish "an immense mutual benefit society for the Jewish tenants of the East Side" to help those who received eviction notices defray expenses and retain legal counsel. As the mutual fund grew, the organization would lease the houses and sublet them to the members at cost,

31. A tenant is evicted from 85 Willett Street. Source: Library of Congress, Prints and Photographs Division, George Grantham Bain Collection, LC-DIG-ggbain-01361.

and then, in time, buy and build its own buildings. It was an exact analogue to the cooperative butcher shops the Ladies' Anti-Beef Trust Association had established in 1902 as a solution to rising meat prices.[11]

Both Joseph Barondess and Abraham Cahan got into the act, just as they had two years earlier. Barondess spoke at a rally of the Social Democrats, though the organizers of the Protective Association doubted whether their involvement would be an asset. And Cahan outlined to the *New York Times* a plan to fight every case in order to tie up eviction proceedings and clog the courts, thus adding to the costs of the "cockroaches."

In a signed editorial in *Worker*, Cahan also provided some genealogical perspective, so to speak, on the rent strike:

> When the Meat Trust raised prices to an unnatural level and the entire ghetto burst into protest, that protest was the child of our trade union movement," he wrote. "The meat strike was the offspring of our trade strikes. This is the case with the present rent strikes. They are the outcome of that same spirit, the offspring of that same struggle against capital.[12]

Indeed, like the meat protesters before them, the tenants borrowed terms from the labor movement, referring to their action as a "strike," calling their tenants' associations "unions," and labeling those who paid their rent increases "scabs."[13]

But it was not only the protesters who drew lessons from the meat strike. The judges seem to have done so, too. They were far more indulgent with tenants than they had been with meat protesters, although clemency was made easier because there was little violence this time around. David Blaustein noted that "the courts showed such leniency to the tenants that even the weakest of them felt a sense of protection. The justices were not able to alter the right of a landlord to raise the rent when he so desires, but they did emphatically put a stop to the eviction of the sick and granted extension of time during the Jewish holidays to so many that it meanwhile became possible to organize a systematic campaign."[14]

On April 9, young Bertha Liebson made a formal request for a parade and a demonstration to Police Commissioner William McAdoo, who had come into office when George B. McClellan, Jr. defeated Mayor Low and took over on the first of the year. She was summarily refused and vowed to appeal to the mayor himself. But like Paulina Finkel, Clara Korn, and Caroline Schatzberg before her, she got only as far as his secretary, who told her the decision was McAdoo's to make.

"I do not see why we should not be allowed to hold parades and open air meetings," she complained to the *New York Times*. "Our people are all law-abiding, and there would be no danger whatever in letting us meet to express our views in this way. We do not advocate violent methods, but are conducting our work along peaceful and orderly lines. I think the Commissioner is unjust in refusing to issue the permit."

It was a speech worthy of the women who had had much the same to say about Police Commissioner Partridge in 1902. Like the Ladies' Association before it, the New York Rent Protective Association foreswore violence. And this time around there had been little of it, although that didn't mean that some lessee landlords didn't peer over their shoulders nervously when they walked the streets of the East Side.[15]

And just as the Ladies' Association had split apart in acrimony, so did the Protective Association. At a meeting at McKinley Hall on Sunday, April 10, it broke up over an argument about money. Samuel Katz turned on Liebson, claiming she was too young to handle the organization's funds; she, in turn, denounced him as a socialist. Before the evening was over, the Katz faction, mostly labor union people, had walked out with the money and rented the hall next door for a meeting of their own. Bertha was eventually ousted by those who remained behind. Even this unpleasantness had a parallel in the exit of Sarah Edelson from the Ladies' Association.[16]

When May 1 came, there were more heartbreaking eviction stories. There was also picketing and deliberate damage done to apartments. There was stone throwing and a few attacks on landlords, but nothing remotely on the scale of the meat protests. The Protective Association offered to engage the landlords in a meeting, even as signs emerged that many of them were starting to capitulate.

"We have the landlords on the run," crowed Samuel Edelstein, secretary of the association. "Since we started to fight them, tenants in eighty houses have gone on strike, refusing to pay the higher rents, and have formed unions to protect themselves. In over 30 percent of the houses where the tenants rebelled, the landlords have signed leases which will prevent them from raising rents for another year," he added. Separately, the *New York Tribune* reported the surrender of landlords who had rented to a group of 150 families pledged to resist eviction.[17]

Some landlords backed down entirely; others reached agreement with individual tenant groups on lesser increments or offered year-long leases that guaranteed against increases. Some tenants left the East Side entirely, heading mostly for Brownsville or Williamsburg. And others just paid the increases. By mid-May it was all over, and people on the East Side went about their lives once again.

"We are greatly pleased with the peaceful ending of this vicious rent war," said an association representative. "It seemed at first as if we had a monster enemy to deal with, but the strength and efficiency of the organized tenants showed our power and compelled the landlords to settle."[18] Indeed, there was reason for celebration. They had managed to avoid the worst aspects of the meat strike and still accomplish their goal.

A second rent strike began at the very end of 1907, the new year being an obvious time for landlords to raise rents. It occurred, however, against the backdrop of the Panic of 1907, an economic recession characterized by runs on banks and a rise in unemployment. The *New York Times* estimated that some 100,000 men and women on the East Side were out of work; they could ill-afford even modest rises in rent, and actually needed reductions.

A twenty-year-old socialist firebrand named Pauline Newman, who would later be remembered as a prominent labor activist and the first female general organizer of the International Ladies' Garment Workers' Union, led the effort to push back on landlords. Although she was employed in a shirtwaist factory on Grand Street by day, she visited tenements in the evenings to organize the housewives.

The plan was for everyone to refuse to pay rent unless it was reduced by 18–20 percent. Once again, it was a page right out of the 1902 meat boycott. And borrowing from the earlier rent strike, Newman and the other organizers urged those who received dispossess notices to take their cases to court, where attorneys would do their best to gum up the system and force delays, thus staving off evictions. They also intended to arrange for families that were ousted to be taken in by neighbors in the same building, thus blunting the effect of the eviction.[19]

What started out as another grass-roots movement of housewives, however, was quickly taken over by the local branch of the Socialist Party, which was heavily Jewish and, of course, male. Tenants of individual buildings were encouraged to negotiate together, but no women's umbrella association emerged this time, or needed to. A male-dominated "Anti-High Rent Bureau" set up *within* the Socialist Party managed everything, and as a result this strike was well organized from the beginning. There was canvassing and leafleting, there were mass meetings, and there was outreach to the labor unions.

Volunteers educated local women on how to present offending landlords with several strong arguments against evicting tenants. They were told to point out that it cost eight dollars to evict one family versus twelve dollars to reduce a family's rent for a year by a dollar a month. And to warn landlords that the Socialist Party would see to it that no one would rent the vacant rooms.

If that didn't work, they could threaten to report the landlord to the authorities. The Tenement House Act had mandated so many improvements that violations could be found in almost any building, and a citation by the Tenement House Commission was essentially a lien on a property. If the landlord could be made to see that his best option was simply to lower rents, he would be asked to sign an agreement committing to do it for a specified period of time—that is, a lease.[20]

There were tussles with the police, who broke up open-air meetings held without permits, and who had no choice but to get involved when crowds interfered with marshals carrying out evictions. But by New Year's Eve, some fifty thousand tenants had signed on, and within the first few days of 1908 the strike had spread to Brooklyn, Harlem, and Newark. The papers began to print news of landlords who capitulated and initialed rent-lowering agreements. Some were willing to deal, provided their tenants kept mum about the agreements. But others were more recalcitrant and set up a fund to fight the strikers, or hired thugs to assault nonpayers.[21]

Past East Side uprisings had, without exception, been the work of obscure women with no claim to fame, who had stood up for themselves and their community when conditions became intolerable, and then faded from public view when their ends had been accomplished. But the 1908 rent strike was notable for the support of a prominent New York power couple who were, and would remain, very much in the public eye: Rose Pastor Stokes, a well-known *Yidishes Tageblatt* columnist, socialist activist, settlement worker, and feminist, and her millionaire Episcopalian husband, James G. Phelps Stokes.

The couple had gained notoriety because of his social status and philanthropy and her activism, not to mention their divergent backgrounds. They visited the strikers' headquarters on January 4 to pledge support, and Rose spoke at several meetings after that. "Rents on the East Side are exorbitant," she told one crowd in a mixture of English and Yiddish. "Two dollars is not enough reduction. Five dollars is a more suitable amount. Stick to your principles and you will win in the end, but be orderly," she exhorted her audience.[22]

The strike reached its crescendo in the second week of January, when some six thousand people were about to be turned out into the streets for nonpayment of rent. Many landlords believed that if this happened, others would capitulate and simply pay what was demanded of them. But the courts moved slowly, and while some tenants gave in or packed up and moved, many landlords came to terms to save the costs of eviction. The Socialists estimated that some 40 percent of the landlords in those tenements they had helped organize had offered rent reductions. And by the middle of January the strike had wound down.[23]

In both 1904 and 1908 the lessons of the 1902 meat boycott had not been wasted on the striking tenants. By organizing early, going house to house to secure grassroots cooperation, and allying with others, they had achieved their objectives with little if any bloodshed. And like the Ladies' Anti-Beef Trust Association before it, the ad hoc vehicles they organized to reach their goals soon faded into history.

20

It Is Not Our Fault That Meat Is So High

It took until January 6, 1905, for the U.S. Supreme Court to hear arguments in the Beef Trust case, but only until the end of that month for it to render a decision.

The court's unanimous opinion was drafted by Associate Justice Oliver Wendell Holmes, who more or less plowed in behind the Seventh Circuit Court. It held that the commerce clause of the Constitution justified regulating the Trust, which was, indeed, an illegal combination in restraint of trade. It enjoined the Trust companies against continuing to suppress competition, fix prices, or press the railroads for preferential rates.[1]

Dissolving the new National Packing Company, however, was not an issue before the court, and this holding company would, for nearly another decade, continue to acquire stockyards, slaughterhouses, and refrigerator cars and place them under its expanding corporate umbrella. It remained an effective vehicle for the three companies that had formed it, and the fourth it had absorbed, to keep abreast of one another's activities and quietly coordinate efforts.

Only the naïve thought the Supreme Court decision would actually put an end to the Beef Trust. These were contentious companies that continued to insist they had not broken the law in spite of the superabundance of evidence to the contrary and the verdicts against them. They were accustomed to being sued, and they were not about to abandon such lucrative cooperation easily. Although some of the more obvious mechanisms for coordination had been dismantled, there were still ways to act together under the radar. Less formally than before, but not much less effectively, they continued to divide territory, pressure cattlemen, and coordinate prices.

As the *Daily People* noted, "the methods and policy of the Trust have in no wise been altered. The livestock man who ships his cattle to the stockyards in Chicago, Omaha, Kansas City or Sioux city will find one price prevailing. No matter what the name of the company he sells to, the cattle find their way into the slaughter pens of the Trust." Something similar could probably also have been said of their efforts to fix the wholesale prices demanded of their customers.[2]

What actually threatened the packers' fortunes more than the Supreme Court's decision was the publication of a novel. In 1904 muckraking journalist Upton Sinclair, who had done his research while living among laborers in the Chicago stockyards, chronicled working conditions and exposed the unsanitary practices of the meat industry in a powerful work of fiction called *The Jungle*. It was published in serial form in 1905 in the socialist newspaper *Appeal to Reason* and as a book in 1906.

Sinclair's narrative was a wholesale indictment of the meat packing industry. His tale of the life of a fictitious Lithuanian immigrant was intended to disparage capitalism and advance the cause of socialism in America, but it was his description of unsafe and unsanitary conditions that most evoked public indignation. Sinclair told of how dirt, rat droppings, and even rats themselves wound up in the ground meat and sausage that ended up on people's plates, and did far more to sully the reputation of the packers than manipulation of prices had ever done.

Sinclair's work was not the first account of questionable food safety practices in the industry; the quality of the food supply had been publicly debated for some time, as had the meatpackers' methods and their relationship to tainted and diseased meat. But Sinclair's work pushed it all squarely into the spotlight.

He sent a copy of his book to President Theodore Roosevelt, who was so horrified by the descriptions in it that he ordered the nation's abattoirs investigated. After Sinclair's allegations were corroborated, Roosevelt raised the revolting conditions his investigators discovered in his December 1905 message to Congress. The Pure Food and Drug Act and the Meat Inspection Act soon followed; both passed in 1906.[3]

The latter law, which took effect that March, mandated inspection of livestock before slaughter and established sanitary standards for abattoirs and meat processing plants. It also added significantly to the cost of meat packing, however, and in so doing gave the industry a new excuse for raising prices.

Sure enough, by late November 1906 the Trust companies were at it again. They raised the wholesale price of beef, which in turn forced kosher butchers to raise retail prices once again. Chuck steak rose from fourteen to sixteen or seventeen cents a pound.

And East Side housewives didn't like it any more than they had in May 1902.[4]

Once again, it was women who took the lead to protest. This time, however, there was no sign of Sarah Edelson, Caroline Schatzberg, or Sarah Cohn. An entirely new cast of characters emerged on November 29. Esther Dolobofsky and Rebecca Reznick, both of East Fourth Street, led the charge.

Just as the 1902 effort had begun abruptly with a meeting at Sarah Edelson's family establishment, the 1906 meat protest began with a gathering of nearly fifty women at the home of twenty-two-year-old, Russian-born Dolobofsky, her out-of-work husband, Max, and their children. A "black-eyed mite of a Jewess" to the *New York Tribune*, the diminutive Dolobofsky advocated a strike. Then, together with twenty-six-year-old Rebecca Resnick, a mother of two who lived in the same tenement, she took to the streets. A gifted orator, she had no trouble attracting crowds wherever she went.[5]

Eventually, they made their way to Lewis Street, where William Ehrenfeld ran a butcher shop and Abraham Brechner did business across the street. They began calling on women to boycott the shops. This was too much for Brechner, an apple-cheeked man with a Van Dyke beard who emerged to shoo them away. He knocked Resnick off of a soap box and punched Dolobofsky. Others rose to their defense and a brawl ensued. Eggs and apples were hurled and clubs were brandished, and both women sustained serious cuts to their faces.

When the police arrived, they made no arrests. That, however, did not stop Dolobofsky. This was not her first rodeo; the *New York Sun* described her as "well-known as an agitator among East Side women." Brechner complained later that she had been a cigar maker before her marriage, and that "she used to lead strikes—she *likes* strikes." Later that day, she sought a warrant for Brechner's arrest, and he was arraigned in Essex Market Court the next day on a charge of assault. There, magistrate Henry Steinert admonished Dolobofsky and Resnick to "mind your own business and keep out of trouble."[6]

An early recruit to the cause was Rebecca Menzen of Madison Street, who parked herself in front of Louis Jeselowitz's shop and took a big bite out of his business. She attracted a crowd, shut him down, and led them to another shop across the street for a repeat performance.

"Look what fools we are to buy meat when fish is cheaper," Menzen told her audience. "Fish is *better* than meat. If you don't know how to make fancy dishes out of fish, I will teach you if you come to my house. When you have it cooked in different styles you can't tell the difference from meat!" She then led them to her home and as many as were able to crowd into her tiny kitchen heard an edifying lecture on preparing fish.[7]

All day long there were demonstrations in front of meat shops, and damage was done to the stock in several of them. By one estimate, more than two thousand people hit the streets, and the butchers, many of whom were veterans of the 1902 strike, were frightened. They hurriedly called a meeting the next day to establish a new organization to represent their interests, the East Side Hebrew Retail Butchers' Association having been rendered defunct after the 1902 strike was over. They named it the Hebrew Retail Kosher Butchers' Protective Association. Louis Kirsch of Rivington Street was chosen as president, and he lost no time in fixing the responsibility for the rise in prices on others.

"We are not to blame for the present high prices of meat," he told the newspapers. "The Beef Trust, the packers, are the ones. We have to pay 10½ to 11 cents wholesale for forequarter beef where we only had to pay 8 and 8½ cents a week ago." But he made it clear that he and his cohorts had no appetite for a return to 1902. "We shall not fight the women," he predicted. "Rather than have meat riots like five years ago, we will close up our shops until the price of meat comes down."[8]

Most of the problem was the high prices demanded by the wholesalers, but the abandonment of a popular Lower East Side custom was also a factor. Over the years, Jewish women had come to expect extra bones and a piece of fat or suet to be thrown in with the purchase of a pound of beef. The wholesalers, however, had always charged the butchers for them. As a result, if a retailer sold 140 pounds of beef, for example, he was actually paid for only about eighty pounds of it. Now, in self-defense, the butchers had taken to charging customers for both soup bones and fat.

Pressed on one side by wholesalers who demanded higher prices and on the other by consumers who insisted on lower ones, many butchers were lucky to net five dollars a week. Some took home less than three dollars and were paying their hired help more than that. They saw no obvious way forward that would stave off eventual bankruptcy.

So they did the only thing they could think of: they appealed to the President of the United States.[9]

Theodore Roosevelt was not a distant figure to those who had been in New York for some years. He had been president of the city's board of police commissioners between 1895 and 1897 before being elected governor of New York in 1898 and vice president of the United States in 1900, and before succeeding William McKinley as president after the latter was assassinated in 1901. And the butchers knew he was an opponent of trusts. He had personally intervened in the Pennsylvania miners' strike, and it had been he who had directed Attorney General Knox to pursue the Beef Trust. It had also been during his tenure as president that the Supreme Court had sustained the verdict against the Beef Trust.

The invitation to Roosevelt was extended informally through the press. The butchers' naïve hope was that he might advise them directly or intercede on their behalf as he had in Pennsylvania. "If President Roosevelt says we should shut our shops up, then we will shut our shops up," one butcher vowed at the meeting, "and then the women will know that it is not our fault that meat is so high."[10]

In early December, fighting broke out in Harlem. Female Jewish pickets made a huge dent in the local kosher meat business. Four butchers had closed by December 3, and others were making no money. At a poorly attended meeting of the butchers' association on December 5, those assembled agreed nearly unanimously to stand by the women and leave the matter up to them.[11]

At a meeting on the Lower East Side that same night, the Meat Consumers' Protective Association was formally established. Those assembled blamed the Beef Trust for the rise in prices; unlike in 1902, the retail butchers were believed and were not considered enemies this time. But nor were they respected. Esther Dolobofsky observed that "they have not the courage that we women have. They are afraid to fight, and they leave it to *us* to begin. Well, we *will* begin, and we will fight and fight until we win. It will be hard. But if we stand together shoulder to shoulder we can accomplish a great deal, as we did before."[12]

It was a tip of the hat to the victory of 1902, still very much in people's consciousness.

The women also decided to appoint some thirty of their number to go from house to house in the tenement district requesting all housewives to join a general boycott, another tactic borrowed from five years earlier.[13]

The conservative English-language weekly *American Hebrew* was sympathetic to the downtown Jews and worried that the city might see a repeat of the earlier unrest. "The poverty of the East Side cannot stand a rise in the price of meats," it declared in an editorial. It, too, accepted at face value the retail butchers' explanation—that the root of the problem was that the wholesalers had raised their prices—and it sent a reporter to two East River slaughterhouses to investigate. Schwarzschild & Sulzberger, which by now was doing relatively little kosher business, denied it had raised prices at all. And United Dressed Beef, now the dominant supplier to the East Side butchers and a part of the National Packing Company, blamed not a shortage of supply, but growing demand for kosher meat.[14]

At a mass gathering on Monday, December 10, more than two hundred Brownsville butchers voted to close their doors indefinitely. While that meeting was going on, five hundred Jewish women met three blocks away. They, too, held the retail butchers blameless, and in fact issued a statement to that effect. But they also vowed to wreck the shops of anyone who sold meat. It was the only way they could see to send a message to the Beef Trust.[15]

While the East Side remained quiet, Brownsville boiled over. Most butchers closed, but those who did not bore the brunt of the anger of protesters, most of whom were female. Women patrolled the streets, goading butchers into closing or delivering summary justice in the form of broken windows and kerosene-soaked meat. Several shops were wrecked, a few people were injured, and a handful were arrested, keeping the police busy. But by the next day there was peace, as almost all of the shops had closed.[16]

Chicago Livestock World echoed the opinion of United Dressed Beef that the cause of the spike in prices was that demand had exceeded supply, and it declared the 1906 meat strike a "tempest in a teapot," which is more or less what it turned out to be. After a dramatic beginning, it did not get much traction, and by the end of December it was a memory.

Nor, as far as is known, was anything ever heard from President Roosevelt.[17]

21

A Great Victory for the American People

The Beef Trust remained capable of collusion and manipulating prices for many years after the Supreme Court decision in *Swift & Co. v. United States*. One key vehicle for coordination was the National Packing Company, described by the federal government as a "strong community of interest among four of the six leading companies in the packing-house business." It came in for Federal Trade Commission scrutiny in 1910 and 1911, and although its directors were absolved of criminal charges, it was finally dissolved under the direction of the Justice Department in 1912.[1]

But even *that* didn't spell the end of the Beef Trust, at least in the public mind. Collusion became more difficult, but not impossible, and hence the price of meat, and therefore that of kosher meat, continued to fluctuate, seemingly independently of the law of supply and demand. When it became too high, as it did from time to time, boycotts were organized by local Jewish communities. These occurred not only in Manhattan and Brooklyn, but also in Philadelphia; Boston; Cleveland; Detroit; Baltimore; St. Louis; Wilmington, Delaware; Providence, Rhode Island; New Bedford and Brockton, Massachusetts; and Newark, Bayonne, and Paterson, New Jersey.

There was a certain sameness to the protests, and most looked a lot like the 1902 New York boycott, only on a smaller scale. They generally pit butchers against wholesalers and women against butchers, and saw women organizing, canvassing, and picketing. They saw committees and mass meetings and butchers closing until prices came down. None of them lasted long, but they could be quite bitter. They usually involved the police, and often degenerated into pulled hair, flesh wounds, broken windows, and kerosene-soaked meat.

In April 1910 a meat riot foreordained by the Chicago meat barons by an arbitrary, two-and-a-half cent per pound jump in prices began in Harlem. It was notable for the leadership of forty-eight-year-old Anna Pastor, the mother of Rose Pastor Stokes, the well-known *Tageblatt* columnist and social activist. At a gathering of Jews on Forsyth Street on April 7, she spoke up for the butchers. "The butchers are *victims* of the Meat Trust," she insisted. "They would like to sell meat cheaper, but I positively know they can't do it at the present wholesale price." She advocated permitting them to dispose of their stocks of meat before joining the boycott. It was agreed they would close the following Monday, April 11, but some were pressured by demonstrators into doing so earlier.[2]

By Monday, there was little daylight between the women and the butchers. The Hebrew Retail Kosher Butchers' Protective Association called a halt to the purchase of meat from the wholesalers, and some twenty-five hundred of the three thousand–odd butchers in greater New York honored it. That in itself didn't stop the breaking of windows and some scattered attacks, but things quieted down once most shops in Harlem, the Bronx, Brooklyn, and the Lower East Side and in Newark and Bayonne in New Jersey were shuttered. A large contingent of butchers even marched on the slaughterhouses to demand lower prices. Abattoir employees shut their doors and windows and stood behind them brandishing knives and cleavers, but there was no violence.[3]

A moratorium on the boycott was called to allow Jewish families to eat kosher meat on the Passover holiday, which began on April 23, and the protest does not seem to have regained much steam after that, though there were outbreaks in other cities throughout the summer.

A Great Victory for the American People

32. A crowd discussing the price of meat in front of East Side shops, 1910.
Source: Library of Congress, Prints and Photographs Division,
George Grantham Bain Collection, LC-DIG-ggbain-04611.

Things heated up in early June 1912 when the wholesale price of chuck rose once again, forcing the retail price up to eighteen cents. This time the first protest action was in Brooklyn, but it eventually spread to the East Side and the tactics were the same: squads of women patrolling the markets with kerosene at the ready. East Siders voted at two neighborhood meetings to support a boycott, and the butchers plowed in behind them a few days after that. By now they knew from bitter experience that there was no percentage in doing anything else. Remaining open was not an option unless they relished having their windows broken and their stock destroyed.

This time the butchers also asked the *shoychtim* and the 150-odd *mashgichim* who worked under them at the abattoirs to walk out in solidarity. The action spread to Chicago, Philadelphia, Boston, and elsewhere before enthusiasm ebbed during the summer.[4]

The butchers took on the wholesalers once again at the end of 1916. The retail prices of *all* foodstuffs had been rising rapidly in the run-up to America's entry into World War I, and as usual, observant Jews were the first to feel the pain because kosher meat was costly and many of its customers were, as one wag put it, "never more than two weeks from the poorhouse." In December, after the price of chuck suddenly skyrocketed, some three thousand butchers refused to deal in it. Many closed their shops or sold only poultry. A truce was declared when the wholesalers agreed to cut prices temporarily, but it didn't last long.[5]

New York was not alone; dealers in Chicago, Boston, Cincinnati, Albany, Philadelphia, and elsewhere were also feeling the pinch. And by February 1917 consumers joined the fray, first in Philadelphia, where protesting women attacked shops and overturned pushcarts, pouring kerosene not just on meat, but also on fish and vegetables. New Yorkers followed shortly.

This time the situation was more desperate than in the past; *everything* had gone up and there was talk of real hun-

A Great Victory for the American People

ger on the East Side. A good deal of the wrath of the *balebostes* was aimed at dealers in kosher poultry, which had risen to twenty-eight cents a pound. But eggs had risen from thirty-two cents a dozen a year earlier to eighty cents; cabbage from two cents a pound to twelve cents. Flour was up more than 200 percent. Violent protests broke out in the Williamsburg neighborhood and on the East Side amid rumors of a conspiracy by retailers to keep prices high.[6]

The Socialist Party, once again sensing an opportunity to further its cause, channeled the women's anger into a series of cost-of-living protests that were about much more than meat. The Socialists organized a mass meeting of five thousand at which the Mothers' Anti–High Price League was established. The group staged a number of demonstrations, and three representatives were granted a meeting with Mayor John P. Mitchel.

After the mayor observed that he felt their distress deeply, one of the women brazenly shot back, "Excuse me, sir, you do *not* feel it. You *think* you feel as we do, but if you are not hungry you cannot. This morning you had your breakfast, today you will have your luncheon, tonight you will have your dinner. How, then, can you feel what it is not to have food?"[7]

The following day the Mothers' League organized a mass meeting in Madison Square. When someone claimed Governor Charles S. Whitman was at the Waldorf-Astoria that day, one thousand people, mostly women, marched up Fifth Avenue to the Waldorf, shouting, "We want bread!" and "Our babies are starving!" They converged on the posh hotel, blocked traffic, defied the police, and would not be moved. But the governor was actually at the St. Regis Hotel on East Fifty-Fifth Street, and eventually he did agree to receive a delegation. Six people attended the meeting, at which he pledged to introduce an appropriation bill in the state legislature to purchase food and sell it to the people of the city at cost.[8]

By early March, the wholesalers had once again raised prices and many butchers more or less declared war on them. The arguments were all the same; only the math was different.

33. East Siders protesting the rising price of food, 1917. Source: Library of Congress Prints and Photographs Division, LC-USZ62–95684.

Butchers were now being charged between seventeen and nineteen cents a pound for beef, and had to add nine cents per pound to turn a profit. But their customers were unwilling to pay more than twenty-three cents a pound.[9]

Like the previous strikes, this one was female-driven. It had been fifteen years since the 1902 meat boycott, and many of those involved had not even been in America back then. But there was a collective memory of 1902 and many of the tactics were from a page torn out of the Ladies' Anti-Beef Trust Association playbook. The women of 1917 reached even further out of the ghetto than their predecessors, however, in their search for a solution. Through sheer pluck, they demanded and were granted meetings with the mayor and the governor, and guided by the Socialists, they asked for direct government relief from high prices.

Predictions that all the stores would stay closed proved too sanguine. By late March, a sizeable number of the five thousand or so kosher butchers had reopened, which forced the others to do the same. Prices had come down slightly, and once again the Passover holiday was on the horizon; it was to begin the following week, so demand for beef was strong. Although food prices would continue to be an issue as they fluctuated throughout the war, there was no further boycott of kosher meat during that period.[10]

History repeated itself in 1919, however, when Anna Pastor presided at a meeting in the Bronx at which yet another boycott was announced. It soon spread to Harlem, where there were a handful of arrests, but it never really got much traction.

And it all happened again during the Great Depression, when, in early 1935 the wholesale price of meat suddenly jumped 50 to 100 percent, ostensibly as a result of a drought. Jewish women in New York believed the wholesalers were stockpiling meat in a deliberate effort to prop up prices. In late May, they shut down most of the kosher butchers in Brownsville and Brighton Beach, while others demonstrated outside the Manhattan abattoirs.

34. Mass demonstration against the rising price of food at East Broadway and Rutgers Streets, 1917. Source: Library of Congress, Prints and Photographs Division, George Grantham Bain Collection, LC-DIG-ggbain-23741.

They were led by radical activist Clara Lemlich, who had risen to prominence in 1909 as an organizer of the Uprising of the Twenty Thousand—the famous New York shirtwaist strike—the largest such action in the nation up to that time. Lemlich had famously called for the strike in a stirring, spontaneous speech to thousands of fellow garment workers at Cooper Union, and over the years she had organized rent strikes, agitated for government-run unemployment insurance, and protested the high cost of staples like bread and milk. She even ran, unsuccessfully, for alderman.

Under the auspices of the Communist-dominated United Council for Working-Class Women, Lemlich and others urged kosher butchers to close. And like their predecessors so many years earlier, they made speeches on street corners and tussled with police. By the time the uprising ended a month later, most shops had closed, and prices at about a thousand of them had been reduced. But this strike spread to half a dozen other cities and reached a level of sophistication unimagined by Lemlich's 1902 predecessors. She led a delegation to Washington, where she urged Secretary of Agriculture Henry Wallace to order wholesalers to stop withholding meat from the market.[11]

In terms of sheer masses of humanity on the streets, none of the subsequent strikes ever reached the magnitude or the fever pitch of the 1902 boycott. But later protesters had learned from the example of their predecessors. Boycotts, whether of meat or rent, could succeed if everyone supported them, which pointed to the need to organize and the imperative of house-to-house canvassing. Alliances were also critical, which meant reaching out to fraternal organizations, unions, and others. And there was no substitute for picketing to keep up pressure. Unfortunately, destruction of property and violence, a negative lesson of 1902, continued to rear its head frequently during these times.

The Beef Trust continued as a malevolent force in the marketplace until 1920, when its constituent companies were compelled by President Woodrow Wilson's government to exit all ancillary businesses. The packers acceded to an injunction ordering them to sell their interests in stockyards and railroads and dissociate themselves from retail business and lines unrelated to meat. That latter list had become a long one, and included groceries, fish, fruits, syrups, coffee, tea, chocolate, cocoa, nuts, flour, sugar, rice, and cereals.

"This decree prevents the defendants from exercising any further control over the marketing of livestock," Attorney General A. Mitchell Palmer said in an official statement. "It forever prevents them from any control over the retailing of meat products. But greater than all, it establishes the principle that no group of men, no matter how powerful, can ever attempt to control the food table of the American people."[12]

The Justice Department earned kudos for divorcing the packers from the other lines of business. "It is a great victory for the American people," Wisconsin's *Manitowoc Pilot* declared, "won through and by their government."[13]

Afterword

Although it was conceived in haste and had its disorderly aspects, the 1902 kosher meat boycott was, from the start, a strategic effort. The women who envisioned it understood that withholding demand was likely to bring prices down. Their challenge was to persuade their neighbors to make short-term sacrifices for long-term benefit.

The only real mistakes they made were to unleash violence against those who continued to patronize the butchers and against the shop owners themselves, and to destroy property. These tactics, which earned them no accolades, were banned by the organizers and condemned by every responsible voice, but they stubbornly reared their heads throughout the effort.

Even here, though, there was discipline. Only butcher shops and, to a much lesser extent, restaurants were ever targeted. Unlike the case in many urban riots, no other establishments suffered collateral damage. Activities, for the most part, ceased from sundown Friday to sundown on Saturday in honor of the Sabbath. And there was never any hint of looting. Confiscated meat was rendered inedible and destroyed, not stolen, taken home, or enjoyed. The women never lost sight of their goal, always tried persuasion first, and did not attack anyone who was not selling or buying meat. It was only the police who were indiscriminate, brutishly clubbing strikers and bystanders alike in their ham-handed efforts to put down the riots.

Resistance in America was a more complex affair than it had been in Russia or Eastern Europe. New York offered a more nuanced legal and economic environment with more stakeholders. To sustain the strike and achieve its goal, the Jewish women needed to break out of their traditional home-maker roles and take radical action. They needed to employ unfamiliar tactics, address a host of audiences, and build coalitions. How they dealt and communicated with their fellow consumers and with the butchers, wholesalers, police, government, media, synagogues, unions, and other allied organizations was of utmost importance. It required planning and creativity.

For ideas, they looked to some extent to the labor unions, which had navigated similar ground in the past. But educating vast numbers of women about supply and demand economics to earn their support for an action that seriously disturbed their families' lives was far more of a challenge than, say, Joseph Barondess had faced a decade earlier when he organized three thousand cloak makers into a union and led them into a strike. Barondess needed to reach a limited universe of people, and he knew where they worked and how to mobilize young workers to recruit them. This could be accomplished by distributing circulars outside of factories and inviting laborers to organizational meetings. And although their jobs were on the line, it was easy for them to grasp the benefits that could accrue through unionizing. Union victories were all around them.

Where Barondess had a *trade* to organize, the women behind the meat boycott had an entire *community* to organize, and in this sense they were pioneers. What is more, it was the largest community of Jews the world had ever seen.

No experiences in Europe prepared these women for a task of this magnitude. If the Jewish population of New York was nearly 600,000 in 1902, then the success of a meat strike probably required reaching a couple of hundred thousand of their women, spread not only throughout the Jewish quarter, but also uptown, in Brooklyn, and in nearby New Jersey.

Balebostes would have to be given a vision of their collective power as consumers to change their situation in order to persuade them to commit their families to immediate sacrifices. A successful boycott also involved the enormous task of organizing a core group and recruiting some three thousand women to picket the butcher shops—all on less than a day's notice.

But that was just the beginning. They had to sustain their effort until their goals were achieved, no mean feat when it meant daily deprivation on the part of their supporters. This required issuing progress reports, reiterating messages, and reaching out to new groups like labor unions and benevolent associations to garner support.

One of the most insidious aspects of the meat riots is that they pitted Jew against Jew. How much the women really understood about who was pulling the strings is debatable; most of their wrath was focused on their neighborhood butchers, who were accused of living luxuriously at their expense. The truth is that, like their customers, most of the retailers were more or less living from hand to mouth. Evidence can be found in the large number of them forced to close their businesses permanently because they lacked the resources to sustain them through a boycott of only a few weeks' duration.

It was probably inevitable that some control over the strike would eventually pass into the hands of men. This was not necessarily because women were doing a bad job of managing things, although there was some public bickering among the females in charge, and the violence in the streets was earning them no friends. It was likely a combination of factors. It did not sit well with men to see their women clubbed in the streets by the police and thrown into jail. Perhaps more importantly, though, it was the males among them who had the most experience handling contentious situations that transcended the Jewish community.

Once the women reached out to other organizations for support, men, for better or worse, became part of the leadership of their movement, and soon they went so far as to organize a coalition, pointedly giving it a new name that omitted the word "Ladies." By the time the strike was ended, a male-dominated Committee of Fifty was calling the shots.

There were certainly examples of male chauvinism in the drama. But it does not appear that it was chauvinism per se that drove the male takeover of the movement, or that this outcome was the object of any nefarious plot to wrest control. Nor do the women appear to have objected to the appropriation of power. It was never doubted that the men who allied themselves with them supported their goals wholeheartedly. And the women seemed accepting of the notion that the men possessed skills, experiences, and connections that they, despite their initial successes, may have lacked.

Indeed, there is no evidence of any dissatisfaction at the direction the movement had taken under the Committee of Fifty until the very end, when Carolyn Schatzberg visited the *Forward* to express her feelings of betrayal. She never explicitly raised the issue of gender in her complaint, but there is no denying that those she accused of losing sight of the goal were male.

It is probably also fair to say that while the women ran their households, they were accustomed to men running organizations and large community efforts, and did not presume, at this early stage, to pose any serious challenge to the status quo in this regard. Jewish women would eventually break down all of these barriers and become active in the suffrage movement, which was nothing if not an attempt to acquire political power, and become far more involved in the labor movement. But this would not happen for several more years.

The Ladies' Anti-Beef Trust Association disappeared as soon as it was no longer needed, but as a short-lived, grassroots community organization movement it was an important milestone as well as a harbinger of things to come. It signaled a new spirit of combativeness and an awakening political consciousness on the part of immigrant Jewish women.

The lessons of the power of community organizing could not be unlearned and, as the vanguard of homemaker-organized Jewish activism in America, the 1902 strike, which was also the high-water mark in terms of sheer numbers of people mobilized, was long remembered, although not to this day. Women needed no further persuading that they were capable of organizing and effecting change; they had already proven that. In subsequent rent strikes, such as those in 1904 and 1908, and when the price of meat went up again in 1908, 1917, and even during the Depression in 1935, copycat tactics could easily be discerned, and the 1902 effort was often explicitly called out as a precedent. Tactics like leafleting, street meetings, and other forms of community organizing also proved handy later in the decade in support of New York Jews' efforts in the women's suffrage movement.

At the end of her 1980 article that explored the implications of the boycott, Professor Paula E. Hyman speculated that "it is likely that the political awareness expressed by boycotters was no isolated phenomenon, but was communicated effectively, if quietly and informally, to their younger sisters and daughters." Hyman was forced to speculate because of the paucity of biographical information available about women who—with apologies to Shakespeare's Hamlet—strut and fret their hour upon the stage and then are heard no more. But we can put a little flesh on those bones today with two examples.

Pauline Newman, a seventy-year veteran of the International Ladies' Garment Workers' Union, may never have met Sarah Edelson, but she owed her a debt. She had lived through the 1902 meat strike, and the subsequent 1908 rent strike, which was the battle that launched her activist career, was a community organization exercise of a piece with the 1902 effort. Her visits to tenements to organize housewives had an analogue in Edelson's pioneer door-to-door effort to build support for her meat boycott.

Similarly, Clara Lemlich, known for her leadership role in the 1909 shirtwaist workers' strike—the largest of its time that involved women—borrowed a page from Caroline Schatzberg's playbook. She didn't arrive in America until

1904, and she was already an experienced activist well before she led the 1935 meat boycott. But like Schatzberg before her, Lemlich sought a meeting with the mayor, headed a committee that demanded that the butchers close up shop, and spoke to the press on behalf of her cohorts. There's no record of her interrupting *Shabbos* services to plead her case, but she did meet with meat wholesalers to demand that they lower their prices.[1]

The women of the 1902 strikes ushered in a new spirit of activism and an awakening among their sisters in the Jewish community. This applied not only to community movements like food and rent strikes; it also applied to labor actions, and was an important factor in the central role that Jewish American women played in the American labor movement well into the twentieth century. That spirit, like their pioneer strategies and tactics, lived on, and was appropriated, as needed, by subsequent generations of Jewish men and women alike to address injustice wherever and whenever they experienced it.

NOTES

1. A City within a City

1. Ancestry.com, 1900 United States Federal Census Online Database.

2. List of Registered Voters in the City of New York for the Year 1880 (New York: Martin B. Brown, 1881).

3. "Fifty Dollars for the Shadchen," *New York Herald*, November 19, 1893; "Business Troubles," *New York Herald*, January 1, 1894.

4. Unpublished memoir of David Ambrose (1872–1965). Collection of the author.

5. "To Let for Business Purposes," *New York Herald*, December 9, 1888.

6. Andrew S. Dolkart, *The South Village: A Proposal for Historic District Designation*. (New York: Greenwich Village Society for Historic Preservation, 2006), 24–35; Alan S. Oser, "Making Tenements Modern," *New York Times*, April 4, 1999; Robert W. de Forest, "Tenement House Regulation—The Reasons for It—Its Proper Limitations," *Annals of the American Academy of Political and Social Science* 20 (July 1902): 83–95.

7. "New York's Big Hebrew City," *New York Sun*, September 14, 1902.

8. Hyman Grinstein, "The Efforts of East European Jewry to Organize Its Own Community in the United States," *Publications of the American Jewish Historical Society* 49, no. 2 (December 1959): 73–74.

9. "New York's Big Hebrew City," *New York Sun*, September 14, 1902.

10. "The Polish Jews of New York," *New York Sun*, June 25, 1875; "The Unions, Free Thinkers and the Meat Strike," *Forward*, May 20, 1902.

11. Bernard Weinstein, *The Jewish Unions in America*, translated by Maurice Wolfthal (1929; Cambridge UK: Open Book Publishers, 2018).

2. Greater Power Than Ten Standard Oil Companies

1. "Immigration to the United States," *Rise of Industrial America, 1876–1900*, Library of Congress, accessed July 31, 2018, http://www.loc.gov/teachers /classroommaterials/presentationsandactivities/presentations/timeline /riseind/immgnts/.

2. "Railroads in the Late Nineteenth Century," *Rise of Industrial America, 1876–1900*, Library of Congress, accessed July 31, 2018, http://www.loc .gov/teachers/classroommaterials/presentationsandactivities/presentations /timeline/riseind/railroad/.

3. Lizabeth Cohen, "A Consumers' Republic," *New York Times*, March 2, 2003.

4. Robert M. Aduddell and Louis P. Cain, "Public Policy toward 'The Greatest Trust in the World,'" *The Business History Review* 55, no. 2 (Summer 1981): 217–42.

5. Maureen Ogle, *In Meat We Trust: An Unexpected History of Carnivore America* (New York: Houghton Mifflin, 2013), 70.

6. Francis Walker, "The 'Beef Trust' and the United States Government," *The Economic Journal* 16, no. 64 (1906): 492.

7. "Meatpacking," *Encyclopedia of Chicago*, accessed August 2, 2018, http:// www.encyclopedia.chicagohistory.org/pages/804.html.

8. Maureen Ogle, *In Meat We Trust* (New York: Houghton Mifflin, 2013), 40.

9. "Career of P. D. Armour," *New York Times*, January 7, 1901.

10. "Hammond (George H.) Co.," *Encyclopedia of Chicago*, accessed August 3, 2018, http://www.encyclopedia.chicagohistory.org/pages/2690 .html; "George H. Hammond," *New York Times*, February 13, 1936; "Nelson Morris Dead," *New York Times*, August 28, 1907; "Nelson Morris," Find a Grave website, accessed August 2, 2018, https://www.findagrave.com /memorial/21928/nelson-morris; "Cudahy Packing Co.," *Encyclopedia of Chicago*, accessed August 3, 2018, http://www.encyclopedia.chicagohistory .org/pages/2635.html.

11. Charles Edward Russell, *The Greatest Trust in the World* (New York: The Ridgeway-Thayer Company, 1905), 5.

3. The Conscience of an Orthodox Jew

1. "City's Beef Supply," *New York Tribune*, June 1, 1902.

2. Paul Ritterband, "Counting the Jews of New York, 1900–1991: An Essay in Substance and Method," *Jewish Population Studies* 29 (Jerusalem: Avraham Harman Institute of Contemporary Jewry, 1997): 202.

3. "New York's Stock Yard," *New York Post*, May 10, 1902.

4. "City's Beef Supply," *New York Tribune*, June 1, 1902.

5. Moses Weinberger and Jonathan D. Sarna, *People Walk on Their Heads: Moses Weinberger's Jews and Judaism in New York* (New York: Holmes & Meier, 1982), 46.

6. "The Kosher Meat War," *Daily People*, June 2, 1902; "City's Beef Supply," *New York Tribune*, June 1, 1902; "Kosher Meat," *Dodge City Times*, August 23, 1883; "Jewish Meat Shops," *Jasper Courier*, June 29, 1888; "Ways of Killing Cattle," *The True Northerner*, June 22, 1887; "Jewish Killing Rites," *New York Tribune*, October 4, 1896; "New York's Stock Yard," *New York Post*, May 10, 1902; "Learned Butchers These," *New York Sun*, April 7, 1901; "Kosher Meat," *Brooklyn Daily Eagle*, May 30, 1902.

7. "Big Kosher Boycott," *New York Tribune*, May 12, 1902.

8. "The Kosher Meat War," *Daily People*, June 2, 1902; "City's Beef Supply," *New York Tribune*, June 1, 1902; "Kosher Meat," *Dodge City Times*, August 23, 1883; "Jewish Meat Shops," *Jasper Courier*, June 29, 1888; "Ways of Killing Cattle," *The True Northerner*, June 22, 1887; "Jewish Killing Rites," *New York Tribune*, October 4, 1896; "New York's Stock Yard," *New York Post*, May 10, 1902.

9. Harry Finkelstein, "The Kosher Meat Industry" (bachelor's thesis, Tufts University, 1926), 51–52; "The Orthodox Hebrews and How Poultry Is Killed," *Truth*, May 13, 1883.

10. "The Real East Side Wife," *New York Sun*, June 29, 1902.

11. "City's Beef Supply," *New York Tribune*, June 1, 1902; "The Real East Side Wife," *New York Sun*, June 29, 1902.

12. Finkelstein, "The Kosher Meat Industry," 55–56, 65–66.

4. Each One Is an Authority unto Himself

1. "Our Orthodox Congregations," *Jewish Messenger*, February 13, 1863.

2. "Kosher Or—," *Jewish Messenger*, April 18, 1879; "A Shechitah Association," *Jewish Messenger*, August 1, 1879.

3. Weinberger and Sarna, *People Walk on Their Heads*, 46–50.

4. Timothy D. Lytton, *Kosher: Private Regulation in the Age of Industrial Food* (Cambridge MA: Harvard University Press, 2013), 14–15.

5. Lytton, *Kosher*, 16–18.

6. "A Chief Rabbi Needed," *New York Herald*, August 4, 1879.

7. Joseph Adler, "Twilight Years of Rabbi Jacob Joseph," *Jewish Frontier* 67, no. 1 (January–August 2000): 639.

8. Abraham J. Karp, "New York Chooses a Chief Rabbi," *Publications of the American Jewish Historical Society* 44, no. 3 (March 1955): 129–98.

9. "Rabbi Jacob Joseph," *Daily People*, August 4, 1902.

10. "A Learned Rabbi Arrives," *New York Sun*, July 8, 1888.

11. "Will He Be an Autocrat?" *New York Herald*, July 21, 1888.

12. "Opposed to the New Rabbi," *New York Sun*, August 12, 1888.

13. "Opposed to the New Rabbi," *New York Sun*, August 12, 1888.

14. "Excited Hebrew Throngs," *New York Herald*, July 22, 1888.

15. "Our Enemy, the Cow," *Rock Island Daily Argus*, September 10, 1888; "Rabbis Carry Quarrel into a Police Court," *New York Sun*, September 20, 1888.

16. Leon Stein, "The Great Flanken War of 1902," (unpublished manuscript, Leon Stein Papers, Kheel Center for Labor-Management Documentation and Archives, Cornell University Library [1978?]), 4.

17. "The Clean and the Unclean: Grand Rabbi Joseph Prescribes Regulations for Kosher Meat," *New York Herald*, October 8, 1888.

18. Isaac Levitats, *The Jewish Community in Russia, 1772–1844* (New York: Octagon Books, 1970), 52–54.

19. Adler, "Twilight Years of Rabbi Jacob Joseph"; "To Indict Rabbi Joseph," *New York Sun*, January 8, 1889.

20. "Among Our Down-Town Brethren," *Jewish Messenger*, January 18, 1889.

21. "A Word of Complaint," *Jewish Messenger*, February 22, 1889.

22. "To the Jewish Public," *Jewish Messenger*, February 15, 1889; "Kosher Meat the Best," *New York Herald*, February 18, 1889.

23. "A Word of Complaint," *Jewish Messenger*, February 22, 1889; Timothy D. Lytton, *Kosher: Private Regulation in the Age of Industrial Food* (Cambridge MA: Harvard University Press, 2013), 23.

24. Lytton, *Kosher*, 23–24.

25. Yitzchok Levine, "The Chief Rabbi Encounters Opposition," *Jewish Press*, accessed July 26, 2018, http://www.jewishpress.com/sections /magazine/glimpses-ajh/the-chief-rabbi-encounters-opposition/2008/06 /04/.

26. Lytton, *Kosher*, 24; Adler, "Twilight Years of Rabbi Jacob Joseph."

5. A Despotic Meat Trust

1. "Beef Trust Puts Up Prices," *New York Sun*, March 29, 1902.

2. "Restaurant Men Protest," *New York Tribune*, April 7, 1902.

3. "Tammany Attacks Beef Trust," *New York Tribune*, April 9, 1902.

4. "Probing the Beef Trust," *New York Tribune*, April 16, 1902.

5. "Denounced the Beef Trust," *New York Tribune*, April 3, 1902; "Meat Prices Condemned," *New York Times*, April 3, 1902; "Against Beef Trust," *Daily People*, April 23, 1902; "To Tackle Beef Trust," *Daily People*, April 19, 1902; "Farmers to Fight Meat Trust," *Daily People*, April 22, 1902; "Farmers v. Beef Trust," *New York Times*, April 22, 1902; "Newark Butchers to Fight," *New York Times*, April 23, 1902; "Aimed at the Beef Trust," *Washington Post*, April 24, 1902.

6. "President Will Probe Beef Trust," *St. Louis Republic*, April 14, 1902.

7. "Congress Won't Act," *Hutchinson News*, April 15, 1902; "Attorney-General Directs the Prosecution of the Beef Trust," *Washington Times*, April 25, 1902; "Will Take Action," *Belleville News Democrat*, April 25, 1902; "Knox Fires First Gun in Open War on Beef Trust," *Philadelphia Inquirer*, April 25, 1902.

8. "Reply from the Beef Trust," *New York Sun*, April 19, 1902.

9. "Not Beef Trust's Work," *Daily People*, April 2, 1902.

10. "Beef Trust Methods," *Daily People*, May 8, 1902.

11. "Herald's Expose Put in the Record," *New York Herald*, April 1, 1902.

12. "Trust Advances Price of Pork, Poultry and Eggs," New York *World*, April 18, 1902.

13. "Trust Advances Price of Pork, Poultry and Eggs," New York *World*, April 18, 1902; "Beef Trust Corners Eggs to Keep Meat Prices Up," New York *World*, April 18, 1902;

14. "Trust Advances Price of Pork, Poultry and Eggs," New York *World*, April 18, 1902.

15. "East Siders Protest," *New York Tribune*, April 19, 1902.

16. "The Fresh Meat Bill," *New York Times*, March 28, 1902; "Hearing on the Adler Bill," *New York Times*, April 30, 1891; "Jewish Butchers' Appeal," *New York Times* April 23, 1901.

6. As Scarce as Ham Sandwiches

1. "Misery on East Side Caused by Meat Trust," New York *World*, April 17, 1902; "Kosher Butchers to Unite," *New York Sun*, May 4, 1902.

2. "East Siders Protest," *New York Tribune*, April 19, 1902.

3. "Meat Trust Drives 200 Men Out of Business," New York *World*, April 17, 1902.

4. "East Siders Protest," *New York Tribune*, April 19, 1902.

5. "Stop! Don't Eat Meat for Breakfast," *Yidishes Tageblatt*, May 6, 1902.

6. "Hebrew Butchers Excited," *New York Tribune*, May 9, 1896.

7. "To Fight Packers," *Wichita Daily Beacon*, April 2, 1902.

8. "Meat Trust Drives 200 Men Out of Business," New York *World*, April 17, 1902.

9. "Ruined," *Yidishes Tageblatt*, May 5, 1902; "Butchers in $1,000,000 Alliance to Resist Beef Trust's Tyranny," *New York Herald*, April 1, 1902.

10. "Jewish Butchers Denounce Trust," *New York Press*, May 5, 1902.

11. "Kosher Butchers May Close," *New York Tribune*, May 5, 1902.

12. "Ruined," *Yidishes Tageblatt*, May 5, 1902.

13. "Kosher Butchers to Unite," *New York Sun*, May 4, 1902; "Jewish Butchers Denounce Trust," *New York Press*, May 5, 1902; "Retail Butchers Combining," *New York Tribune*, May 28, 1891.

14. "War to Death on Beef Trust," *New York Sun*, April 20, 1902; "Official Figures Prove the Beef Trust's Arguments False," *New York Herald*, May 5, 1902; "High Price of Meat Stirs Kosher Butchers," *San Francisco Chronicle*, May 5, 1902; "Kosher Butchers in Session," *New York Times*, May 5, 1902.

15. "Kosher Butchers to Close Sundays," *New York Herald*, May 6, 1902; "Kosher Butchers to Close," *New York Sun*, May 6, 1902; "Jews to Fight Beef Trust," *Daily People*, May 7, 1902.

16. Ancestry.com, 1900 United States Federal Census Online Database.

17. "Mobbed a Kosher Butcher," *New York Times*, May 11, 1902; "Kosher Butchers Kept Open," *New York Sun*, May 11, 1902; "Attacked by a Mob of Butchers," *New York Press*, May 11, 1902.

18. "East Side Is without Meat," *New York Sun*, May 12, 1902.

19. "Big Kosher Boycott," *New York Tribune*, May 12, 1902.

20. "Big Kosher Boycott," *New York Tribune*, May 12, 1902; "East-Side Boycott on 'Kosher' Meat," New York *World*, May 12, 1902; "East Side Butchers Will Boycott Meats," *New York Times*, May 12, 1902; "East Side Is without Meat," *New York Sun*, May 12, 1902.

21. "East-Side Boycott on 'Kosher' Meat," New York *World*, May 12, 1902; "East Side Butchers Will Boycott Meats," *New York Times*, May 12, 1902; "East Side Is without Meat," *New York Sun*, May 12, 1902.

7. Let the Women Make a Strike

1. "War on the Beef Trust," *Scranton Tribune*, May 12, 1902; "Government Bill against Beef Trust," *Washington Times*, May 10, 1902; "Complaint against Beef Trust Filed," *Washington Times*, May 11, 1902.

2. "Agents Everywhere Pursue the Beef Trust," *New York Herald*, May 17, 1902.

3. "State Officials Follow the Federal in Prosecuting the Rapacious Beef Trust," *New York Herald*, May 12, 1902.

4. "Boycott by East Side Butchers Is Spreading," *New York Times*, May 13, 1902.

5. "East Side Eats Meat Again," *New York Sun*, May 15, 1902.

6. "Kosher Boycott Called Off," *Washington Post*, May 14, 1902.

7. "Jewish Butchers to Reopen," *New York Times*, May 14, 1902; "Kosher Strike Ended," *New York Tribune*, May 14, 1902.

8. "Kosher Butchers to Resume," New York *World*, May 14, 1902.

9. "East Side Eats Meat Again," *New York Sun*, May 15, 1902; "Disorder in the Ghetto," *Daily People*, May 17, 1902.

10. "Meat Riots on the East Side," *New York Post*, May 15, 1902.

11. Hyman Grinstein, "The Efforts of East European Jewry to Organize Its Own Community in the United States," *Publications of the American Jewish Historical Society* 49, no. 2 (December, 1959): 81; Ancestry.com, 1900 United States Federal Census Online Database and 1905 New York State Census Online Database; "Women's Revolution," *Yidishes Tageblatt*, May 15, 1902.

12. "Fierce Meat Riot on Lower East Side," *New York Times*, May 16, 1902.

13. "Women's Revolution," *Yidishes Tageblatt*, May 15, 1902; "Butchers and Women Shout That They Have Been Swindled," *Forward*, May 14, 1902.

14. "Retail Kosher Butchers Win," *New York Press*, May 14, 1902; "Meat Riots on the East Side," *New York Press*, May 15, 1902; "Butchers and Women Shout That They Have Been Swindled," *Forward*, May 14, 1902; "Meat Riots on the East Side; Mobs Charged by Police Army and Fifty-Four Women Arrested," *New York Press*, May 16, 1902.

15. [Title Unclear], *New York Sun*, May 16, 1902.

16. "Butchers and Women Shout That They Have Been Swindled," *Forward*, May 14, 1902.

8. If We Cry at Home

1. [Title unclear], *New York Sun*, May 16, 1902; "Kosher Meat Causes Small Riot in New York," *Pawtucket Times*, May 16, 1902.

2. "Brava, Brava, Jewish Women," *Forward*, May 15, 1902, trans. Chana Pollack, as quoted in Liza Schoenfein, "120 Years of the Forverts: The Great Kosher Meat Strike of May 1902," *Forward* website, accessed August 12, 2018, https://forward.com/food/371997/120-years-of-the-forverts-the-great-kosher -meat-strike-of-may-1902.

3. "Meat Riots on East Side," *New York Post*, May 15, 1902.

4. "Women Rioters," *Boston Morning Journal*, May 16, 1902.

5. "Police Club Meat Rioters on East Side," New York *World*, May 16, 1902.

6. "Riot Preceded the Parade," *New York Times*, October 12, 1894.

7. "Meat Riots on East Side," *New York Post*, May 15, 1902.

8. "Brava, Brava, Jewish Women," *Forward*, May 15, 1902.

9. [Title unclear], *New York Sun*, May 16, 1902.

10. "Meat Riots on the East Side," *New York Post*, May 15, 1902; "Fierce Meat Riot on Lower East Side," *New York Times*, May 16, 1902; "Turmoil in the Ghetto," *New York Post*, May 16, 1902.

11. "Women's Revolution," *Yidishes Tageblatt*, May 15, 1902.

12. "Brava, Brava, Jewish Women," *Forward*, May 15, 1902.

13. "Scores Arrested," *Boston Daily Globe*, May 16, 1902; "Brava, Brava, Jewish Women," *Forward*, May 15, 1902.

14. "Brava, Brava, Jewish Women," *Forward*, May 15, 1902.

15. "Meat Riots on the East Side: Mobs Charged by Police Army and Fifty-Four Women Are Arrested" *New York Press*, May 16, 1902; "Women Driven to Desperation by the Meat Trust," New York *World*, May 15, 1902; [Title unclear], *New York Sun*, May 16, 1902.

16. "Thousands in Riots in Streets of East Side over Meat Prices," *New York Herald*, May 16, 1902.

17. Melech Epstein, *Profiles of Eleven* (Detroit: Wayne State University Press, 1965), 113–20.

18. "Mobs in Meat Riots," *New York Tribune*, May 16, 1902.

19. "Boycott! Boycott! Boycott!" *Forward*, May 16, 1902.

20. "Mobs in Meat Riots," *New York Tribune*, May 16, 1902.

21. "Boycott! Boycott! Boycott!" *Forward*, May 16, 1902.

22. "Mobs in Meat Riots," *New York Tribune*, May 16, 1902; "Police Club Meat Rioters on the East Side," New York *World*, May 16, 1902.

23. "Mobs in Meat Riots," *New York Tribune*, May 16, 1902.

24. "Police Club Meat Rioters on the East Side," New York *World*, May 16, 1902.

25. "Jerome's East Side Home," *New York Tribune*, January 22, 1902; "Jerome and Jewish Meat," *Forward*, May 24, 1902.

26. "Police Club Meat Rioters on the East Side," New York *World*, May 16, 1902; "Mobs in Meat Riots," *New York Tribune*, May 16, 1902.

27. "Fierce Meat Riot on Lower East Side," *New York Times*, May 16, 1902.

28. "Food Riots and the Beef Combine," *New York Times*, May 17, 1902.

29. "Fierce Meat Riot on Lower East Side," *New York Times*, May 16, 1902; "Police Club Meat Rioters on the East Side," New York *World*, May 16, 1902; "It Will Not Do," New York *World*, May 16, 1902.

30. "Meat Riots in the Ghetto," *Brooklyn Standard Union*, May 16, 1902; "Meat Riots and Liberty," *Brooklyn Daily Eagle*, May 16, 1902; Stein, *Great Flanken War of 1902*, 15.

31. "Fierce Meat Riot on Lower East Side," *New York Times*, May 16, 1902; "Police Club Meat Rioters on the East Side," New York *World*, May 16, 1902; "It Will Not Do," New York *World*, May 16, 1902; "Meat Riots and Liberty," *Brooklyn Daily Eagle*, May 16, 1902.

32. "Women's Revolution," *Yidishes Tageblatt,* May 15, 1902.

33. "Brava, Brava, Jewish Women," *Forward* , May 15, 1902; "Our Jewish Women," *Forward,* May 16, 1902, trans. Chana Pollack, as quoted in Liza Schoenfein, "120 Years of the Forverts: The Great Kosher Meat Strike of May 1902," *Forward* website, accessed August 12, 2018, https://forward.com/food/371997/120-years-of-the-forverts-the-great-kosher-meat-strike-of-may-1902.

34. "Meat Riots in the Ghetto," *Brooklyn Standard Union,* May 16, 1902; "Thousands in Riots over Meat Prices," *New York Herald,* May 16, 1902.

35. "Thousands in Riots over Meat Prices," *New York Herald,* May 16, 1902; "Rioters Use the Torch," *New York Tribune,* May 17, 1902.

36. Stein, *Great Flanken War of 1902,* 15.

9. They Never Saw Such Assemblages

1. "Cheerful Pants Makers Strike," *New York Tribune,* July 25, 1900; "Strike at an East Side Theater," *New York Tribune,* January 1, 1900; "Strike of Hebrew Bakers," *New York Tribune,* December 30, 1900; "The Bakers' Strike," *Daily People,* January 14, 1901; "The Tailors' Strike," *Worker,* July 28, 1901.

2. Bernard Weinstein, *The Jewish Unions in America* [1929], trans. Maurice Wolfthal (Cambridge UK: Open Book Publishers, 2018).

3. "Big Crowds Out," *Boston Globe,* May 22, 1902.

4. "Recognizing Women's Right to Vote in New York State," New York Heritage Digital Collections, accessed November 9, 2018, https://nyheritage.org/exhibits/recognizing-womens-right-vote-new-york-state.

5. "When Jewish Workmen Strike," *New York Sun,* August 11, 1896.

10. Hebrews with Shaved Beards

1. "Boycott! Boycott! Boycott!" *Forward,* May 16, 1902.

2. "Disorder in the Ghetto," *Daily People,* May 17, 1902.

3. "Rioters Use the Torch," *New York Tribune,* May 17, 1902; "Trouble Renewed on Lower East Side," *New York Times,* May 17, 1902.

4. "One Woman's Protest Started Big Meat Strike," New York *World,* May 17, 1902.

5. "Mob Tries to Storm Jail for Women," New York *World,* May 17, 1902; "Sabbath Makes Rioters Pause," *New York Press,* May 17, 1902; "Trouble Renewed on Lower East Side," *New York Times,* May 17, 1902.

6. "Rioters Use the Torch," *New York Tribune,* May 17, 1902.

7. "Trouble Renewed on Lower East Side," *New York Times,* May 17, 1902.

8. "Disorder in the Ghetto," *Daily People,* May 15, 1902.

9. "Sabbath Makes Rioters Pause," *New York Press,* May 17, 1902; "Brava, Brava, Jewish Women" *Forward,* May 15, 1902, trans. Chana Pollack, as quoted in Liza Schoenfein, "120 Years of the Forverts: The Great Kosher Meat Strike of May 1902," *Forward* website, accessed August 12, 2018, https://forward.com/food/371997/120-years-of-the-forverts-the-great-kosher-meat-strike-of-may-1902; "Truce in Kosher Meat War," *New York Times,* May 17, 1902; "Rioters Use the Torch," *New York Tribune,* May 17, 1902.

10. "'We Want Kosher Meat!' Scream Pious, Poor Jews," *Forward*, May 17, 1902; "Rioters Use the Torch," *New York Tribune*, May 17, 1902.

11. "Mob Tries to Storm Jail for Women," New York *World*, May 17, 1902; "Trouble Renewed on Lower East Side," *New York Times*, May 17, 1902.

12. "Rioters Use the Torch," *New York Tribune*, May 17, 1902.

13. "Sabbath Makes Rioters Pause," *New York Press*, May 17, 1902.

14. "Petition the Mayor to Restrain Police," *New York Post*, May 16, 1902; "Women Ask Permit for Meeting," *New York Tribune*, May 17, 1902; "Sabbath Makes Rioters Pause," *New York Press*, May 17, 1902; "Rioters Use the Torch," *New York Tribune*, May 17, 1902.

15. "Mob Tries to Storm Jail for Women," New York *World*, May 17, 1902.

16. "The East-Side Meat Trouble," New York *World*, May 17, 1902.

17. "The East Side Riot," *New York Sun*, May 17, 1902.

18. "Boycott! Boycott! Boycott!" *Forward*, May 16, 1902.

19. "In the Name of the Chief Rabbi," *Forward*, May 17, 1902.

20. "Sabbath Makes Rioters Pause," *New York Press*, May 17, 1902.

11. And He Shall Rule over Thee

1. Hyman Grinstein, "The Efforts of East European Jewry to Organize Its Own Community in the United States," *Publications of the American Jewish Historical Society* 49, no. 2 (December, 1959): 76.

2. "Women Agitate in the Synagogues for Boycott," *Forward*, May 18, 1902.

3. "Women Agitate in the Synagogues for Boycott," *Forward*, May 18, 1902.

4. "Beef Riots Spread in Three Boroughs," *New York Herald*, May 18, 1902; "Women Agitate in the Synagogues for Boycott," *Forward*, May 18, 1902; "Protests of Hebrews against High Prices," *New York Herald*, May 19, 1902; "Barondess as a Pleader," New York *World*, May 19, 1902; "Butchers Give in to Rioting Women," *New York World*, May 19, 1902.

5. "Beef Riots Spread in Three Boroughs," *New York Herald*, May 18, 1902.

6. "Calm. Riots Are Ending," *Yidishes Tageblatt*, May 18, 1902.

7. "Will Not Give Up Meat," *New York Tribune*, May 19, 1902.

8. "Beef Riots Spread in Three Boroughs," *New York Herald*, May 18, 1902; "In Three Boroughs, Meat Riots Raged Fiercely All Night, Women Leading the Attacks," *New York Press*, May 18, 1902.

9. "The Majority of the Butcher Shops are Closed," *Forward*, May 18, 1902; "East Side Butchers Close," *New York Sun*, May 18, 1902.

10. "The Majority of the Butcher Shops Are Closed," *Forward*, May 18, 1902.

11. "The Majority of the Butcher Shops Are Closed," *Forward*, May 18, 1902.

12. "Calm: Riots Are Ending," *Yidishes Tageblatt*, May 18, 1902.

13. "Brooklyn Meat Riots over Kosher Shops: Twenty-Two Arrests," *Brooklyn Standard Union*, May 18, 1902; "Women Attack Butchers in a Kosher Meat Riot," *Brooklyn Daily Eagle*, May 18, 1902; "In Three Boroughs, Meat Riots Raged Fiercely All Night, Women Leading the Attacks," *New York Press*, May 18, 1902.

14. "Riots in the Bronx," *Brooklyn Daily Eagle*, May 18, 1902; "Beef Riots Spread in Three Boroughs," *New York Herald*, May 18, 1902.

15. "In Three Boroughs, Meat Riots Raged Fiercely All Night, Women Leading the Attacks," *New York Press*, May 18, 1902; "East Side Butchers Close," *New York Sun*, May 18, 1902.

12. No Industry in the Country Is More Free

1. "How the War on the Beef Trust Has Spread," *New York Herald*, May 19, 1902.

2. "The State after Beef Trust," *New York Sun*, May 16, 1902.

3. "Meat Inquiry Is Begun," *Chicago Tribune*, May 16, 1902; "Butcher Was Blacklisted," *Daily People*, May 16, 1902; "Probing the Beef Trust," *New York Times*, May 16, 1902.

4. "Ways of the Beef Trust," *Washington Post*, May 16, 1902; "War on the Beef Trust," *New York Tribune*, May 16, 1902; "Will File Proof of Beef Trust," *Chicago Tribune*, May 17, 1906.

5. "State Inquiry Today," *Daily People*, May 15, 1902; "War on Beef Trust," *New York Tribune*, May 16, 1902.

6. "Beef Trust Men Missing," *New York Tribune*, May 17, 1902.

7. "Postponed Beef Trust Case," *New York Times*, May 17, 1902.

8. "Beef's Record-Breaking Price," New York *World*, May 17, 1902; "Figures Show High Prices Are Not Due to Shortage of Cattle," New York *World*, May 17, 1902.

9. "Letter books of Armour & Co. Unveil the Beef Trust, Expose Its Machinery and Prove Price Agreements: Managers and Arbitrator Flee New York with Books," *New York Herald*, May 18, 1902; "Meat Combine Now Proven by Armour Letters," *Chicago Tribune*, May 18, 1902.

10. "The Herald's Campaign Splendid, Says Former Judge W. A. Day," *New York Herald*, May 19, 1902; "Tribune Exposé Stirs Capital," *Chicago Tribune*, May 19, 1902.

11. "Letter Books of Armour & Co. Unveil the Beef Trust, Expose Its Machinery and Prove Price Agreements: Managers and Arbitrator Flee New York with Books," *New York Herald*, May 18, 1902; "Beef Trust Agents Flee from the State of New York," *New York Herald*, May 18, 1902.

12. "Beef Trust Agents Flee from the State of New York," *New York Herald*, May 18, 1902; "Removal Is Confession," New York *World*, May 20, 1902.

13. "Letters Force Change in Packers' Plans," *New York Herald*, May 19, 1902.

14. "Injunction for Beef Trust," *New York Sun*, May 21, 1902.

15. "Injunction Granted against Beef Trust," *New York Times*, May 21, 1902.

16. "Court Forbids Beef Trust to Juggle Prices," New York *World*, May 21, 1902.

17. "Attorney for Packers Offers No Defense, But Pleads to Retain the Blacklist Club," *New York Herald*, May 21, 1902.

18. "Court Forbids Beef Trust to Juggle Prices," New York *World*, May 21, 1902.

19. "Attorney for Packers Offers No Defense, But Pleads to Retain the Blacklist Club," *New York Herald*, May 21, 1902.

20. "Beef Trust Enjoined," *Washington Post*, May 21, 1902.

13. It Is a Fight among Ourselves

1. "Brownsville Meat Riot Nipped by Police," *Brooklyn Daily Eagle*, May 19, 1902; "Protests of Hebrews against High Prices of Kosher Meat in Co-operative Shops," *New York Herald*, May 19, 1902.

2. "Help from Gentile Butchers," *New York Sun*, May 19, 1902; "East Side Boycotters Meet and Organize," *New York Times*, May 19, 1902.

3. "A Boycott Is a Boycott," *Forward*, May 19, 1902.

4. "Anti-Beef Society in New York," *Ft. Wayne Journal-Gazette*, May 19. 1902.

5. "Meat Rioters Rest," *New York Tribune*, May 19, 1902.

6. "Boycott upon Meat Dealers," *New York Press*, May 19, 1902.

7. "Meat Boycott Grows Stronger," *New York Press*, May 20, 1902.

8. "Butchers Give in to Rioting Women," New York *World*, May 19, 1902; "Boycott upon Meat Dealers," *New York Press*, May 19, 1902; "A Boycott Is a Boycott," *Forward*, May 19, 1902.

9. "Butchers Give in to Rioting Women," New York *World*, May 19, 1902; "Protests of Hebrews against High Prices of Kosher Meat in Co-operative Shops," *New York Herald*, May 19, 1902; "A Boycott Is a Boycott," *Forward*, May 19, 1902.

10. "East Side Boycotters Meet and Organize," *New York Times*, May 19, 1902; "Calm: Riots Are Ending," *Yidishes Tageblatt*, May 18, 1902.

11. "Eloquent Woman Leads War on High-Priced Meat," New York *World*, May 19, 1902.

12. "Trust Raises Price of Cheaper Meats," *New York Herald*, May 20, 1902. "Meat Riots Laid to Trust Agents," *New York Herald*, May 20, 1902; "Raises Prices on Poor Man's Meat," New York *World*, May 20, 1902.

13. "The *Karobke* in Russia and Here," *Forward*, May 18, 1902.

14. "Women's Revolution," *Yidishes Tageblatt*, May 15, 1902.

15. "Meat Boycott Grows Stronger," *New York Press*, May 20, 1902.

16. "Meat Riot in Brooklyn," *Washington Post*, May 20, 1902; "Women Fight to Be Beef Boss," *New York Sun*, May 20, 1902.

17. "Women Rioters in a Family Battle," New York *World*, May 20, 1902.

18. "Women Fight to Be Beef Boss," *New York Sun*, May 20, 1902; "Beef Riots Continue," *New York Times*, May 20, 1902.

19. "Women Rioters in a Family Battle," New York *World*, May 20, 1902; "Meat Riots Laid to Trust Agents," *New York Herald*, May 20, 1902.

20. "Beef Riots Continue," *New York Times*, May 20, 1902; "Women Rioters in a Family Battle," New York *World*, May 20, 1902.

21. 2 Kings 17:14.

22. "The Beef Trust and New York Jews," *Chicago Tribune*, May 20, 1902.

14. Vein Him as He Veins His Meat

1. "Meat Up Again," *Daily People*, May 21, 1902.

2. "Beef Fighters Can't Agree," *New York Sun*, May 22, 1902.

3. "War on Beef Trust Shows No Abatement," *New York Press*, May 21, 1902.

4. Untitled editorial, *Daily People*, May 21, 1902.

5. "Split in the Anti-Beef Ranks," *New York Sun*, May 21, 1902.

6. "Kosher Riots in Newark," *Daily People*, May 21, 1902.

7. "Kosher Meat Riot," *Lowell Sun*, May 21, 1902; "Many Beaten in the North End Meat Riots," *Boston Post*, May 21, 1902.

8. "Kosher Dealers Take Up Boycott and Attack Retailers Who Buy," *New York Herald*, May 22, 1902.

9. David Blaustein and Miriam Blaustein, *Memoirs of David Blaustein, Educator and Communal Worker* (New York: McBride, Nast, 1913); Cyrus Adler and Benuel H. Brumberg, "David Blaustein," in *Jewish Encyclopedia*, ed. Isidore Singer (New York, Funk & Wagnalls, 1906), 238–39.

10. "Meat Rioters Organize," *New York Tribune*, May 22, 1902.

11. "East Side Anti-Beef Action," *New York Times*, May 22, 1902.

12. "Beef Fighters Can't Agree," *New York Sun*, May 22, 1902; "Kosher Meat Rioters in Newark Enforce Boycott with Force," *New York Herald*, May 21, 1902; "Kosher Dealers Take Up Boycott and Attack Retailers Who Buy," *New York Herald*, May 22, 1902; "Organized," *Yidishes Tageblatt*, May 22, 1902; "East Side Anti-Beef Action," *New York Times*, May 22, 1902.

13. "No Chaos," *Yidishes Tageblatt*, May 21, 1902.

14. "Everyone Is United against the Jewish Butchers' Trust," *Forward*, May 20, 1902; "The Unions, Free Thinkers and the Meat Strike," *Forward*, May 20, 1902.

15. Patience Will Win the Battle

1. "East Side Shop Wrecked," *New York Times*, May 23, 1902; "Meat Riots Everywhere," *Yidishes Tageblatt*, May 23, 1902.

2. "Brooklyn Mob Loots Butcher Shops," *New York Times*, May 23, 1902; "More Kosher Meat Riots," *Daily People*, May 24, 1902.

3. "Meat Riots Everywhere," *Yidishes Tageblatt*, May 23, 1902.

4. "A Yelling, Howling Mob of Five Thousand," *Boston Morning Journal*, May 23, 1902; "Kosher Rioters in Boston Beat Policemen with Meat," *New York Herald*, May 23, 1902; "Meat Riots in Boston," *New York Times*, May 23, 1902; "Police Guard Boston Shops," *New York Times*, May 24, 1902; "Pres. Pike's Statement," *Boston Globe*, May 23, 1902.

5. "Pres. Pike's Statement," *Boston Globe*, May 23, 1902.

6. "Meat Shops All Open," *Boston Globe*, May 25, 1902.

7. "1,500 in Kosher Riot Defy the Police Force," *Brooklyn Daily Eagle*, May 24, 1902.

8. "A Real Police Problem," *New York Times*, May 24, 1902.

9. Herbert G. Gutman, "Work, Culture and Society in Industrializing America," *American Historical Review* 78, no. 3 (June, 1973): 575–76.

10. Editorial, *Jewish Messenger*, May 30, 1902.

11. Jack Glazier, *Dispersing the Ghetto: The Relocation of Jewish Immigrants across America* (Ithaca NY: Cornell University Press, 1998), 1–40.

12. "Mobs Pelt the Police," *Brooklyn Daily Eagle*, May 25, 1902; "Meat Mob on Rampage," *New York Tribune*, May 25, 1902.

13. "Anti-Beef Trust Conclave," *New York Times*, May 25, 1902; "Organize for War on Kosher Butchers," *New York Herald*, May 26, 1902; "Will Open Shops Today," *New York Tribune*, May 26, 1902.

14. "Agree to Sell Meat at Lower Prices," *Chicago Tribune*, May 27, 1902.

15. "New Move vs. Meat Shops," *New York World*, May 26, 1902.

16. "Organize for War on Kosher Butchers," *New York Herald*, May 26, 1902; "Will Open Shops Today," *New York Tribune*, May 26, 1902.

17. "License Anti-Trust Butchers," *New York Sun*, May 27, 1902.

18. "Not Cheap, But Kosher, Is the Cry," *Arbeiter Zeitung*, May 31, 1902.

19. "The Struggle," *Yidishes Tageblatt*, May 28, 1902; "Kosher Butchers Resuming Business," *New York Sun*, May 28, 1902; "Butchers Resume: Kosher Meat War Appears to Be Over," *Daily People*, May 27, 1902.

16. Disregard All Agreements

1. "Writ Mailed by Packers," *Chicago Tribune*, May 23, 1902.

2. "Beef Trust Witnesses," *New York Times*, May 23, 1902.

3. "Get Facts about Beef Trust," *Chicago Tribune*, May 28, 1902.

4. "The Meat Trust," *New York Tribune*, May 27, 1902; "Beef Packers' Agreement," *New York Tribune*, May 28, 1902; "Beef Trust Quits State," New York *World*, May 28, 1902.

5. "Beef Packers' Agreement," New York *World*, May 28, 1902.

6. "End of Blacklist the Climax in the Herald's War on Trust," *New York Herald*, May 28, 1902.

7. "A Meat Famine Threatened," *Watertown (NY) Daily Times*, May 29, 1902, quoting the *New York Herald*.

8. "End of Blacklist the Climax in the Herald's War on Trust," *New York Herald*, May 28, 1902.

9. "Beef Trust Men Enjoined," *New York Sun*, June 4, 1902.

10. "Meat Firms Enjoined," *New York Tribune*, June 5, 1902.

11. "'Kosher' Riots and Meat Price," *National Provisioner*, May 31, 1902.

17. This Cooperative Shop Is Here to Stay

1. "Victory Is Near," *Yidishes Tageblatt*, June 5, 1902; "Wholesalers Agree to Sell at 9 or 9½ Cents a Pound—Retailers to get 14," *New York Sun*, June 4, 1902; "Ghetto Meat Shops Reopen," *Philadelphia Times*, June 5, 1902; "Kosher Meat Cheaper, But Boycott Remains," *New York Herald*, June 6, 1902.

2. "Kosher Meat Committee Fails to Decide," *Chicago Tribune*, June 6, 1902.

3. "Victory is Near," *Yidishes Tageblatt*, June 5, 1902; "Beef Trust Enjoined Here: Effect of Order Doubtful," *New York Press*, June 5, 1902.

4. "What's New," *Arbeiter Zeitung*, June 7, 1902.

5. "The Meat Strike and the Worker," *Forward*, June 4, 1902.

6. "Appeal to Kosher Butchers," *New York Times*, June 8, 1902; "Plan for Cheap Kosher Meat," *New York Sun*, June 9, 1902.

7. "Plan for Cheap Kosher Meat," *New York Sun*, June 9, 1902.

8. "'Kosher' Meat from Canada," *National Provisioner*, June 7, 1902.

9. "'Kosher' Eyes Opening," *National Provisioner*, June 14, 1902.

10. "Anti-Trust Women," *New York Tribune*, June 15, 1902.

11. "Women Open Shops to Beat Butchers," New York *World*, June 10, 1902; "New Co-operative 'Kosher' Meat Shops Open and Are Overrun by Eager Customers," *New York Herald*, June 10, 1902; "Women Selling Trust Beef," *New York Sun*, June 12, 1902.

12. "Women Selling Trust Beef," *New York Sun*, June 12, 1902.

13. "Anti-Trust Women," *New York Tribune*, June 15, 1902.

18. There Was Never Such an Outrage

1. "Meat Destroyed as Shops Reopen," *New York Herald*, June 19, 1902.

2. "Kosher Cooperative Troubles," *National Provisioner*, June 28, 1902.

3. "People in the Public Eye," *New York Tribune*, August 6, 1902.

4. "Pray for Dead Rabbi," *New York Tribune*, July 29, 1902; "Death of Chief Rabbi Jacob Joseph," *New York Times*, July 29, 1902; "Reverent Throngs Kneel in Street in Front of Dead Rabbi's Home," New York *World*, July 29, 1902.

5. "Fierce Riot Marks Funeral Service of Rabbi Jacob Joseph," *St. Louis Republic*, July 31, 1902; "Full Text of the Report," *New York Times*, September 16, 1902; "Riot Mars Funeral of Rabbi Joseph," *New York Times*, July 31, 1902; "Riot at Funeral," *Daily People*, July 31, 1902; Edward T. O'Donnell, "Hibernian versus Hebrews? A New Look at the 1902 Jacob Joseph Funeral Riot," *Journal of the Gilded Age and Progressive Era* 6, no. 2 (April 2007): 209–25.

6. "Jews Denounce the Police," *New York Times*, July 31, 1902; "Mayor and Aldermen to Avenge Hebrews," New York *World*, July 31, 1902.

7. "Jews Offer Reward," *New York Tribune*, August 1, 1902.

8. "Police Denounced by Jews in Mass Meeting," *New York Times*, August 2, 1902.

9. "Mayor Low Starts Riot Investigation," *New York Times*, August 1, 1902; "Mayor Orders Probing," *New York Tribune*, August 1, 1902.

10. "Full Text of the Report," *New York Times*, September 16, 1902.

11. "Rabbi Jacob Joseph," *Weekly People*, August 16, 1902.

12. "New York's Disgrace," *American Israelite*, August 7, 1902.

19. We Don't Feel Like Paying

1. *The Trow Business Directory of Manhattan and Bronx* (New York: Trow Directory, Printing and Bookbinding, 1903, 1904, 1905, 1906).

2. David Gordon, "Swift & Co. v. United States: The Beef Trust and the Stream of Commerce Doctrine," *American Journal of Legal History* 28, no. 3 (July 1984): 262–66; "Complete Rout for the Beef Trust," New York *World*, May 26, 1902.

3. "Completing Meat Trust," *Rock Island Argus*, March 25, 1903; "Beef Trust Merger," *Evening Times-Republican* (Marshalltown IA), March 25, 1903; "Start of Beef Trust," *New York Tribune*, March 25, 1903; *Report of the Commissioner of Corporations on the Beef Industry: March 3, 1905* (Washington DC: U.S. Government Printing Office, 1905), 26–27.

4. "Start of Beef Trust," *New York Tribune*, March 25, 1903; "War in Beef Trust," *Washington Evening Star*, April 9, 1903.

5. "Conference on Beef Trust," *New York Sun*, November 11, 1904.

6. "Rise in Rentals on the East Side," *New York Tribune*, January 31, 1904; "60,463 Evictions in This City in One Year," New York *World*, January 21, 1904; "1,000 Families to Be Evicted," New York *World*, April 4, 1904.

7. "1,000 Families to Be Evicted," New York *World*, April 4, 1904.

8. For an excellent discussion of the 1904 and 1908 rent strikes, see Jenna Weissman Joselit, "The Landlord as Czar: Pre–World War I Tenant Activity," *The Tenant Movement in New York City, 1904–1984*, TenantNet, accessed October 12, 2018, http://www.tenant.net/Community/history/hist01.html.

9. *Forward*, March 18, 1904, as quoted in Joselit, "Landlord as Czar."

10. "Fears East Side Rent Riots," *New York Sun*, April 6, 1904.

11. "Tire the Landlords Out," *New York Sun*, April 8, 1904.

12. "Ghetto Has Plan to Defeat the Landlords," *New York Times*, April 8, 1904; Abe Cahan, "What Sense Is There in These Rent Strikes?" *Worker*, April 17, 1902.

13. "Tenants Wreck Their Rooms," *New York Sun*, April 27, 1904; "Landlords Invited to Talk," *New York Sun*, May 9, 1904.

14. David Blaustein, "Cockroach Landlords," *New Era Illustrated Magazine* 4, no. 6 (May 1904), 379.

15. "East Side Dwellers Carrying on the Fight," *New York Times*, April 10, 1904; "Ghetto Tenants Fight Eviction with Delay," *New York Times*, April 9, 1904.

16. "Anti-Landlord Unions Split," *New York Sun*, April 11, 1904; "C.F.U. May Cooperate," *New York Tribune*, May 9, 1904.

17. "Landlords Invited to Talk," *New York Sun*, May 9, 1904; "Rent War Surrender," *New York Tribune*, May 10, 1904.

18. "Rent War Surrender," *New York Tribune*, May 10, 1904.

19. "New Joan of Arc Leads Rent Strike," *New York Times*, December 27, 1907.

20. "Rent Strike Spreads on the East Side," *New York Times*, December 28, 1907.

21. "Rent Strikers Rejoice over Great Victory," New York *World*, January 3, 1908; "Says Landlords Are Resorting to Thugs' Ways," New York *World*, January 4, 1908.

22. "Many Landlords Yield in Rent War," *New York Times*, January 5, 1908; "Rent Strike Is Dying Down," *New York Tribune*, January 10, 1908.

23. "Rent Strike Crisis at Hand for 6,000," *New York Times*, January 8, 1908; "Both Sides See End to Rent War," *New York Times*, January 9, 1908.

20. It Is Not Our Fault That Meat Is So High

1. *Swift and Company v. United States*, 196 U.S. 375 (1905).

2. "Probing, a Farce," *Daily People*, October 2, 1907.

3. Maureen Ogle, *In Meat We Trust* (New York: Houghton Mifflin Harcourt, 2013), 64–67; "Probing, a Farce," *Daily People*, October 2, 1907; "Upton Sinclair Tells More about Beef Trust Horrors," New York *World*, June 11, 1906.

4. "War on the Kosher Butchers," *New York Sun*, November 30, 1906.

5. "Women on Strike," *New York Tribune*, December 1, 1906.

6. "Women Cause Riot over Kosher Meat Prices," *New York Herald*, November 30, 1906; "Women on Strike," *New York Tribune*, December 1, 1906; "City News in Brief," *New York Tribune*, December 2, 1906.

7. "East Side Women Riot over High Meat Rates," *New York Times*, November 30, 1906.

8. "Women Cause Riot over Kosher Meat Prices," *New York Herald*, November 30, 1906; "War on the Kosher Butchers," *New York Sun*, November 30, 1906.

9. "Free Meat Scraps Cause of Strike," *New York Herald*, December 5, 1906; "East Side Butchers Appeal to Roosevelt," *New York Times*, December 3, 1906.

10. "Butchers Call on Roosevelt," *New York Sun*, December 3, 1906.

11. "On Verge of Riot over Meat Prices," *New York Herald*, December 4, 1906; "Boycott of Butchers," *Salt Lake Tribune*, December, 5, 1906.

12. "East Side Women Start a Big Meat Boycott," *New York Times*, December 6, 1906; "East Side Women Organize," *New York Tribune*, December 7, 1906.

13. "East Side Women Start a Big Meat Boycott," *New York Times*, December 6, 1906.

14. "Meat Disturbances on the East Side," *American Hebrew*, December 7, 1906.

15. "Kosher Butchers Shut Shop To-Day," *New York Herald*, December 11, 1906.

16. "Fear More Riots over Kosher Meat," *New York Telegram*, December 12, 1906; "Kosher Meat Riots," *New York Tribune*, December 12, 1906; "Kosher Rioting Less, but Butchers Shut Up," *Brooklyn Daily Eagle*, December 12, 1906; "Women Raid Meat Shops in Bands," New York *World*, December 12, 1906.

17. "Tempest in a Teapot," *Chicago Livestock World*, December 13, 1906.

21. A Great Victory for the American People

1. U.S. Bureau of Corporations, *Report of the Commissioner of Corporations on the Beef Industry, March 3, 1905* (Washington DC: Government Printing Office, 1905), 27; Robert M. Aduddell and Louis P. Cain, "Public Policy Toward 'The Greatest Trust in the World,'" *Business History Review* 55, no. 2 (Summer 1981): 228–29.

2. "Meat Boycott Declared," *New York Tribune*, April 8, 1910; "Woman Is Leader of Fight against High Meat Prices," *Mitchell Capital*, April 14, 1910; "More Kosher Meat Riots," *New York Tribune*, April 13, 1910.

3. "Kosher Butchers Now Refuse to Buy," *New York Times*, April 11, 1910; "The East Side Meat Riots," *American Hebrew*, April 15, 1910.

4. "Women in Battle with Policemen to Destroy Meat," New York *World*, June 7, 1912; "Women Ruin Kosher Food," *New York Tribune*, June 8, 1912; "East Side Meat Strike," *New York Sun*, June 12, 1912; "900 Butchers Vote a Dear Meat Strike," *New York Times*, June 15, 1912.

5. "High Living Cost Hits City," *New York Times*, December 27, 1916; "Two Days Truce in Meat Boycott," *New York Sun*, December 27, 1916; "The Food Demonstrations in New York," *Outlook*, March 7, 1917.

6. "Women in Riot Pour Oil on Meat in Philadelphia," *New York Sun*, February 23, 1917; "Kosher Poultry Shops Closed in Price Boycott," *New York Tribune*, February 26, 1917; Dana Frank, "Housewives, Socialists, and the Politics of Food: The 1917 New York Cost-of-Living Protests," *Feminist Studies* 11, no. 2 (Summer 1985): 255–85.

7. "The Food Demonstrations in New York," *Outlook*, March 7, 1917.

8. "Crowd Besieges Waldorf-Astoria," *Washington Evening Star*, February 25, 1917; "'Give Us Bread' Slogan of Mob Along 5th Avenue," *New York Sun*, February 25, 1917.

9. "Kosher Butchers, 5,000 Strong, Wage War on Meat Price," New York *World*, March 24, 1917; "Jewish Butchers Boycott Packers," *New York Times*, March 25, 1917.

10. "Kosher Meat Strike Fails; 3,000 Butchers Keep Open," New York *World*, March 26, 1917; "Meat Boycott Closes Shops of 3,000 Butchers," *New York Tribune*, March 27, 1917.

11. Annelise Orleck, *Common Sense and a Little Fire* (Chapel Hill: University of North Carolina Press, 2017), 235–37; Beth S. Wenger, *New York Jews and the Great Depression: Uncertain Promise* (Syracuse: Syracuse University Press, 1999), 125–27.

12. "The Big Five Is Enjoined," *Glasgow (MT) Courier*, January 2, 1920.

13. Editorial, *Manitowoc (WI) Pilot*, January 1, 1920.

Afterword

1. "Women of 1936," *Daily Worker*, May 15, 1936.

FURTHER READING

Contemporaneous accounts published in local English- and Yiddish-language newspapers, documented in the notes, have informed much of this work, but several secondary sources also shed light on the events chronicled. Here is a selection of them, organized by subject.

On the Beef Trust

Aduddell, Robert M., and Louis P. Cain. "Public Policy toward 'The Greatest Trust in the World.'" *Business History Review* 55, no. 2 (Summer 1981): 217–42.

Ogle, Maureen. *In Meat We Trust*. Boston: Houghton Mifflin Harcourt, 2013.

Russell, Charles Edward. *The Greatest Trust in the World*. New York: Ridgway-Thayer, 1905.

Sinclair, Upton. *The Jungle*. New York: Doubleday, 1906.

Walker, Francis. "The Beef Trust and the United States Government." *Economic Journal* 16, no. 64 (December 1906): 491–514.

On Immigrant Jewish Women

Ewen, Elizabeth. *Immigrant Women in the Land of Dollars*. New York: Monthly Review Press, 1985.

Glenn, Susan A. *Daughters of the Shtetl: Life and Labor in the Immigrant Generation*. Ithaca NY: Cornell University Press, 1990.

Gurock, Jeffrey S. *Orthodox Jews in America*. Indianapolis: Indiana University Press, 2009.

Howe, Irving. *World of Our Fathers: The Journey of the East European Jews to America and the Life They Found and Made*. New York: Harcourt, Brace, Jovanovich, 1976.

Kosak, Hadassa. *Cultures of Opposition: Jewish Immigrant Workers, New York City, 1881–1905*. Albany: State University of New York Press, 2000.

Nadell, Pamela S. *American Jewish Women: A History from Colonial Times to Today*. New York: W. W. Norton, 2019.

———, ed. *American Jewish Women's History*. New York: New York University Press, 2003.

Orleck, Annelise. *Common Sense and a Little Fire: Women and Working-Class Politics in the United States, 1900–1965*. Chapel Hill: University of North Carolina Press, 1995.

On Kosher Meat

Finkelstein, Harry. "The Kosher Meat Industry." Bachelor's thesis, Tufts University, 1926.

Fishkoff, Sue. *Kosher Nation*. New York: Schocken, 2010.

Lytton, Timothy D. *Kosher: Private Regulation in the Age of Industrial Food*. Cambridge MA: Harvard University Press, 2013.

On the Lower East Side

Polland, Annie, and Daniel Soyer. *Emerging Metropolis: New York Jews in the Age of Immigration, 1840–1920*. New York: New York University Press, 2012.

Richlin, Moses. *The Promised City: New York's Jews, 1870–1914*. Cambridge: Harvard University Press, 1962.

Weinberger, Moses. *People Walk on Their Heads: Jews and Judaism in New York*. Translated by Jonathan D. Sarna. New York: Holmes and Meier, 1982.

Ziegelman, Jane. *97 Orchard: An Edible History of Five Immigrant Families in One New York Tenement*. New York: HarperCollins, 2011.

On New York Kosher Meat Boycotts

Frank, Dana. "Housewives, Socialists and the Politics of Food: The 1917 New York Cost-of-Living Protests." *Feminist Studies* 11, no. 2 (Summer 1985): 255–85.

Hyman, Paula E. "Immigrant Women and Consumer Protest: The New York City Kosher Meat Boycott of 1902." *American Jewish History* 70, no. 1 (September 1980): 91–105.

Lichaw, Eden. "Got Meat? The Kosher Meat Boycott of 1902." Bachelor's thesis, Tufts University, 2018.

Orleck, Annelise. "'We Are That Mythical Thing Called the Public': Militant Housewives during the Great Depression." *Feminist Studies* 19, no. 1 (Spring 1993): 147–72.

Rockmore, Marlene. "The Kosher Meat Riots: A Study in the Process of Adaptation among Jewish Immigrant Housewives to Urban America, 1902–17." Master's thesis, University of Massachusetts, 1980.

Stein, Leon. "The Great Flanken War of 1902." Unpublished manuscript, collection number 5780/087. Kheel Center for Labor-Management Documentation and Archives, Cornell University Library [1978?].

On Rabbi Jacob Joseph

Adler, Joseph. "Twilight Years of Rabbi Jacob Joseph." *Jewish Frontier* 67, no. 1 (January–August 2000).

Karp, Abraham J. "New York Chooses a Chief Rabbi." *Publications of the American Jewish Historical Society* 44, no. 3 (March 1955): 129–98.

Levine, Yitzchok. "The Chief Rabbi Encounters Opposition." *Jewish Express*, June 4, 2008.

On New York Rent Strikes

Day, Jared. *Urban Castles: Tenement Housing and Landlord Activism in New York City, 1890–1943.* New York: Columbia University Press, 1999.

Josselit, Jenna Weissman. "The Landlord as Czar: Pre–World War I Tenement Activity." In *The Tenant Movement in New York City, 1904–1984.* Edited by Ronald Lawson. New Brunswick NJ: Rutgers University Press, 1986.

INDEX

Page numbers in italics indicate illustrations

Beef Trust Case. See *United States v. Swift & Co. et al.*

Beis Hamidrash HaGadol Synagogue, 3, 39, 43, *44*, 124

Bernstein, Raphael, 131

Bethea, Solomon H., xx, xxii, 73, 135, 139

Bible, ix, 3, 31

Big Six: background of, 22; cooperatives and, 188; legal proceedings against, 73–74, 77, 135–36, 179, 181, 182–83; members of, 55; price-fixing by, 151; reorganization of, 208–9. *See also* Beef Trust

blacklisting, 52, 136, 153, 180, 181, 182, 211

Blaustein, David, xxvii, 161, 163, *164*, 173–74, 177, 185–87, 188, 215

Blumenthal, Isaac, xxvii, 66, 75, 77

Blumenthal, Maurice, 144, 147

Board of Aldermen (New York City), 52, 201

Board of United Building Trades, 52

Boston, MA, xxii, xxv, 52–53, 133, 159, *160*, 168, 170, 232

Boston Globe, 170

Boston Tea Party (1773), xxxii, 100–101

boxcars, refrigerated. *See* refrigerated boxcars

boycotts, ix, xi, xx–xxi, xxii–xxiii, xxv, xxvii–xxviii, xxxii, *169*; butchers and, 68–70, 74–75, 81–82, 95–96, 112, 152–53, 183, 195, 223–24, 226–27, 229–30, 232; delicatessens and, 115; in Jewish history, 106–7; need for, 70; opposition to, 125–26; Orthodox Jews and, 176; overview of, 239–44; planning for, 94–95, 144, 226, 237; price issues in, 186–87, 195; as rent strike model, 212, 218, 220; results of, 69, 78, 101, 185, 192–93, 207–8; rumors of, 47; Sabbath services and, 123–24; socialists and, 156–57; strikes compared to, 107, 109, 148; union support for, 148; wholesalers and, 75, 77; women important to, 110, 235

Brechner, Abraham, 223–24

Breckstein, Mrs., 163

Bronx NY, 68, 131, 133

Brooklyn Daily Eagle, 100–101, 170

Brooklyn NY, xxiv, xxv, 68, 130–31, *132*, 133, 170, 219

Brooklyn Standard Union. See *Standard Union*

Brownsville NY, *145*, 151, 227

butchers, kosher, xix–xxiii, xxv, xxxi–xxxii, *35*, *71*, *97*, *160*; Beef Trust and, 66–68, 181, 183–84; boycotts and, 68–70, 74–75, 81–82, 95–96, 112, 152–53, 183, 195, 223–24, 226–27, 229–30, 232; buying by, 32–33, 52; conscience of, 34; cooperatives and, 191, 192–93; discord among, 150; fraud by, 38–39; housewives protesting, 79, 81–83, 105–6, 112–14, 117, 223–24, 227; housewives trusting, 36; low sales of, 63; in negotiations, 156–57, 173–74; organizing, 224–25; oversight of, 37–38, 43, 46–47, 48, 49; post-boycott, 207, 208; press on, 118–19, 149, 177; price increases and, 51, 223; religious schedules and, 33, 59–60, 62, 143; reopening by, 170, 175, 186, 235; role of, 33; Samuel Solomont & Son and, 168, 170; slaughterhouses and, 38–39, 64, 66, 72; Theodore Roosevelt and, 225–26; wholesalers and, 77–78, 233, 235

butchers, non-Jewish, 60, 66, 75

butcher shops, 34–36, *35*, *71*, *87*, *97*, *132*, *145*. *See also* cooperatives

Cahan, Abraham, xxvii, 102, 119–21, *120*, 165–66, 202, 215

capitalism, 18, 148, 222

Carnegie, Andrew, 17–18

cartoons, *54*, *90*

cattle: for cooperatives, 187–88; price of, 55, 75, 77, 137, 149; purchase of, 57–58; shipment of, 20, 21, 26, 182; slaughter of, 28, 30–31; supply of, 157, 183

Central Federated Union, 147–48

Central Labor Union, 52–53

certificates, of kosher preparation, 48

certificates, of price reduction, 174, 175, 187, 207

Cherry Street (Manhattan), 85–86

Chester, Alden, xxiii, 135, 136, 137, 138, 179, 182

Chicago: butchering in, 25, 26; demonstrations in, 232; legal proceedings in, 73, 136; as livestock market, 20–21, 24, 137, 209, 222; strikes in, 108

Wexelman, Mrs., 211

Whitman, Charles, 223

wholesalers, xix, xx, xxii, xxiii, xxv, xxviii; agreements by, 207; boycotts against, 69–70; butchers and, 75, 77–78, 82, 89, 91, 156–57, 170, 225, 230, 232, 233; Clara Lemlich and, 244; cooperatives and, 190; credit policy of, 180; Great Depression and, 235; independent, 153; meat withheld by, 237; of poultry, 34; press investigating, 227; religious authorities and, 185–86; speculators and, 32–33; threats by, 69

Wigdorowitz, Morris, 151

Willett Street (Manhattan), *214*

Williamsburg NY, xxii, 151, 167–68, 170, 233

Wilson, Woodrow, 237–38

Wolf, Charles, 45

women's suffrage movement, 109, 242, 243

Worker, 215

working conditions, 11, 18–19, 107–8, 222–23

World: on Beef Trust, 52, 57, 101, 137, 138; on boycotts, 70; on Carolyn Schatzberg, 148; on food costs, 58–59, 64, 66, 149; on police, 88, 96; on riots, 100, 118–19; on Sarah Edelson, 112; women activists and, 81, 112, 148, 151–52, 189–90

Wurtzel, Annie, 192

Yiddish language, 9–10

Yidishes Tageblatt: on Beef Trust, 66; on boycotts, 101–2, 150, 176, 177, 185; on court proceedings, 91; Orthodox perspective of, 10; on police, 103–4, 168; on protests, 130; on women's meetings, 79, 81, 165

Zeff, Joseph, xxi, 93, 94, 195–96